Chuck,

Thank you for your passion for LIFE!!

For Life,

Billy

Why Overturning Roe versus Wade Will Have Little Impact on Ending Abortion

YOUR PRO-LIFE BOTTOM LINE

How You Can Help End Abortion by
Investing in Groundbreaking
Consumer Marketing Strategies
that Encourage Women to Choose Life

BRETT ATTEBERY

Print ISBN: 978-1-66782-526-7
eBook ISBN: 978-1-66782-527-4

Printed in the United States of America

THIS BOOK IS DEDICATED TO:

Jesse, my child in Heaven

TABLE OF CONTENTS

FOREWORD

"God bless, Brett" was the way Brett Attebery signed an email to me about fifteen years ago. You may think "What's the big deal?" since you are probably a Christian if you're reading this book. There's a story behind that "big deal." Before I tell you that story, let me tell you briefly what this book is about. In short, it's a radical rethinking of how to save lives that would otherwise be lost to abortion.

An enormous amount of money is poured into the pro-life movement every year. Some of it is effective and well spent, but much of it isn't. Otherwise disciplined donors who might set clear expectations for their for-profit business initiatives end up checking that discipline at the door when it comes to measuring the effectiveness of their pro-life activities and donations. Or perhaps they don't even know what to measure.

The Holy Grail of many pro-life donors would be overturning *Roe v. Wade*. But what if that goal, while certainly important, wouldn't make much of a dent in reducing the actual number of abortions in our country? That's where this book comes in. This book opens up a new way of thinking about pro-life through the lens of basic business principles: a deep understanding of the "consumer" (an abortion-seeking pregnant woman), the cost/benefits in the consumer's mind of aborting her child or choosing life, an understanding of the marketplace and available "product options," measuring success/market share, and more.

Have you ever read a book or seen a movie that permanently changed the way you thought about something? *Toxic Charity* by Bob Lupton and *A Billion Bootstraps* by Phil Smith and Eric Thurman did that for me. Both books apply principles of human behavior and economics to traditional nonprofit organizations made up of well-intentioned donors—donors who often enable others.

The book you're holding has the potential to, in a similar way, teach principles that will motivate you to think differently about pro-life and give you ways to allocate your resources to save human lives lost to abortion. My journey through this discovery, led by Brett, has certainly done so for me.

When Brett asked me to write the foreword to his book, my first thought was I'm not an expert enough on the topic to add much value. A foreword should be written by someone who lends credibility to the message of the book. Sure, I have some knowledge of the pro-life industry, and I have supported it and donated to it. I've even worked closely with Brett on the development of consumer-based testing of pro-life messaging in the Oklahoma City market. We both have backgrounds in economics and consumer products, so we speak the same business language, and I served as a sounding board of sorts for Brett's ideas. But still, I'm no expert on the pro-life issue.

What I am an expert on, however, is the life and witness of Brett Attebery.

So let's get back to how this book came about. The story behind this book is remarkable. In fact, I truly believe it is God's handiwork, as you shall see.

It's true that Brett is a polyglot (he speaks both Japanese and French), earned an MBA from Wharton, has years of experience living overseas in different cultures, and has spent many years professionally in international marketing, consumer products, and technology. He's also had exposure to private equity. All of this has deeply shaped Brett, and the insights he shares in this book naturally well up from these deep and rich experiences. But what makes Brett's life truly remarkable, and his credibility on the topic of this book even more robust, is his "Fiat!" ("Yes!") to God.

Brett and I met at Putnam City North High School in Oklahoma City in the summer of 1980 when this spunky underclassman showed up for a preseason cross-country workout. From that day we were fast friends (Brett was fast anyway, winning the 800-meter state championship his senior year and then going on to become a scholarship runner at Tulane).

While we have not lived in the same city since high school, Brett and I have remained very close friends. We kept in touch while both of us attended different universities, MBA programs, and work. We even wrote an occasional longhand letter back and forth in the days before e-mail. (I suppose we could have talked on the phone every now and then, but the guy lived in Japan for five years for heaven's sake, and neither of us could afford that call!)

Brett was raised by loving parents (Ray and Sharon never missed a track meet!), but a life of faith was not part of the family dynamic. I, on the other hand, was raised in a faithful Roman Catholic family, never missing Sunday mass, even on vacation, and praying the occasional rosary with my mom. Brett and I had many shared interests, but faith in Christ was not one of them. Over the many years after college, as my faith grew, I would share an occasional message or book on faith with Brett, generally with no response.

So, as you might imagine, when I saw that "God bless, Brett" sign-off, I was stunned! What had happened to my friend? Was it just a throw-away line, or had the Hound of Heaven finally somehow "gotten ahold of him"? I was so shocked that I immediately called Brett and just asked him point-blank what was up with the "God" thing.

What had happened to Brett was a deeply personal encounter with the living God. I hope he doesn't mind me sharing this, but as he was struggling with something we Christians call "sin," Brett said there was something "not right" about his life. He had run across a TV evangelist—probably while flipping between NFL games—who suggested giving prayer a try. Brett thought "Why not?" so he did, and God, that very day, did indeed "get ahold of him."

I was blown away and suggested he go the nearest Catholic Church and tell the priest the exact same thing he told me! He did, and the following spring at the Easter Vigil, Brett was baptized and welcomed into the Catholic Church. Shortly after, he began leading faith-formation classes at his local parish, became involved in pro-life work, started *Pro-Life Magazine*, and eventually left for-profit work entirely, devoting himself full-time to saving lives from abortion.

As Brett involved me more in his pro-life work, our friendship grew deeper. We began a targeted online advertising campaign in the Oklahoma City market and performed consumer research to measure its impact. We fleshed out the distinction in the abortion industry between "demand" (the abortion-determined woman's demand for abortion) versus "supply" (the availability/legality of the abortion "product"). Brett is a thought leader who has taught me how to think about—not just give to—pro-life causes.

I have been privileged to share a pilgrimage with this remarkable man. I believe God handpicked Brett to share the message of this book. It is a book that will change the way you think about the effectiveness of your pro-life efforts, and encourage you to apply disciplined, measurable expectations toward the organizations receiving your pro-life donations.

Brett Attebery is a highly educated man, had a powerful midlife conversion, understands the topic of abortion from the inside out, and serves as CEO of one of the country's leading organizations committed to reducing demand for abortion. When I think about whether God had a hand in Brett's journey, I sense God asking, "Haven't you noticed—everything?"

Don Greiner

Cofounder and President, One Heartbeat Foundation

PROLOGUE: ASK AND IT WILL BE GIVEN TO YOU

Ask and it will be given to you; seek and you will find; knock and the door will be opened to you. Matthew 7:7

In the first draft of this book, I did not include this prologue. The reason? This prologue is about me, but I want this book to be about *you* and what *you* can do to shut down Planned Parenthood and the abortion industry. Not about *me*.

However, several reviewers of early drafts of the book who know well my personal pro-life journey gave me feedback something to this effect. "Brett, people who decide to read this book are going to want to know why they should trust what you have to say, and what motivates you to do the pro-life work you do. They will want to know *your* story!"

Those reviewers strongly encouraged me to share my journey with you at the beginning of the book. After some initial hesitation about the idea, I began to see some merit to it.

So here goes. I'll try to keep it short so we can quickly get back to *your* story—the story *you* have the potential to write about the role you played in helping shut down Planned Parenthood and the abortion industry.

What Do I Know?

Let me briefly make a case for why you should trust what I have to say in this book, which as you will soon see, even though it is a book about pro-life, it is at its core a book about business strategy. First, I do not come from the world of social work, or faith-based ministry, or anything like that. I am a businessman. Specifically, I am a marketing professional.

I began my marketing career in 1990, securing my first marketing and sales job working in the international division of Komatsu at its headquarters in Tokyo, Japan. So I have been practicing all aspects of marketing, with a particularly heavy focus on product marketing, for more than thirty years.

After three years in Tokyo, I made my way back to the United States, but before joining a company here I decided to first upgrade my business skills through formal education. I applied and was accepted into the Wharton School of the University of Pennsylvania, where I received my MBA in 1995. I then entered the high-tech world, working for Motorola's cell phone division in their international marketing department. I spent the next seventeen years working in cell phone consumer product marketing, primarily on the manufacturing and technology development side, with management roles at Motorola (1995–98), running marketing and helping raise capital for a dotcom wireless start-up called Clariti Telecommunications (1998–2001), and strategy development roles for wireless tech development and patent licensing company InterDigital Communications (2004–12).

Note that in the middle of that seventeen-year run, I had a brief two-year "non-high-tech" stint from 2002 to 2003 when I tried my hand at an entrepreneurial retail start-up in partnership with a Japan-based product design firm. When that business failed, I returned to the wireless product marketing world.

In 2012, I was let go from InterDigital and instead of seeking work in the high-tech corporate world, I decided to take another shot at an entrepreneurial venture. As a side gig to my full-time work in high tech, starting in 2007, I had already been developing my consumer internet marketing skills while helping my wife expand her internet-based "how to make jewelry" video tutorial business called Jewelry Making Professor. It seemed logical to pursue an entrepreneurial venture in which I already had some experience, so with my wife's jewelry-making instruction business as the base, I started a digital internet publishing business. One of the great fruits of that was publishing a digital magazine called *Jewelry Designer Magazine*, which led to co-creating a handmade jewelry marketing course that we successfully sold on Jewelry TV for many years.

Now I'm going to throw a major surprise at you that you won't understand until you read more about my motivations for doing pro-life work, but within three years after starting this new entrepreneurial venture, I had abandoned it and completely committed myself to full-time pro-life work. I know. When people hear the details of my professional background, they often can't fathom why I decided to work full-time in pro-life. Then I tell them what happened to me, which you will read about in what follows, and they understand.

Before we get to that, though, I want to address one more element in the "why you should trust me" category, and that is that throughout this book, I will make many claims about the pro-life world and the pro-life organizations that operate within that world that you should probably only trust if made by someone who has significant "on the ground" experience in that world. And I do.

As you'll read, I began full-time pro-life work in April 2013, first starting two of my own pro-life projects, *Pro-Life Magazine* and Maria's Choice, under a nonprofit I created, and then starting in February 2015 working full-time with a nonprofit organization called Heroic Media—where as of this writing I serve as president, CEO and a member of the board of directors. In my work at Heroic Media, now approaching seven years, I interact very often with those team members at pro-life pregnancy centers who daily fight the frontline battles against Planned Parenthood and the abortion industry. I have had a front row seat to see what that battle looks like, and what works and what doesn't work, when it comes to successfully encouraging women facing the fear of an unexpected pregnancy to choose life instead of abortion. In addition, as executive editor of *Pro-Life Magazine*, I have had the privilege of interviewing many of the leaders of the top pro-life organizations in the country on a host of pro-life issues.

All this is to say I have had my hands on the pulse of the pro-life world in the United States for nearly a decade. So my hope is that as you read some of the controversial things I have to say in this book, please know that my claims are born of firsthand experience, not based on abstract theory. With that, let's move on to my motivations, my "why" of committing myself to full-time pro-life work.

A Mistake That Can't Be Undone

In the predawn hours of Sunday, April 28, 2013, I sat alone in an adoration chapel at Our Lady of Czestochowa Catholic Church in Doylestown, just outside of Philadelphia. With tears streaming down my face, I looked at Jesus present in the Blessed Sacrament, and I prayed. *Lord, please use me to help young women and men not make the same mistake I made.* What "mistake" was I talking to Jesus about? Decades earlier, in the 1980s, I, together with my girlfriend at the time, made a terrible decision. My girlfriend was pregnant with our child, and she and I decided to abort our child.

So how did I go from the terrible mistake I made three decades earlier to looking right at Jesus and asking Him, *Lord, please use me to help young women and men not make the same mistake I made*? In one sense, you could say my journey to that moment began three decades earlier when I consented to the abortion of my own child. I think deep down there was always something inside of me that knew what I did was grievously wrong. My conscience just wasn't formed enough in virtue to know better. But that would eventually change, and in dramatic fashion. As they say, better late than never.

The Lord Comes Knocking

In 2002, at the age of thirty-seven, I had a powerful mystical experience. I was so moved by what happened to me I felt there was only one thing to do, and I did it: I gave my life to Christ. Two years later, at the Easter Vigil on Saturday evening, April 10, 2004, I entered into full communion with the Catholic Church at Mary Mother of the Redeemer parish in North Wales in the suburbs of Philadelphia.

Thank You Jesus! Now What?

Not unlike many converts, I was on fire for the faith! I threw myself into learning everything about the teachings of the Church. Of course that included studying the Church's teachings on the sanctity of life. And from the beginning, I never questioned that *all* the Church's teachings on the sanctity of life were true. In addition, and this is very important for what happened in the years to follow, I believed without reservation God had completely forgiven me for my role in the abortion of my own child many years earlier.

When I emerged from the baptismal waters on that grace-filled evening in April 2004, I believed with absolute certainty and confidence God had forgiven me for **EVERYTHING**. I was a new creation. So if I believed I was completely forgiven by God, that I was a new creation in Christ, again the question, why was I on my knees nine years later, crying out to Jesus, *Lord, please use me to help young women and men not make the same mistake I made*?

I Didn't Know What I Didn't Know

It took me a very long time to understand that the Lord's forgiveness included a great desire to heal me of the wounds I experienced from having agreed to the abortion of my own child. The problem was that I wasn't even aware I had those wounds. But as time moved on following my baptism, I began experiencing deeper stress about the role I played in the abortion of my child. I thought the cause of my stress was that I didn't really believe God had forgiven me. I believed I was suffering from a case of Catholic scrupulosity!

Of course, the Lord knew that wasn't the real cause. He knew what I didn't know—that deep in my heart, I was experiencing profound REGRET for having done such a terrible thing to my own child. In baptism, my relationship with God the Father had been restored, but I had yet to make amends with my child who had lost his life because of my actions. The Lord knew I needed healing in order to restore a relationship with my child. So as He often does, God took the initiative.

There Are No Coincidences

Driving home from work one day in early April 2013, I was listening to Catholic radio, and heard a short announcement about a Rachel's Vineyard abortion healing retreat scheduled to take place two weeks later at Our Lady of Czestochowa in Doylestown, just about five miles up the road from where I lived. As soon as I arrived at my house, I ran upstairs and called the retreat director. I remember clearly making the point to her that "I know I'm forgiven by God, but something is wrong and I don't know what it is. Do you think the retreat can help me?"

The retreat director responded, "Absolutely."

The Big Reveal

When I arrived at the retreat two weeks later, I was nervous. Part of me anticipated that something profound might happen at the retreat, but another part of me was skeptical the retreat would result in anything other than temporary relief from whatever was causing my stress. I didn't have to wait long to discover that I should have trusted the part of me that anticipated something profound would happen.

On the first evening of the retreat, we watched a short film about a woman who had lived a somewhat "out of control" life when she was young. She frequented bars, slept with many different men, became pregnant several times, and had an abortion each time she became pregnant. Then she met a godly man, put her former way of life behind her, became a Christian, and married.

Fast-forward to years later. The woman had a stable family life and was raising a number of young children with her husband. Then one night, soon after she went to bed, the Holy Spirit showed up in this woman's life in a powerful way. Led by the Spirit, she got up out of bed, went downstairs to a desk in her living room, pulled out some paper, and began writing personal letters to each one of the children she had chosen to have aborted years earlier, giving first names to each one of her children as she wrote to them.

The Scales Fall from My Eyes and My Heart

I don't think I can adequately describe in words what happened to me at that moment of the film. You see, I had always viewed the abortion of my child so many years earlier as an "event" that just happened, not as something that I actively *did* to a person, and what's more, a very special person—my own child.

Through this woman's story in the short film, the Lord suddenly tore down a wall that had blocked my heart from seeking what it truly desired for many years—first, to ask my child for forgiveness for the role I had played in unjustly taking his life, and second, to tell him how deeply I desired to start our relationship anew, to build a spiritual relationship with him.

For the rest of the retreat, I put myself completely in the Lord's hands and let Him begin to heal me of deep wounds of regret, a process that continues to this day. In one of many grace-filled moments during the abortion healing retreat, each retreatant named the child or children he or she had lost to abortion. I decided on a name that kept coming to mind during my prayer time—Jesse.

Jesus, Jesse, and Me

The night before the final day of the retreat, the retreat team offered me the opportunity to spend an hour alone in Eucharistic Adoration. I jumped at the chance. I was beyond **GRATEFUL** to the Lord for what he had done for me during the retreat, so I couldn't wait to spend time alone with Him in praise and adoration. But I knew it wouldn't be just the two of us. Jesse would be with us. As I entered the chapel for the sacred hour, I brought pen and paper with me. Following some quiet time thanking Jesus, I took out the pen and paper and wrote a letter to Jesse. I had no plan for what I would write. I just let the Holy Spirit guide me. Of course, I still have the letter I wrote and I treasure it. I still take it out from time to time and read it.

It's short, but it starts with this: "Jesse, I love you." Does a child want to hear anything more from his father than that? I go on in the letter to tell Jesse how deeply sorry I am for what I did to him. But I recognized then, as now, there isn't a word in English that can adequately express the depth of repentance required to atone for having done such a thing to one's own child. I wrote to Jesse, "Even the word sorry seems so inadequate to describe what I want to say to you. I know you can feel my soul crying out to you to forgive me for what I deprived you of."

Then the letter turns positive. "And Jesse, by the Lord's grace I just learned in the past two days that you not only forgive me, but that you love me and are constantly praying for me. That is such a blessing, so astounding that I can't even describe how beautiful it is to me. I'm so proud that I can talk to you as a father to a son. I'm so proud to call you my son. You are so beautiful in my sight. I am just now starting to see you with my heart, and, God, I'm just so grateful."

As I looked at the words I had just written to Jesse, I experienced an intense epiphany: *I have to do everything I can so others don't decide to abort their babies and then have to experience this profound regret.* I fell to my knees, looked at Jesus, and said, *Lord, please use me to help young women and men not make the same mistake I made*. And I would add, I think Jesse was asking Jesus as well, *Lord, please use my dad to help young women and men not make the same mistake he made*.

"Ask and it will be given to you … "

I was in such an emotional state when I made that prayer to Jesus, I would understand if others discounted it as nothing more than intense sentimentality. I didn't even really know what I was asking the Lord—it was a prayer from the heart, not the head. But as subsequent events in the weeks, months, and years that followed would show, I think there's strong evidence the Lord granted my prayer. I believe one of the fruits of the prayer I made to Jesus that day is this book you hold in your hands.

If you use any of the recommendations I offer in the pages to come, and as a result of that, if even just *one* young woman decides to choose life instead of getting an abortion, then together you and I will know the Lord has not only connected us as a result of my prayer that day, but that He has accomplished a *very* good work through us. Of course, even just one life saved from abortion would be amazing, but the numbers-driven businessman part of me hopes you will desire to do even more—to let the Lord work through you to help *many* young women change their minds about aborting their babies. That may be greedy, but I hope you'll agree it's a very good kind of greedy.

There is more to the story of my pro-life journey, but I will save that for the epilogue. (I encourage you to read the book in its entirety before reading the epilogue.) It's now time to move on from my story so we can get to the story *you* have the potential to write within the bigger pro-life drama. Let's talk about how *you* can play a role in shutting down Planned Parenthood and the abortion industry.

Glossary of Terms

I use some terms in this book that may be unfamiliar to you, so I have listed them here for your reference.

3T assets: Your **T**ime, **T**alent, and **T**reasure.

Abortion facility: A facility where medication and surgical abortions are conducted.

Abortion industry: All the facilities in aggregate that conduct abortions in any way, surgical or medication abortions, plus any and all organizations that support those facilities.

Abortion pill: The combination of two medications, mifepristone and misoprostol, that cause an abortion. An abortion option for women who are eight weeks pregnant or less.

Abortion-determined: The mindset of a woman facing an unexpected pregnancy who has a very strong desire to get an abortion.

Brand marketing: The practice of a company educating its prospective customers/clients about the benefits of the category in which its products/services fit, and then working to associate the company's particular brand name or product/services names with the category.

Business model: A company's core strategy for doing business. It identifies the products or services the business sells, its target market, and any operating expenses.

Capital: The money a business has available to pay for its day-to-day operations and to fund its future growth.

Caveat emptor: Latin phrase for "Let the buyer beware." Describes the concept of placing the burden of due diligence on the buyer of a good or service.

Choose abortion services: The "product" offered by abortion facilities operating in the abortion industry.

Choose life services: The "product" offered by pro-life pregnancy centers operating in the Pro-Life Business Industry.

Demand: A consumer's desire to purchase goods and services and willingness to pay a price for those goods and services.

Direct response marketing: A type of marketing designed to elicit an instant response by encouraging prospects to immediately take a specific action.

Feelgoodism: A feeling of happiness or satisfaction, often superficial.

IRS Form 990: A tax form most tax-exempt organizations must file annually that gives the IRS an overview of the organization's activities, governance, and detailed financial information.

Key Performance Indicator (KPI): A measurable value that demonstrates how well a company is achieving a key business objective.

Key Success Factor (KSF): The combination of important factors that are required in order to accomplish desirable business goals.

Linear thinking: The process of thinking in a sequential manner, like a straight line.

Market positioning: A strategy that focuses on creating a unique image or perception of a brand, product, or service in the consumer's mind.

Market share: Out of total sales (either by dollar value or by volume) of a product or service, the percentage of sales that go to an organization.

Marketing: The activity and processes for creating, communicating, delivering, and exchanging offerings that have value for consumers. These activities and processes are described using the 4 Ps of marketing: Product, Price, Placement (i.e., Distribution), and Promotion.

Maslow's hierarchy of needs: A theory of psychology explaining human motivation based on the pursuit of different levels of needs in a hierarchical order, beginning with the most basic needs before moving on to more advanced needs. The ultimate goal is to reach the fifth level of the hierarchy: self-actualization.

Nonlinear thinking: Not thinking in a sequential manner or along straight lines.

OAASYS™ (On-demand Alternatives to Abortion SYStem): An advertising system that offers pro-life philanthropists the opportunity to sponsor direct-response internet ads that redirect abortion-seeking women away from Planned Parenthood, connecting them instead to highly skilled pro-life pregnancy centers.

Pregnancy Resource Center (PRC): Center whose primary mission is to provide material assistance to those women who are already likely to carry their pregnancies to term.

Product mix: The complete set of products and services offered by an organization.

Pro-Life Business Industry (PLBI): All of the pro-life pregnancy centers in aggregate that offer women life-giving alternatives to abortion, plus any and all organizations that support those centers. Competes against the abortion industry for the same clients: women seeking an abortion because they are experiencing profound fear due to an unexpected pregnancy.

Pro-Life demand-side investments: Pro-life philanthropic investments in organizations operating in the Pro-Life Business Industry.

Pro-Life Movement: A human rights movement whose primary objective is to influence the overturning of laws that allow legal human abortion, eliminating the abortion industry's ability to supply abortion services.

Pro-Life pregnancy center: Pro-life facilities that offer women life-giving alternatives to abortion.

Pro-Life supply-side investments: Pro-life philanthropic investments in organizations operating in the Pro-Life Movement.

Repositioning: The process of changing a target market's understanding or perception of a product or service.

Return on investment (ROI): How profitable an activity is, calculated by looking at the activity's up-front cost versus the net profit it produced.

Roe v. Wade: A US Supreme Court legal decision issued on January 22, 1973, that struck down a Texas statute banning abortion, effectively legalizing abortion across the United States. The Supreme Court held that a woman's right to an abortion was implicit in the right to privacy protected by the Fourteenth Amendment to the Constitution.

Scalable: The ability of a business to efficiently ramp up operations and increase sales when there is a rise in demand, based on a business model that can be easily replicated without incurring high additional costs.

Self-actualization: The final stage of development in Maslow's hierarchy of needs. Self-actualization is the ability to become the best version of oneself. Maslow stated, "This tendency might be phrased as the desire to become more and more what one is, to become everything that one is capable of becoming."

Self-managed abortion: A common term used within the abortion industry to describe the abortion pill. Also known as a "DIY abortion" or a "self-administered abortion."

Supply: A fundamental economic concept that describes the total amount of a specific good or service that is available to consumers.

Total Available Market (TAM): The total market demand, measured in unit sales or total revenue, for a product or service.

Turnkey business system: A business that is ready to use, existing in a condition that allows for immediate operation.

WIIFM: Acronym for "**W**hat's **I**n **I**t **F**or **M**e?" The question human beings naturally ask themselves either consciously or unconsciously when presented with choices: "Will the thing being proposed improve my life, or not improve my life?"

INTRODUCTION

If the ladder is not leaning against the right wall, every step we take just gets us to the wrong place faster. Stephen R. Covey

This is a book about business, with a specific focus on marketing strategies in what I call the **Pro-Life Business Industry** (PLBI) (much more on that later). If you are an experienced business professional, then the concepts I present in this book will be very easy for you to understand. But what if you are not an experienced business professional?

Not to worry. By virtue of the fact that you yourself have been a consumer for a long time, and have been marketed to daily over many years by companies and organizations that want you to buy what they offer, you already possess a keen understanding of *consumer marketing* from being on the receiving end of that marketing, even if you are not professionally involved in marketing to consumers.

So this book is for you as well. That said, as you will soon notice, my writing style is to address my readers as if they are already experienced business professionals. Please don't take offense. Writing that way simply helps me focus my arguments. I don't believe there is anything in the book that is too complicated for the nonbusiness professional to grasp. In addition, for experienced business professionals as well as for nonbusiness folks, I want to make a quick comment on my writing style.

I find that my writing becomes sharper when I write not in an academic tone, but instead in a conversational tone, as if you are sitting right in front of me and we are discussing pro-life issues over coffee. This writing style can come off as a bit "salesy," as one book reviewer put it. I don't disagree with that feedback, but please understand that writing in a conversational tone versus a traditional academic style is just a personal preference, so I hope that even if you find the more traditional writing approach more appealing, you'll still read through the book in its entirety, including the epilogue.

The Bottom Line

With that understanding in hand, in the spirit of the title of this book, let me make a bold **BOTTOM LINE** statement: If you are pro-life and are one or more of the following—a successful business owner, business executive, marketing and sales professional, or investor—then you already possess *assets* that, if deployed thoughtfully and strategically, have the potential to play a key role in shutting down Planned Parenthood and the abortion industry.

What do I mean by your "assets"? You often hear at church about giving your Time, Talent, and Treasure. Those are the assets I'm talking about. Let's call them your 3T assets.

If you're like most busy business professionals, you primarily use your assets of Time and Talent in the so-called real world, which earns you an income—your asset of Treasure—a portion of which you then give to your church. This is the most common process for faith-based philanthropy. And since you are pro-life, you likely view your faith-based philanthropy to pro-life organizations in the same way you view your philanthropy to church: you use your Time and Talent in the business world to earn Treasure, and then give a portion of that Treasure to pro-life organizations.

Of course, investing your asset of Treasure in pro-life organizations is important. However, as I argue in the pages that follow, if you are a typical pro-life philanthropist, then you are likely investing your asset of Treasure in the least impactful part of the pro-life world. Let's assume for a second that I successfully convince you of this and as a result you decide to reallocate your pro-life philanthropy investments to organizations that prove, through verifiable results, that they are succeeding at hurting Planned Parenthood's business.

Planned Parenthood will not be happy with you. But Planned Parenthood still won't fear you. At least not yet. Why not? Because the asset you possess that can inflict the greatest damage on Planned Parenthood is not your Treasure—as important as that asset is—*it's your Talent*. If you are the typical pro-life philanthropist, you are giving generously of your asset of Treasure, but it's very unlikely you are currently leveraging your asset of Talent—your business skills and experience—to fight Planned Parenthood on the battlefield it wants to dominate more than any other—*the battlefield of business*.

On the battlefield of business, for decades, Planned Parenthood has implemented powerful marketing programs to successfully persuade millions of American women that abortion is the best "product" for them to choose if they face an unexpected pregnancy that causes them fear. The results? Planned Parenthood can claim business "success" at having aborted *tens of millions* of preborn human beings. In 2019 alone, Planned Parenthood reported 354,871 abortions. That's one abortion every eighty-nine seconds on average!

Get in the Fight

If you are pro-life, that reality—354,871 preborn human lives forcefully taken by abortion—should motivate you to fight. And perhaps you are fighting. However, if you are the typical pro-life philanthropist, you are likely not engaging Planned Parenthood on the battlefield of business, but instead on the battlefield of *human rights advocacy*.

For example, if I asked you what you are doing to fight Planned Parenthood, you are all in on the battlefield of human rights advocacy if you reply something like, "I march in the March for Life. I frequently serve as a sidewalk advocate in front of a local Planned Parenthood abortion facility. I am active in my church's Right to Life group. When I vote, I make pro-life my number one issue and I call and send emails to local, state, and national lawmakers asking them to support pro-life laws."

First of all, I sincerely thank you if you are doing any of those things. They *are* important activities in the fight to shut down Planned Parenthood. But I didn't claim you're not fighting Planned Parenthood on *a* battlefield. Clearly, you are. My assertion is you're not fighting Planned Parenthood on *the* battlefield that matters to it *the most*—the battlefield of business.

We'll get into this at a deeper level in the first section of this book, but let me briefly explain what I mean when I make the following claim: If you have a successful track record of business achievement, and your current pro-life efforts are focused primarily on the human rights aspect of pro-life, then you are engaged against Planned Parenthood on the wrong battlefield.

Embrace Your Highest and Best Use

Think about it. If you are engaged in numerous human rights advocacy pro-life activities, all of those activities can be done by pro-lifers who do not possess the business skills you have honed over many years working in the for-profit world. Therefore, when it comes to how you engage Planned Parenthood, you, and many successful business professionals like you, are furiously climbing a ladder that is leaning against the wrong wall.

I know this because, like you, I come from the for-profit business world, and I also first battled Planned Parenthood *exclusively* on the battlefield of human rights advocacy. Then in 2013, frustrated by not knowing if my pro-life efforts in human rights advocacy were actually making any difference, I decided to try a new approach. I put to work business skills I had developed over twenty-five years as a professional product marketer in the for-profit world.

The results? Since 2013, business strategies and tactics I developed and implemented have *verifiably* resulted in more than two thousand pregnant women changing their minds about getting an abortion and choosing life instead. I intentionally emphasized that word, *verifiably*, because verifiable impact is something that is sorely missing in the pro-life world. I talk more about that problem in Part II of this book.

My job in this book is to show you how to move your ladder to the right wall, to redirect your focus to the battlefield of business, where the Goliath of the abortion industry, Planned Parenthood, currently reigns supreme. And by the way, I'm not necessarily talking about you abandoning your current career to work full-time battling Planned Parenthood, though of course that is an option. As you will see in later chapters, you can continue to work full-time in your current profession and still bring your business skills and experience to bear on taking down Planned Parenthood.

It's All about Leverage

Before we get you onto the battlefield of business to take on Planned Parenthood, I want to address a thought that may have crossed your mind when I claimed the business strategies and tactics I developed and implemented have verifiably resulted in more than two thousand pregnant women changing their minds about getting an abortion and choosing life instead.

I'll wager you did a little math in your head because, well, you're a business professional! Perhaps you thought, "Brett, two thousand client wins over seven years averages to about three hundred wins per year.

That pales in comparison to Planned Parenthood's approximately three hundred and fifty thousand abortion client wins per year." Right you are! Look, to win three hundred and fifty thousand clients away from Planned Parenthood every year, it will require *business leverage*.

To me, business leverage means having *real-world, proven turnkey business systems* that professionals can invest in (either their human capital of time and talent, or their financial capital of money) instead of taking on excessive risk by building a new unproven business system from the ground up. In the for-profit world, well-known franchise models such as McDonalds and Subway are examples of such proven turnkey business systems.

With that in mind, let me return to my two thousand client win number. Here's the key: of those two thousand women, only for the first two or three women would I take most of the credit for achieving those wins—using almost exclusively my own assets of time and talent, plus my own treasure. Those two or three client wins *verified* for me that I had successfully developed a cost-effective business system that could turn abortion-seeking women away from Planned Parenthood. Once I had that verification in hand, I quickly turned my focus to leveraging that system by showing other pro-lifers how they could use the same system to achieve verifiable client wins against Planned Parenthood.

By using a proven system that I had already developed, those pro-lifers didn't have to figure out on their own how to take abortion-seeking clients away from Planned Parenthood. I had already done the work for them. They could just invest in *a proven business system*. And many did just that, resulting in the more than two thousand client wins against Planned Parenthood.

The Multiplier Effect

My purpose for this book is to show more successful businesspeople like you how to win against Planned Parenthood on the battlefield of business. Here's the good news. Effective pro-life turnkey business systems already exist that are inflicting significant damage on Planned Parenthood's business—even to the point of shutting them down in certain locations.

Now the bad news. Those successful pro-life business systems are currently grossly underutilized. Why? I believe it's because tens of thousands, perhaps hundreds of thousands, of successful business professionals like you are not even aware those business systems exist. And without that awareness, it's unlikely you have even considered that your hard-earned business skills could be put to use to enhance and expand those systems in order to inflict massive damage on Planned Parenthood's business operations.

In this book, I will make you aware of those systems and show you how to put your 3T assets to use to successfully shut down Goliath Planned Parenthood. Now you may be thinking, "Brett, wait a minute. I can't shut down Planned Parenthood on my own!" You are right about that. But consider the following simple math. Let's say you invest your 3T assets in the proven-effective pro-life turnkey business systems I reveal to you in this book. Further, let's say that over time, the return on your investments results in one incremental client win (defined as an abortion-seeking woman choosing life instead of abortion) per week versus Planned Parenthood, or about fifty client wins per year. Now think about this. If other successful pro-life business professionals like you *also* achieved fifty incremental client wins per year, how many successful business professionals would it take to redirect *all* abortion-seeking women away from Planned Parenthood?

Let's do the math. Planned Parenthood reported 354,871 abortions for the year 2019. Again, assuming a pro-life business professional like you could achieve 50 client wins per year, in other words take away 50 of Planned Parenthood's abortion-seeking clients, it would take 7,097

(354,871 divided by 50) pro-life business professionals to take away *all* of Planned Parenthood's abortion clients.

Notes: (1) I realize it's an overly simplistic example, but my point is to make clear that most successful business professionals who are pro-life have no idea the massive impact they could exert on Planned Parenthood's business operations. (2) Yes, I'm aware Planned Parenthood accounts for less than half of all abortions in the United States. However, it is the flagship for the abortion industry, and I believe when we shut down Goliath Planned Parenthood, the rest of the abortion industry will fall with it. Are there at least 7,097 talented, experienced business professionals in our country who could put their 3T assets to use to each win 50 abortion-seeking clients away from Planned Parenthood every year?

I believe the answer is a resounding **YES**! When you, me, and thousands of other successful business professionals who are pro-life implement the strategies contained in this book, we will engage Planned Parenthood with an overwhelming show of force, and the day will come when we will shut down Planned Parenthood on the battlefield of business. When we do that, at long last, the stone from David's sling will lodge deep into Goliath Planned Parenthood's forehead, and Planned Parenthood will crash to the ground in a humiliating *final* defeat.

Time is of the essence. Let's get to it!

Brett Attebery

December 8, 2021

Dallas, TX

P.S. You are a busy professional, so I created an executive summary for you that immediately follows this introduction. In the executive summary, I attempted to capture the essence of the key concepts contained in each chapter of this book. I recommend you study the executive summary first to quickly gain a basic understanding of the arguments presented in the book.

Executive Summary

In what follows, you will find the Bottom Line summaries of each chapter.

Chapter One

The primary objective of the Pro-Life Movement is to influence the overturning of laws that allow human abortion. Successfully overturning such laws impacts Planned Parenthood's ability to *supply* abortion services, but has less impact on the *demand* for abortion services.

Chapter Two

It is unlikely that overturning *Roe v. Wade* will have a large impact on reducing the number of total abortions nationwide.

Chapter Three

The abortion pill is gradually replacing first-trimester surgical abortions (aspiration abortions) as Planned Parenthood's core product offering. It is plausible that current legal restrictions on the sale and distribution of the abortion pill could be lifted in the future. If that happens, Planned Parenthood could convert its abortion pill business into a mail-order business, possibly circumventing much of the expected negative impact the overturning of *Roe v. Wade* would have on Planned Parenthood's traditional brick-and-mortar surgical abortion business.

Chapter Four

You should continue investing (time, talent, treasure) in organizations leading the Pro-Life Movement because they impact Planned Parenthood's ability to supply abortion services—what I call the supply side of the business equation. However, you can achieve greater return on investment (ROI) by concentrating your investment capital (time, talent, treasure) on the demand side of the business equation.

Chapter Five

Pro-life pregnancy centers have the potential to beat Planned Parenthood at business, but currently lose the vast majority of client prospects to Planned Parenthood. The cause for this massive competitive underperformance is that the typical pro-life pregnancy center does not compete against Planned Parenthood as a business.

Chapter Six

The fact that pro-life pregnancy centers significantly outnumber abortion facilities isn't very meaningful from a business perspective because the typical abortion facility has a dominant market share versus the typical pro-life pregnancy center. Pro-life pregnancy centers in general, from the first locations established in the 1970s to new centers built recently, were not established based on business principles of serving clients and competing to win clients away from abortion facilities. Instead, pro-life pregnancy centers operate principally on the same fundamentals that motivate the Pro-Life Movement: the right to life for preborn human beings.

Chapter Seven

In a certain sense, the Pro-Life Movement can claim it is "winning" because abortion numbers have dropped by about half in the past thirty years. But total annual abortion numbers are still almost 1 million, so it's probably more accurate to say the Pro-Life Movement is "not losing as badly" as in the past. The conclusion for the Pro-Life Business Industry (PLBI), on the other hand, is clear: the PLBI is losing, badly, as measured by market share. The PLBI must stay focused on one key performance indicator (KPI)—market share—measured by how many women who wanted an abortion ultimately choose the services of a pro-life pregnancy center versus how many women choose the abortion services of a facility like Planned Parenthood.

Chapter Eight

To win the market share battle against Planned Parenthood and the abortion industry, pro-life pregnancy centers must hire team members who are effective at selling—meaning successfully *encouraging* women who want an abortion to instead become clients of a pro-life pregnancy center and then choose life instead of abortion. One of the main reasons typical pro-life pregnancy centers suffer from low market share is because they are not clear about who they actually serve. In answering the question "What problem do you solve and for whom do you solve it?" they will answer that they serve both the preborn baby and the pregnant woman. The first step pro-life pregnancy centers in the PLBI must take to eventually achieve significant market share gains against Planned Parenthood and the abortion industry is to focus solely on solving problems for pregnant women who want an abortion.

Chapter Nine

A pro-life pregnancy center's client **IS NOT** the preborn human being. A pro-life pregnancy center's client **IS** the woman who experiences fear because of an unexpected pregnancy and then seeks to abort her preborn baby. The majority of individuals on the teams of pro-life pregnancy centers are overly focused on the moral issue of killing a preborn human in its mother's womb. In order to have increased success—as measured by market share—against Planned Parenthood and the abortion industry, a pro-life pregnancy center should singularly and obsessively focus its marketing and sales efforts on answering a woman's WIIFM question in a way that leads her to say, "Now I see that what you're offering is the best option *for me.*"

Chapter Ten

Planned Parenthood's product, abortion services, is so attractive to women because **it gives them exactly what they think they want**: to return to the way things were before they became pregnant. One of the reasons Planned Parenthood's abortion product wins in the market, as measured by market share, is because on a subconscious level, it clearly answers the question on the woman's mind: **What does getting an abortion mean for** ***me*****? Pro-life pregnancy centers can counter that by** answering, in a compelling way, the competing question that is on the woman's mind: **What does choosing life for this baby mean for** ***me*****?** Offering a pro-life product that gives an attractive answer to that question moves a pro-life pregnancy center from having a marketing and sales approach that is defensive in orientation, to putting an offense on the field that seeks to empower women. Pro-life pregnancy centers in the PLBI will win more battles against Planned Parenthood to the extent they can reposition pro-life services as meeting a woman's physiological and safety needs *and also* empower her by meeting her needs for love and belonging, esteem, and self-actualization.

Chapter Eleven

To gain market share against Planned Parenthood and the abortion industry, pro-life pregnancy centers in the PLBI need to excel at the four fundamental elements of marketing known as the 4 Ps: Product, Price, Placement (i.e., distribution), and Promotion.

Currently, most centers don't commit to excellence at all of the 4 Ps, believing that the attractiveness of their "choose life" services (our product saves lives!) will make them successful. Pro-life pregnancy centers fail to promote because they typically consider advertising an unnecessary expense instead of a nonnegotiable investment.

Chapter Twelve

ThriVe Women's Express Healthcare, a pro-life pregnancy center in St. Louis, Missouri, has proven that it is possible to compete against and beat Planned Parenthood, *even without* Roe v. Wade *being overturned*. The foundation of ThriVe's success is excellent marketing—all 4 Ps of ThriVe's marketing are congruent with a young woman's mindset that abortion is a medical choice, not a moral one. The foundation of the foundation of ThriVe's excellent marketing is authentic, empowering Christ-centered LOVE offered to young women who become ThriVe clients. ThriVe offers its investors a superior ROI in both *effectiveness* and *cost-effectiveness*. In 2019, for example, ThriVe saved 1,692 babies from abortion at a cost of $1,200 per life. ThriVe's business model is designed to be easily expanded to other cities.

Chapter Thirteen

Most pro-life pregnancy centers are not staffed with team members who possess the marketing skills and experience necessary to win the market share battle against Planned Parenthood. To solve this problem, a center's board of directors should find team members who are skilled at marketing.

Chapter Fourteen

You must carefully discern between pro-life pregnancy centers whose "why" clearly indicates they are all in on empowering women experiencing unexpected pregnancies, versus centers that are so enamored with "what" they do, they can't even clearly articulate their why. Many pro-life pregnancy centers have "gone medical," meaning they have converted their operations from only providing young women with "resources" to providing them with comprehensive women's healthcare services. However, *if not marketed based on a compelling why* that resonates psychologically and spiritually with what young women really desire—the things at the top of Maslow's hierarchy of needs: freedom, happiness, success, self-actualization—it's unlikely the medical model will succeed as a competitive counter to Planned Parenthood.

Chapter Fifteen

Effective brand marketing is a two-way street whereby companies must bring the voice of the customer (VOC) into the brand creation process. However, before creating your company's brand, your prospective client must first know *the kind of thing you offer* and how that thing can improve his or her life—in other words, your product or service must fit into a *category* that is known by your prospective client. Remember: *If women don't know about pro-life pregnancy centers before they face an unexpected pregnancy, then women won't go to pro-life pregnancy centers when they face an unexpected pregnancy.* If a viable national pro-life pregnancy center brand or brands emerged, they could run brand marketing campaigns for their centers that achieve two goals through one campaign: raising awareness about the pro-life pregnancy center category and the women-empowering benefits centers offer, and at the same time branding their business names as the leading centers that actually provide the services—two birds with one stone.

Chapter Sixteen

Most young women have already been "pre-sold" on abortion services offered by Planned Parenthood and the abortion industry, but some women will still use their cell phones to search the Internet for additional information about how to get an abortion. When they do, pro-life pregnancy centers can use direct-response marketing to intervene and redirect abortion-seeking women away from Planned Parenthood and into the compassionate empowering care offered by the centers. The pro-life organization Heroic Media (https://heroicmedia.org) offers a direct response marketing service—**OAASYS**™ (**O**n-demand **A**lternatives to **A**bortion **SYS**tem)—that gives pro-life philanthropists the opportunity to sponsor direct response internet ads that redirect abortion-seeking women away from Planned Parenthood, connecting them instead to highly skilled pro-life pregnancy centers.

Chapter Seventeen

In general, pro-lifers praise those who work full-time in the pro-life movement based on how hard they try (intentions) to stop abortion, rather than how measurably successful (results) they are at actually stopping abortion. A pro-life pregnancy center's board of directors tends to evaluate the center's performance based on how hard the center's team members are *trying* rather than using objective analytical measurements such as market share that would reveal whether the team at the center is actually *succeeding*. The antidote to remedy investing based on intentions rather than results is for pro-life philanthropists to only invest in centers that show the most promising potential for saving the greatest number of babies' lives at the lowest cost possible.

Chapter Eighteen

The PLBI is not currently structured in a way that holds pro-life pregnancy centers accountable to winning the market share battle against Planned Parenthood. For the typical pro-life pregnancy center, both the board of directors and the team operating the center are *deeply emotionally invested* and passionate about the pro-life cause—not necessarily about measuring success by keeping score using market share metrics. However, remember that almost all of a center's revenue comes from investments (e.g., donations) by committed pro-life philanthropists. Therefore, those philanthropists can yield tremendous influence over a center. If a group of a center's philanthropists—a group that accounts for a substantial amount of the center's donation revenue—has the courage to demand the center change its strategy to the point of being willing to pull its investments, then there is a chance that the center's board of directors will implement a new strategy that focuses on the center achieving a *consistent increase in market share*, as measured by the number of lives saved from abortion relative to the number of abortions performed at Planned Parenthood.

Chapter Nineteen

Currently there is no objective source of information revealing the market share performance of individual pro-life pregnancy centers. If such an objective source of information existed, then pro-life philanthropists could direct their philanthropic capital into high-performing pro-life pregnancy centers, as well as take their money out of pro-life pregnancy centers that consistently perform poorly. Such a change would transform the PLBI from a conglomeration of thousands of very small, independent, single-facility, pro-life pregnancy center nonprofit organizations into one or perhaps several multilocation pro-life pregnancy center nonprofit organizations that could successfully compete against Planned Parenthood on a national scale.

Chapter Twenty

Supply-side investments that seek to restrict access to abortion by way of electing legislators to change abortion laws are *extremely risky from an ROI perspective*—it is likely your investment will achieve very little return. On the other hand, demand-side investments in the right pro-life pregnancy centers will give you *a guaranteed ROI* whereby you will receive frequent proof of lives saved from abortion—sometimes even on a weekly basis. Therefore, you should *rebalance your pro-life philanthropic investment portfolio* to put the majority of your investments in the demand side—the PLBI—rather than the supply side. Frequent and verified ROI from your pro-life demand-side investments can provide you with both the emotional satisfaction and the logical justification to not grow weary with your long-term, speculative, pro-life supply-side investments.

Chapter Twenty-One

The vast majority of the twenty-five hundred to three thousand pro-life pregnancy centers in the United States are not really competing against Planned Parenthood. Most centers are actually what we call Pregnancy Resource Centers (PRCs), and their primary mission is to *provide material assistance to those women who are already likely to carry their pregnancies to term*. You must weed out PRCs until you find "investable" pro-life pregnancy centers that are actually having success encouraging abortion-determined women to change their minds and choose life for their preborn babies. Do not use a center's IRS Form 990 data as a factor in your analysis, as a center's financial accounting results, especially its "program" spending, may not be relevant at all to its actual success at competing against Planned Parenthood for abortion-determined clients. After conducting thorough due diligence, you may find that no competitive centers exist in your local community. If so, you have three choices: (1) Easiest: Invest in a center outside your local community, (2) Harder: Organize philanthropists who fund a center in your local community to leverage their influence to demand the center's board of directors change the center's strategy to become more competitive (3) Hardest: Start your own pro-life pregnancy center using an existing, proven successful pro-life pregnancy center turnkey business system. *Remember that you must view pro-life pregnancy centers as competitive organizations if you want to help them win, as measured by market share, against Planned Parenthood.*

PART I:
WHY THE PRO-LIFE MOVEMENT WILL NOT END ABORTION

You want to end abortion, as do I. This book is going to show you how you can put your 3T assets (Time, Talent, and Treasure) to use to do exactly that.

But before we get into those details, I need to shift your perception a bit. You see, it's likely you already consider yourself a card-carrying member of the Pro-Life Movement. Congrats! I am a proud card-carrying member myself! However, I strongly believe *the Pro-Life Movement, by itself, will not end abortion*.

I know this is a controversial position, so in Part I, I want to present you with the reasons for my stance. Please do not misunderstand: I believe the Pro-Life Movement plays an indispensable role in ending abortion in our country. That said, I believe the Pro-Life Movement is very good at doing certain things, but is not so good at doing many other things that will be required to shut down Planned Parenthood and the abortion industry.

Even so, I think there is a tendency for pro-lifers to expect the Pro-Life Movement to lead on *all* the battlefields in the war against Planned Parenthood. That expectation is rarely questioned, but in Part I, I reveal to you why I believe asking the Pro-Life Movement to lead the fight against abortion on all battlefields is a serious strategic blunder.

CHAPTER ONE: THE *PRIMARY* OBJECTIVE OF THE PRO-LIFE MOVEMENT

> *We hold these truths to be self-evident, that all men are created equal, that they are endowed by their Creator with certain unalienable rights, that among these are life, liberty, and the pursuit of happiness.* US Declaration of Independence

In 1973, the Supreme Court of the United States blew it. Somehow, it found in the US Constitution a "right" to intentionally kill preborn human beings in their mothers' wombs. In the *Roe v. Wade* decision, the Supreme Court decreed that federal statutes took legal precedence over state laws concerning abortion. No sooner was this egregiously immoral law imposed on Americans than the Pro-Life Movement was born with the express goal of overturning it. And the Pro-Life Movement's work of overturning *Roe v. Wade* continues to this day.

A Right to Life

The central theme that guides the Pro-Life Movement's strategies is that all human beings have a *right to life*. This right to life is the Pro-Life Movement's calling card, and it is a truth that is self-evident to many American citizens, particularly, but not exclusively, to those who are faith based. Here's the key: declaring that all human beings have a right to life is a *moral argument about human rights*. As such, the Pro-Life Movement is a human rights movement. Therefore, the *primary* objective of the Pro-Life Movement is first, to overturn all existing laws that allow abortion, and, second, to establish new laws that provide unequivocal legal protection to preborn humans.

Getting Started in the Pro-Life Movement

For many pro-lifers, making a public stand against unjust laws that allow the killing of preborn humans is the entryway into active participation in the Pro-Life Movement. The premier event for publicly expressing one's opposition to pro-abortion laws and support for pro-life laws is the annual March for Life in Washington, DC. Perhaps you too first engaged in pro-life by participating in this event or a local one like it, or by supporting the event in some way. Marching in the March for Life was how I got started in pro-life advocacy back in 2010.

Of course, publicly advocating for overturning unjust laws and replacing them with just laws is highly admirable. However, as I cover in the next chapter, overturning laws that allow abortion and passing laws that protect a preborn human's right to life are *only part of the equation* pro-lifers need to solve in order to end abortion in our country. I didn't understand this initially, but as my involvement in the Pro-Life Movement deepened, I came to see that there is another critical part of the equation we pro-lifers must solve. In particular, we have to address how to effectively outcompete the business responsible for almost half of the abortions in the United States: Planned Parenthood.

They Are All Business

The more I learned about Planned Parenthood and its operations, it became clearer to me that, while it's true Planned Parenthood invests significantly in advocating for pro-abortion laws, it does so *primarily* to advance its own *business interests*. The "my body, my choice" slogan—or whatever catchy phrase of the day is promulgated by advocates of human abortion—may display a veneer of human rights advocacy by promoting the advancement of women's rights, but consider this: Planned Parenthood regularly pushes the directors of its clinics to meet or exceed *abortion quotas*.

As a business professional, you know what that means—Planned Parenthood clinic directors have to "make their numbers." That is the language of business. *Planned Parenthood's primary strategic thrust is to grow its abortion business*. Its seeming concern about advancing women's rights ("my body, my choice," etc.), is a public relations tactic. Through its well-funded public relations programs, Planned Parenthood seeks to influence both the passing and the maintenance of laws that support its business interests—specifically, its ability to *supply* abortion services without restriction.

To the extent the Pro-Life Movement is successful in its mission to overturn laws that allow abortion, it impacts Planned Parenthood's ability to *supply* abortion services. Of course, the passing of laws that restrict Planned Parenthood's ability to supply abortion services is important. However, you, as an experienced business professional, know that supply is only part of the business equation.

There is also *demand*. My contention is that Planned Parenthood's *primary* strategy to grow its abortion business is to increase demand for its abortion services, and its *secondary* strategy is to use its public relations programs to influence the passing or maintenance of laws that protect its ability to supply abortion services.

On the other hand, the Pro-Life Movement's primary strategy is to restrict or eliminate abortion services, and its secondary strategy—as I argue in this book, a strategy it pursues very poorly—is to decrease demand for abortion services. *To shut down Planned Parenthood, you can't focus only on restricting supply of abortion services. You also have to decrease demand for abortion services.*

Cutting Off Supply

But for the moment, let's stay focused on the issue of supply. Remember: when the Pro-Life Movement successfully overturns laws that allow abortion, it restricts Planned Parenthood's ability to *supply* its abortion services. The question is to what extent overturning abortion laws will impact Planned Parenthood's ability to supply abortion services. A little? A lot? Total? Partial?

The Pro-Life Movement works incessantly to overturn any and all pro-abortion laws. Some of the laws it overturns have a small impact on restricting supply and some have a large impact. But the prize the Pro-Life Movement pursues with the greatest enthusiasm is the overturning of the US Supreme Court decision known as *Roe v. Wade*. If the US Supreme Court overturns *Roe v. Wade*, that would unquestionably have a disruptive impact on Planned Parenthood's ability to supply abortion services.

However, that disruptive impact would very likely *not* be as earth-shattering as many pro-lifers believe. In my early days of participation in the Pro-Life Movement, when I was just trying to figure out what was going on, I too believed overturning *Roe v. Wade* would be all-encompassing—it would end abortion in our country. As we will see in the next chapter, this is *not* the case. Not even close.

Chapter One BOTTOM LINE

The primary objective of the Pro-Life Movement is to overturn pro-abortion laws. Successfully overturning such laws impacts Planned Parenthood's ability to *supply* abortion services, but has less impact on the *demand* for abortion services.

CHAPTER TWO: OVERTURNING *ROE V. WADE* WILL NOT SHUT DOWN PLANNED PARENTHOOD

We sometimes cannot see the forest for the trees.
Based on a sixteenth-century English proverb

Overturning *Roe v. Wade* would send the issue of legal abortion back to the states, where each state government would establish abortion laws that applied within its own borders. In other words, overturning *Roe v. Wade* would *localize*, in a sense, the legality of abortion, instead of a federal mandate that applies nationwide. You may have already known this, and if so, congratulations!

Does It Really Matter?

But do all pro-lifers know? I don't think so, because I know I wasn't aware of this when I first became active in the Pro-Life Movement. These days, at the conclusion of the annual March for Life, or any of the other pro-life marches that take place in cities around the country, a question always comes into my mind as I view the throngs of passionate pro-lifers advocating for the "right to life." The question is, "How many of those marching truly understand what the impact of overturning *Roe v. Wade* would be?"

I would wager more than half of those marching believe that overturning *Roe v. Wade* would completely end legal abortion in the United States. I wish that were correct, but alas, it isn't so. Why are so many unaware of what would actually happen should *Roe v. Wade* be overturned? Now that I've been active in the Pro-Life Movement for about a decade, one of my criticisms of the movement is that while going all in on overturning *Roe v. Wade*, the movement rarely clarifies for pro-lifers exactly what the impact would be in terms of the number of human lives that would be saved from abortion.

There is little doubt that it would have a significant impact, but you, as a business professional, would like that impact quantified. Quantified scenarios are little discussed within the Pro-Life Movement. Why not? I don't know the exact reasons, but I can offer a guess. I believe it's because, as discussed in the previous chapter, the Pro-Life Movement is fighting a *moral* battle. And overturning *Roe v. Wade* would undoubtedly be an enormously significant moral win. But again, an inquiring business mind like yours wants to know how many preborn human lives it would save.

Can You Quantify That for Me, Please?

How many lives would actually be saved from abortion if *Roe v. Wade* was overturned? Unfortunately, research suggests not as many as you might think. In a 2019 article on *National Review*'s website titled, "In a Post-*Roe* World, Pro-Lifers Would Still Have a Lot of Work Left to Do," David French refers to a study by researchers from Middlebury College, the Guttmacher Institute, and the Bixby Center for Global Reproductive Health. The study found that in "more than half of states, including the entire West Coast and Northeast," overturning *Roe* would have no real effect on abortion access.

Let that sink in for a moment. Still, even that statement doesn't quantify how many lives would be saved. I will let David French answer by directly quoting from his article:

> So, what does this mean in terms of real numbers? The study estimates that post-*Roe*, the abortion rate would be 32.8 percent lower "for the regions at high risk of banning abortions" and 12.8 percent lower nationwide. In raw numbers that's more than 100,000 fewer abortions per year, a pro-life triumph. But am I the only pro-lifer who is sobered rather than enthused by the idea that ending Roe would cut nationwide abortions by less than 13 percent? How could that be? Haven't states passed waves of pro-life legislation? Wouldn't abortion bans have greater effect? Not really. A glance at state-by-state Guttmacher data on abortion rates tells us why. The states that have sought to ban or dramatically restrict abortion generally already have extremely low abortion rates. The big states of the West and Northeast that don't restrict abortion have much higher rates of the procedure.

I share French's sentiments that a reduction of only 13 percent is a sobering reality. I invite you to read the study for yourself. You can find the report by searching online using the title, "Changes in Abortion Access and Incidence in a Post-*Roe* World."

It Matters. A lot. But ...

Returning to the question of how many lives would be saved from abortion by overturning *Roe v. Wade*, according to the research, it would be *around 100,000 lives per year*. That's 274 lives saved from abortion *every day* on average. Now that would be an amazing achievement! So absolutely, making our voices heard through marching and other forms of pro-life advocacy matters, a lot.

But if the researchers are correct in their forecast, the lives saved from *overturning* Roe v. Wade *would still account for less than 13 percent of the total number of abortions* in the United States. A reduction of only 13 percent seems a little depressing considering how much time and talent (human capital), plus treasure (financial capital) the Pro-Life Movement invests every year in an effort to bring about laws that will protect the right to life of preborn humans. Now you may argue that the study is just a model based on many assumptions that could turn out to be wrong. I would agree with you, but wrong to what degree?

If *Roe v. Wade* is overturned, even if abortions are reduced by *triple* the number forecasted in the report, it would still mean a reduction of less than half of abortions nationwide.

And That's Not All

In addition, there are other scenarios to consider. These are the ones I think are most important.

1. **SCENARIO: Political winds blow back the other direction**

You have likely noticed how pro-abortion advocates push fervently for laws that will keep abortion "accessible." Even if *Roe v. Wade* is overturned, who's to say that eventually the political winds won't blow back hard the other direction, and a law similar to *Roe v. Wade* will be reinstated at the federal level? The same could be said even if the Pro-Life Movement takes it a step further than overturning *Roe v. Wade* and successfully influences the passing of a law at the federal level that protects all preborn human life. While such a law would undoubtedly save millions of preborn human lives, remember that if *Roe v. Wade* can be overturned, so can any national pro-life law.

2. **SCENARIO: Federal defunding of Planned Parenthood doesn't work**

If *Roe v. Wade* is overturned, it will likely bring with it total "defunding" of Planned Parenthood at the federal level. Would that have a significant impact on Planned Parenthood's business? Indeed it would, causing Planned Parenthood to lose as much as 40 percent of its total annual income. Such a sudden, large loss of income would be devastating to most businesses. But again, I think the Pro-Life Movement's focus on defunding Planned Parenthood, even though it would indeed impact its business, is more of a moral victory than a practical one.

Why? For the simple reason that Planned Parenthood has multiple streams of income. To illustrate, in its most recent annual report (2019–20) at the time of this writing, Planned Parenthood's primary income streams, amounts, and percentages were as follows:

Government:	**$618 million, 38%**
Fees for Patient Services:	**$370 million, 23%**
Private Donations:	**$510 million, 31%**
Other:	**$143 million, 8%**

For arguments sake, let's say the income stream from government sources consisted of all federal funding. (It doesn't, by the way. There are also state and local government components.) Much of that loss of funding could potentially be made up for by the pro-abortion states that would legislate to keep abortion services legal within their own borders. Pro-abortion state governments could use tax increases to force citizens of those states to pay for increased funding to Planned Parenthood. In addition, for the private donations income stream, it is likely Planned Parenthood could substantially increase donations from private citizens and foundations.

Consider the following: Planned Parenthood claims to have more than 1.1 million active individual donors. If *all* of Planned Parenthood's $618 million from government sources suddenly dried up, it would require $562 annually per donor on average, or $47 per month, from Planned Parenthood's active donor pool to make up for that loss. Achieving that sounds plausible to me. Imagine the power of a Planned Parenthood marketing campaign to its existing donors stating that so-called reproductive rights were under attack and increased financial support was required to defend those rights and launch a counteroffensive.

Not only do I believe such a campaign would motivate substantial increased giving by current Planned Parenthood donors, but I think it would also attract a large number of new donors to Planned Parenthood's cause. And don't forget such a campaign would likely also attract substantial increased giving from wealthy politically left-leaning philanthropists.

3. **SCENARIO: Planned Parenthood goes all in on medication abortion (aka the "abortion pill")**

From a business perspective, I believe this scenario is the most impactful in terms of its potential to blunt the life-saving impact of the overturning of *Roe v. Wade*. If *Roe* is overturned, the Pro-Life movement generally assumes that it will *immediately* have a devastating impact on Planned Parenthood's abortion business. In my view, that assumption is not necessarily true. I think the Pro-Life Movement's view is based on *linear thinking*—meaning the Pro-Life Movement forecasts the impact of overturning *Roe v. Wade* based on the way Planned Parenthood has *historically* offered its abortion services.

What will happen if Planned Parenthood completely shifts its product strategy? For example, what if Planned Parenthood can offer women an "enhanced" abortion product? And what if that enhanced abortion product effectively circumvents many of the restrictions the overturning of *Roe v. Wade* would place on the abortion product Planned Parenthood currently offers most often? In fact, that shift in product strategy has already been in process for many years, and has been accelerating in the past few years. The enhanced abortion product? Medication abortion, more commonly known as the "abortion pill."

The Newcomer Is Gaining Ground. Fast.

In the past five years, use of the "abortion pill" has increased substantially relative to other abortion methods (details in the next chapter). In business terms, this is simply a shift in Planned Parenthood's "product mix" to increase the use of one method of abortion while decreasing the use of another. From a product marketing perspective, the abortion pill would be considered an important "innovation" for Planned Parenthood and the abortion industry. While Planned Parenthood's increased use of the abortion pill has not gone unnoticed by the Pro-Life Movement, from a business perspective, I don't think the movement has carefully thought through the long-term implications. I believe the impact of this product shift to the abortion pill could be substantial. We explore the implications of this in the next chapter.

Chapter Two BOTTOM LINE

It is unlikely that overturning *Roe v. Wade* will have a large impact on reducing the number of total abortions nationwide.

CHAPTER THREE: THE EVOLUTION OF THE ABORTION "PRODUCT"

A good hockey player plays where the puck is. A great hockey player plays where the puck is going to be.
Wayne Gretzky

As you've undoubtedly picked up on by now, from a business perspective, I think the Pro-Life Movement vastly overestimates the impact overturning *Roe v. Wade* will have on Planned Parenthood's business operations. From a strategic planning perspective, the main culprit affecting the Pro-Life Movement is *linear thinking*—or, as Wayne Gretzky might say in the quote that begins this chapter, playing where the puck *is*, instead of playing where the puck *is going to be*.

As a successful business professional, you have likely experienced or witnessed what can happen to a business if it gets stuck competing where the puck is while its strongest competitor quickly moves to where the puck is going to be. It's not a pretty outcome. For example, think about what has happened to big-box department stores like Sears in their competition with Amazon.com. Amazon.com skated to where the puck was going to be, while Sears and other department stores got stuck playing where the puck was.

We've all seen the result: It's game, set, and match to Amazon.com. Successful businesses never stop trying to understand what their customers will want in the future—where the puck is going to be—in order to start developing, *right now*, products that will successfully meet their customers' desires.

Where Is the Puck Going to Be?

How does this concept apply to Planned Parenthood? Planned Parenthood has not been sitting still, embracing a strategy of wishful thinking, hoping *Roe v. Wade* won't be overturned. On the contrary, it has made strategic moves in many areas of its business because it knows overturning *Roe v. Wade* is a plausible scenario. But I believe one strategic move Planned Parenthood made will have the largest impact on its future business prospects: its strategic shift toward conducting more abortions by use of the abortion pill than by surgical abortion.

I believe the abortion pill, not in-clinic surgical abortions, represents the future of Planned Parenthood's abortion services. And, in a sense, that future is already here. As I stated in the previous chapter, the shift in the abortion industry's "product mix" from surgical abortion to abortion pill has been going on for some time. According to research from the Guttmacher Institute, the number of abortions completed by use of the abortion pill increased 73 percent between 2008 and 2017. The same research reveals that in 2017, the abortion pill accounted for 39 percent of all abortions (www.guttmacher.org/evidence-you-can-use/medication-abortion#) (www.guttmacher.org/article/2020/09/20th-anniversary-medication-abortion-antiabortion-politicians-are-trying-ban-it). Following the trend of those historical data, I think it's fair to say that the abortion pill now likely accounts for more than 40 percent of all abortions.

A No-Brainer Product

What is Planned Parenthood's thinking behind this product shift? From a product marketing perspective, I think the abortion pill is a no-brainer for Planned Parenthood. Why? Because I think it's a reasonable assumption that most people would prefer taking a pill to undergoing an invasive surgical procedure.

Imagine if a major pharmaceutical company announced tomorrow it had developed a pill that replaced the need for quadruple bypass surgery for those suffering from serious heart disease. Assuming the price for the pill was the same as the price for the surgery, which do you think most heart disease patients would choose? Easy decision, right? The same goes for the choice between the abortion pill and surgical abortion. Abortion delivered in the form of a pill offers a woman a much more private option compared to a surgical abortion.

And, of course, in its marketing programs, the abortion industry emphasizes the privacy aspect of the abortion pill. It uses terms such as "self-managed abortion" and "DIY abortion" when describing the "benefits" of a woman using the abortion pill. Therefore, from a marketing perspective, it seems obvious to me an overwhelming majority of young women would find the abortion pill a much more attractive product option than surgical abortion.

It's Not Personal. It's Just Business.

Even so, just because a woman will likely prefer the abortion pill over surgical abortion, we can't assume the abortion pill is better for Planned Parenthood's business from a financial perspective. For example, of all of the women who seek an abortion, what if the number of women eligible to use the abortion pill (what we call the Total Available Market [TAM]) is small? Or even if the TAM is large, what if the profit margins are much lower for the abortion pill than for surgical abortion?

You can be sure Planned Parenthood takes all factors concerning "profit potential" into consideration when developing its product strategy because *Planned Parenthood is a business, and it plays to win*. And like all successful businesses, Planned Parenthood seeks to offer products with proven potential to accelerate growth of its sales and profits.

A Big Market ...

With that in mind, what is the TAM of abortion-seeking women eligible to use the abortion pill? Eligibility to use the abortion pill is determined by how far along a woman is in her pregnancy. Currently the abortion pill can only be used up to the tenth week of pregnancy. The tenth week time limitation means the abortion pill must only be used for first-trimester abortions. Of all abortions, how many are first-trimester abortions? According to the Centers for Disease Control and Prevention (CDC), 88 percent of all abortions occur during the first trimester. That means almost nine out of every ten abortion-seeking women are eligible to use the abortion pill instead of undergoing a first trimester surgical abortion (an aspiration abortion). Clearly, nine out of ten is a large market, so that checks the TAM box.

... With Big Profits

But what about profit margins? According to the Guttmacher Institute, Planned Parenthood sells the abortion pill to women for about $530 on average—a five-to-six-time markup on its product cost of $90. So each sale of an abortion pill generates around $440 in profit for Planned Parenthood. That is a *very* healthy profit margin. But is the abortion pill as profitable as the type of surgical abortion (an aspiration abortion) Planned Parenthood would typically offer a woman in the first trimester of her pregnancy?

It's very likely at least as profitable. Planned Parenthood charges about the same price for the two products—aspiration abortion and medication abortion—and I don't think I would be going too far out on a limb to say that Planned Parenthood's total costs to provide an aspiration abortion are likely significantly higher than the costs to provide an abortion pill. Why? The labor costs of a first-trimester aspiration abortion (the total labor costs of the abortionist plus attending assistants) are likely significantly more than the $90 product cost of the abortion pill.

But Isn't There More to the Bottom Line?

You would be right to point out this example represents only gross profit because we haven't included other operating costs (i.e., overhead). I would agree with you. We need to go a level deeper and compare not just gross profits but also the required overhead expenses for Planned Parenthood to operate its abortion pill business versus its first-trimester surgical abortion (aspiration abortion) business.

Watch Out Overhead!

To kick off that analysis, I'll ask you the following: in your business experience, what overhead cost line item on the profit and loss (P&L) statement typically accounts for the largest percentage of total operating costs? The answer is labor expenses. Recall that a surgical abortion requires a physical medical facility and people to manage it.

How does that compare to the overhead expenses required to offer the abortion pill? Planned Parenthood could operate its abortion pill business by simply taking orders on a website or by phone and shipping those orders to customers. Under that scenario, labor costs would consist primarily of laborers required to pick, pack, and ship the abortion pill to a woman's residential address, and a low-cost warehouse operation to store inventory of the pill.

Thus, I believe total overhead costs for Planned Parenthood to operate its abortion pill business could be substantially lower than the overhead costs to operate its surgical abortion business. If I'm right, then the two key drivers of overall company profit for Planned Parenthood—gross profit and low overhead expenses—are heavily in favor of the abortion pill business versus the surgical abortion business.

But Wait! That's Not How It Works!

Okay. You caught me! I tried to slip one past you! I presented what the overhead costs of the abortion pill business *could be* for Planned

Parenthood *if* it ran its abortion pill operations as a mail-order business. But *currently*, it doesn't do that because it can't, not necessarily because it doesn't want to. Many legal restrictions substantially limit how Planned Parenthood can distribute the abortion pill. And those legal restrictions place significant operating burdens on Planned Parenthood's abortion pill business, leading to an increase in overhead expenses that would not be necessary if those legal restrictions were lifted.

Here is a quick overview of some of those legal restrictions:

1. The US Food and Drug Administration (FDA) does not *currently* allow the abortion pill to be sold at retail pharmacies as a prescription drug. Women must pick up the abortion pill in person at a limited number of qualified clinics.

2. Thirty-two states *currently* require the person administering the abortion pill be a licensed physician.

3. Eighteen states *currently* prohibit the provision of the abortion pill via a virtual online visit. Women must see someone in person to receive the abortion pill.

In these examples, I emphasized the word *currently* for good reason. Go back through those legal restrictions now and ask yourself how Planned Parenthood's abortion pill business could be transformed if those restrictions were lifted. Think about the business impact if the abortion pill were available anywhere prescription drugs are sold, if prescription privileges were expanded to include licensed nurses and physician's assistants, if the abortion pill could be prescribed during a quick online teleconference instead of an in-person visit.

Is it likely the current legal restrictions on the sale and distribution of the abortion pill will be lifted? Perhaps not in the near future. But is it *plausible* those restrictions will be lifted or relaxed at some time in the future? Absolutely. Anyone who says it's not plausible is simply thinking in a linear fashion and engaging in wishful thinking.

You are a successful business professional, and like many, you have likely made business mistakes in the past that, on reflection, you can attribute to linear thinking. There aren't many highly successful business professionals who became successful by embracing the belief that "it will be that way in the future because that's the way it's always been in the past." Disruption happens in business, as in life, when things go nonlinear.

Of course, successful business professionals understand the linear flow of events in the markets in which they compete. But they *plan for the nonlinear events*. And should *Roe v. Wade* be overturned, I believe the nonlinear event that would have the greatest impact on blunting the negative impact on Planned Parenthood's business operations would be the lifting of legal restrictions on the sale and distribution of the abortion pill.

The Abortion Pill Does an End-Around on *Roe*

Why? Because it is much easier to regulate, control, and place restrictions on an abortion procedure conducted by specific people (an abortionist) at a defined location, in this case, an abortion facility. Think about how much more difficult it is to regulate, control, and place restrictions on an abortion "procedure" that no longer requires people to conduct it and doesn't have to take place in a defined location like an abortion facility. That's what you have with the abortion pill.

The abortion pill effectively frees the abortion procedure from a defined time (an appointment), at a defined place (an abortion clinic), by a defined person (an abortionist). And the scenario of governments lifting legal restrictions on the abortion pill is not as far-fetched as you might think. In fact, there are indicators it's already happening. For example, in an October 11, 2019, article in the *Los Angeles Times* titled "Abortion Medication to Be Available at California's College Health Centers under New Law" (www.latimes.com/california/story/2019-10-11/

abortion-medication-california-college-health-centers-legislation), the final paragraph in the article, in reference to Governor Gavin Newsom, reads as follows: "Newsom also signed legislation that streamlines access to birth control medication provided by Planned Parenthood, allowing women to be prescribed the drugs through an app on a smartphone. Prior to the signing of the bill, the assumption was that California law required use of videoconferencing for long-distance prescriptions."

Please note the phrase "the assumption was" in that last sentence. That is a classic example of linear thinking. And that last paragraph is not even the main point of the article! The main story in the article is about the successful passage of California Senate Bill 24, which will go into effect in 2023. California Senate Bill 24 effectively requires public universities in California to offer students the abortion pill *on campus*.

Today's "Unthinkables" Are Tomorrow's Realities

Skate to where the puck *is going to be*. And where is it going to be in terms of abortion services? We can gain insight into that by thinking about what a typical abortion-seeking woman wants. What a typical abortion-seeking woman who is early in her pregnancy wants is an easy way to conduct an affordable, "self-administered" abortion in the privacy of her own home. If Planned Parenthood could provide that, it would be a very attractive product offering.

I submit to you that, over time, it is plausible that demand for the abortion pill will be so great that both federal and state government officials will face tremendous pressure to lift many, if not all, of the current restrictions on the sale and distribution of the abortion pill. When we abandon linear thinking, it becomes clear that it is plausible to envision Planned Parenthood's abortion business becoming primarily virtual—serving the majority of its abortion customers by prescribing the abortion pill online by either an online app or live chat. This would make access to an abortion "portable" for a woman, meaning she can access the means of an abortion, the abortion pill, at any local pharmacy or Planned Parenthood office.

Under that scenario, a woman's abortion takes place wherever the woman chooses—no longer does she have to go get an abortion at an abortion facility. Again, this is a powerfully attractive product offering, and it is a scenario the Pro-Life Movement should be better preparing for to become a reality, but for the most part, it isn't. Where does that leave you? Should you pull the investment of your 3T assets out of the Pro-Life Movement and invest them elsewhere? It's an excellent question. We consider it in the next chapter.

Chapter Three BOTTOM LINE

The abortion pill is gradually replacing first-trimester surgical abortions (aspiration abortions) as Planned Parenthood's core product offering. It is plausible that current legal restrictions on the sale and distribution of the abortion pill could be lifted in the future. If that happens, Planned Parenthood could convert its abortion pill business into a mail-order business, possibly circumventing much of the expected negative impact overturning *Roe v. Wade* would have on Planned Parenthood's traditional brick-and-mortar surgical abortion business.

CHAPTER FOUR: SHOULD YOU STOP INVESTING IN THE PRO-LIFE MOVEMENT?

Wide diversification is only required when investors do not understand what they are doing. Warren Buffett

I want to pose a question to you. Assume the one thing you want to achieve more than anything with the pro-life investments of your 3T assets is to take down Planned Parenthood. Further assume that you have only one day left in your life to make investments in order to achieve your ultimate goal. In other words, you really have to make your investments count.

Now with those assumptions in mind, here's my question: what investments would you make, and how do you know those investments would have the best chance of shutting down Planned Parenthood compared to other investments? Tough question, right? Ask a random sample of one hundred pro-lifers this question, and I'll wager you'll get a hundred different answers. And that is how I view the Pro-Life Movement: millions of passionately pro-life individuals running in many different directions when it comes to their investments of Time, Talent, and Treasure, a lot of diffused energy. It's why I have, not what I would call a "love-hate" relationship with the Pro-Life Movement, but more like a "love, but frustrated" relationship. It's probably controversial to say this, but I believe the Pro-Life Movement is dominated by too much hype and sentimentality and not enough *direct evidence* of its actual impact at ending abortion.

But We're Winning! How Could You Say That?

When I criticize the Pro-Life Movement for not showing enough direct evidence of impact, the retort by pro-life advocates is often something like, "How could you say that? The Pro-Life Movement is winning because the number of annual abortions has dropped by half since their peak around 1988!" They want to know what I'm missing, and you might be thinking the same thing when you hear the impressive statistic of the number of annual abortions dropping by half over a thirty-year period. So let's dive in a little deeper so that you understand why I don't agree with the "we're winning" claim made by many leaders in the Pro-Life Movement.

First off, let's look at the data. It is true that the number of annual abortions is much lower now than it was thirty years ago in the late 1980s. You can find data on annual abortions listed on Abort73.com's website (www.abort73.com/abortion_facts/us_abortion_statistics). To calculate historical annual abortions, Abort73.com uses a combination of the two most comprehensive sources on national abortion statistics: the CDC, which publishes abortion statistics annually, and the Guttmacher Institute, which publishes abortion statistics every three years (the most recent report covers the number of annual abortions through the year 2017).

So if we take annual abortion data from Abort73.com's website and create a graph showing annual abortions over the past thirty years, here's what we see:

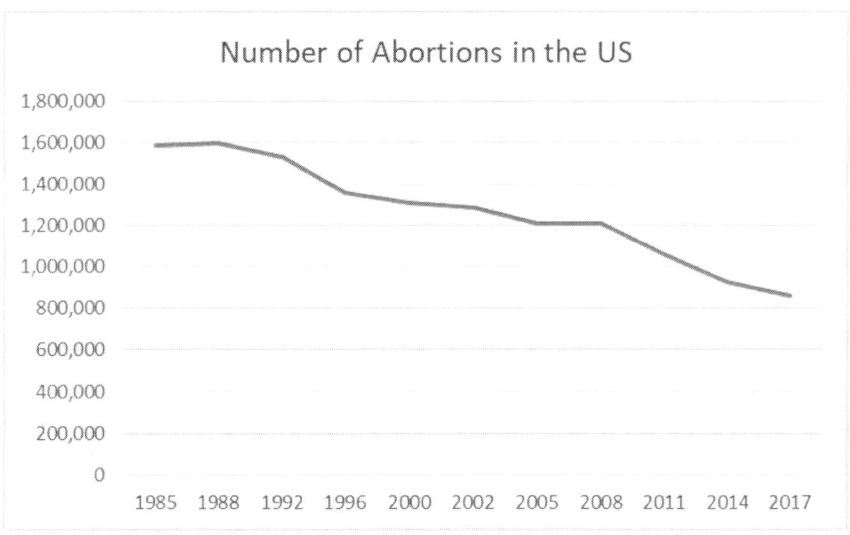

The graph visually demonstrates a very hopeful trend: annual abortion numbers have dropped from about 1.6 million in 1988 to about 850,000 in 2017. So what would happen if annual abortion numbers continued to follow the same trend line into the future? If that happened, we would expect to see a reduction in annual abortions by another 850,000 over the next thirty years, and if we started in the year 2018, that would get us to zero annual abortions starting in the year 2048!

How awesome would that be?! Even so, that would still mean many innocent preborn lives lost over the next thirty years. To estimate how many lives would be lost to abortion, I calculated how many total abortions would take place over that thirty-year period if annual abortions were reduced by exactly 28,333 each year for the next thirty years starting in 2018. The cumulative number of abortions over that thirty-year period would be 13,175,145. This is a terrible tragedy for sure, but looking at the trend line on the graph, it would seem my claim that the Pro-Life Movement is not demonstrating enough direct evidence of impact is off base.

But will that same downward sloping trend line continue? There is already evidence that it will not. Consider this cautionary note from the CDC. "From 2009 to 2018, the number, rate, and ratio of reported abortions decreased 22%, 24%, and 16%, respectively. In 2017, the total number, rate, and ratio of reported abortions decreased to historic lows for the period of analysis for all three measures. However, compared with 2017, in 2018, the total number and rate of reported abortions increased by 1%, and the abortion ratio increased by 2%" (www.cdc.gov/reproductivehealth/data_stats/abortion.htm).

Something else that doesn't seem to add up is that Americans' beliefs about abortion have not changed in a favorable pro-life direction during the thirty-year time frame in question. Consider the results of this Gallup poll (https://news.gallup.com/poll/1576/abortion.aspx):

According to Gallup's research, the number of Americans who believe abortion should be legal under any circumstance has *increased* from 24 percent in 1988, when abortion numbers hit their peak, to 32 percent in the year 2020. The number of Americans who believe abortion should never be legal under any circumstance has only increased two percentage points from 17 percent in 1988 to 19 percent in 2020. Yet we have a 50 percent drop in annual abortions over that same thirty-year period. What gives?

Of course, no one knows exactly. However, I think it makes sense to ask the question, "Is it plausible that other factors unrelated to the work of the Pro-Life Movement have contributed to the drop in the number of annual abortions?" I will offer just one example of what I think is likely a major contributing factor, but I believe there are probably others. It seems to me that one obvious variable contributing to unexpected pregnancies that could lead to a decision to pursue an abortion is frequency of sex among young people—an important consideration because approximately 70 percent of all abortions are by women between the ages of eighteen and twenty-nine years old.

Now I don't want to take us too far down a rabbit hole here, so let me cite the results of just one study, and then I invite you to do some internet research on your own. According to research carried out by Indiana University and Sweden's Karolinska Institute, the percentage of sexually *inactive* eighteen to twenty-four-year-old men increased from 18.9 percent between 2000 and 2002 to 30.9 percent between 2016 and 2018 (www.cnn.com/2020/06/12/health/young-americans-less-sex-intl-scli-wellness/index.html). That is a big increase in sexually inactive young men.

Now if research showed the reason for that increase was because young people were embracing chastity and saving sex until marriage, we would all praise God for that because that would indicate a very pro-life trend of our culture healing from a culture of death to a culture of life. But as you dive deep into the research, unfortunately that doesn't appear to be the case.

Also, you interact with our current culture every day in your own life, so you probably have already sensed that we are not exactly living within a new dawn of the expansion of a culture of life. I'll offer just one article on the topic of frequency of sex among young people, but

I invite you to do your own research and you will find an abundance of content on this topic. In the December 2018 issue of *The Atlantic* magazine, Kate Julian, in her article "The Sex Recession," offers reasons why young people today are having sex less frequently than young people of previous generations (www.theatlantic.com/magazine/archive/2018/12/the-sex-recession/573949).

The significant drop in sexual activity among young people is just one hint that the Pro-Life Movement should not claim responsibility for all of the drop in annual abortion numbers over the past thirty years. I think it is clear that other factors have played a role. And interestingly, even in the midst of the drop in overall abortion numbers, Planned Parenthood's reported abortion numbers have continued to increase year after year—reaching 354,871 abortions (one every eighty-nine seconds) reported in 2019.

Planned Parenthood and the Pro-Life Movement can't both be winning. The numbers seem to indicate Planned Parenthood is winning. Nonetheless, let's pause to give credit where credit is due. I don't think there is any doubt the activities of the Pro-Life Movement contributed to some of the drop in annual abortion numbers, and I praise God for all of those pro-life advocates who let God work through them to make that happen. We all owe those pro-life warriors an enormous debt of gratitude.

Is the Pro-Life Movement Still "Investable"?

With everything I have said so far in this book about the Pro-Life Movement, you might think I don't believe the Pro-Life Movement is worthy of your investment. That's not exactly right, but let me focus for a second on that word "worthy." If you've ever watched the TV show *Shark Tank*, you've heard celebrity investors discussing whether certain business ideas presented by entrepreneurs are "worthy" of the Sharks' investments.

The Sharks often use the phrases "investable" and "not investable" to describe various business opportunities that come before them. In the same way, I believe the Pro-Life Movement is investable, and I recommend you continue investing your 3T assets in specific organizations that lead the Pro-Life Movement. My purpose in heaping criticism on the Pro-Life Movement is to open your eyes to the fact that, while the Pro-Life Movement plays a vital role in shutting down Planned Parenthood, it can't shut it down by itself. Why not?

Because the Pro-Life Movement's primary role of advocating for "changing abortion laws" limits its influence to placing restrictions on Planned Parenthood's ability to supply abortion services. Of course, that is very important. But as I have argued in the first few chapters, even in the best-case scenario of overturning *Roe v. Wade*, I believe the negative impact on Planned Parenthood's overall business would be minimal. And because I am operating on the assumption you want the investment of your pro-life 3T assets to play a significant role in taking down Planned Parenthood and the entire abortion industry—and the sooner the better—I know that making a "minimal" impact is not what you're interested in.

Investing for Maximum Pro-Life Impact

I want to equip you with an investment plan that empowers you to wield maximum impact on shutting down Planned Parenthood and the abortion industry. What does such an investment plan look like? First, as I said earlier in this book, an important part of the plan is continued investment of *some* of your 3T assets in organizations that spearhead the Pro-Life Movement.

I use that word "some" deliberately, because if you are like many pro-lifers, it is likely you currently have *all* of your pro-life 3T assets invested in the Pro-Life Movement. As you will see, starting in the next chapter and continuing for the remainder of this book, I recommend you make a major change to your pro-life investment strategy. I make a case that you should invest the majority of your pro-life capital in an industry that, unlike the Pro-Life Movement, actually has the potential to eventually shut down Planned Parenthood, not in part, but in whole. I'm sure you want to know what that industry is, like right now! I don't blame you! Eight years ago, when I learned about this industry, I got fired up to be part of it.

What motivated me? As an experienced business professional, I immediately saw, as I believe you will soon see, the potential of this industry to become the David that could eventually shut down Goliath Planned Parenthood on the battlefield of business. Why do I believe this particular industry has that potential? Think of it this way. In business, there is always a formula for winning against your competition.

In the same way, because Planned Parenthood is a business, there is a *business formula*—a business equation for winning, if you will—that a competing company can use to shut down Planned Parenthood. For certain, part of that formula rests on the supply side of the business equation. The Pro-Life Movement impacts the supply side of that equation, but as I have argued in previous chapters, the impact is limited.

In contrast, the industry I am excited for you to learn more about impacts the demand side of the business equation. As such, this industry competes directly against Planned Parenthood for the same clients. Who are those clients? Simple: pregnant women who *demand* abortion services. These women are the clients who drive the growth and profitability of Planned Parenthood's business.

Now imagine this. What if an industry existed made up of nonprofit organizations competing directly against Planned Parenthood for those same women? And what if the fundamental difference between these companies and Planned Parenthood is these companies offer "choose life" services, not abortion services. Well I have good news for you: that industry exists! And the major competitive advantage of companies in this industry is grounded in this: they endeavor to *empower* women in their unexpected pregnancies, whereby both the woman and the preborn human growing in her uterus win.

In other words, these companies offer a pregnant woman a very compelling benefit: the opportunity to choose a win-win arrangement that benefits not just one, but two human beings—the woman *and* the preborn human. When such a "product" is packaged and marketed skillfully, it offers an enormous competitive advantage over Planned Parenthood's abortion product—a product that can only offer a woman a decidedly win-lose arrangement: the woman wins (supposedly), and the preborn human growing in her uterus loses (literally loses its life).

Said another way, Planned Parenthood's abortion offering permits one human being (the woman) to "win" at the expense of another human being (the preborn human). How *objectively disempowering* the abortion product is for a woman, to tell her that another human being has to lose (giving its very life) in order for her to win! What a defective product! In any case, I hope I have you excited to learn more about this industry that I am certain has great potential to ring Planned Parenthood's bell in the marketplace—and I'm talking about a decisive knockout! I dive into that in the next chapter.

But before we go there, let's return to the supply side discussion for just a moment, and conclude this chapter with my recommendations for where you should consider placing your supply-side investments in the Pro-Life Movement.

Laser-Focused, Effective Supply Siders

Whether you follow my recommendations for your pro-life supply-side investments or follow your own, please keep this important fact in mind as you compare investment opportunities: there are practically no barriers to entry for starting a pro-life nonprofit organization. That reality is both a blessing and a curse. It is a blessing because it paves the way for rapid ascension of innovative, effective pro-life organizations led by strong, results-focused leaders. A number of these organizations have great potential to help the Pro-Life Movement make meaningful, measurable progress in its efforts to influence the passing of laws that restrict Planned Parenthood's ability to supply abortion services.

But it's also a curse because it facilitates the emergence of too many pro-life organizations in the Pro-Life Movement—and all of those organizations compete for the attention of pro-lifers, asking them for investments of both human and financial capital. The problem is twofold. First, many of those organizations are led by people who are very passionately pro-life but don't have the experience or skills required to achieve *quantifiable* results. Second, it spreads the total available pro-life investment of 3T assets too thin instead of funneling those assets into the organizations and programs that have the greatest likelihood of bringing about measurable impact on successfully restricting the supply of abortion services.

To place in your mind a real-world example of how "focused" investment of assets can remarkably transform a competitive landscape, recall from many years ago how you had to make several trips to a handful of different stores in order to get all of the things you needed for your daily life. Then Walmart came on the scene and changed the landscape by putting under one roof all of the things you needed, and lowered the prices on all those goods to boot. Walmart clearly had a better business model that not only attracted many more customers to its stores but also attracted many more investors who supplied investment capital that enabled Walmart to expand its retail operations. Competitively weaker, inefficient general stores could no longer attract customers and therefore could no longer attract investment capital, so they went out of business. Walmart achieved greater overall positive impact on consumers' lives and therefore attracted both consumers and investor capital away from the general stores that couldn't match that impact.

Many pro-life organizations are similar to those general stores. The Pro-Life Movement will not be as successful as it could be until pro-life investors stop investing in the less impactful pro-life organizations and move their investments to the pro-life organizations that are having greater measurable impact at taking down Planned Parenthood and the abortion industry.

My List of "Investable" Supply Siders

But in the midst of so many pro-life organizations clamoring for attention, how can you discern which organizations in the Pro-Life Movement are actually "investable?" It's not easy. After all, you want to make sure your investments are focused on organizations that are achieving actual impact—measurably moving the ball forward, not just talking a big game. Of course, you can do your own due diligence looking into these organizations. However, I know you are a busy professional, so you may not have the time to invest sifting through and prioritizing the organizations in the Pro-Life Movement that are having real impact on restricting the supply of abortion services, versus those organization that aren't.

I can help. Though my expertise is grounded primarily on the demand side of the business equation, I know quite a bit about both the organizations and the people leading them on the supply side. For your reference and consideration, I share with you the organizations I invest in. For each organization, I also include a short, bottom-line reason explaining why.

Before I share the list, a few things to note:

1. The leaders of all of these organizations would claim they also have an impact on the demand side of the business equation, not just the supply side. And I would agree with them. My point is that these organizations *primarily* influence the supply side of the business by bringing to the attention of pro-lifers and society at large the damaging effects Planned Parenthood's abortion

services exact on preborn humans, women, and society. These organizations do not compete directly against Planned Parenthood by offering competing "choose life" services by way of brick-and-mortar healthcare clinic operations, as do the organizations that make up the industry I discuss in the next chapter.

2. The organizations on my list are national organizations. Local and state-based pro-life organizations also exist that are effective at fighting Planned Parenthood on the supply side of the business equation. For example, in the state of Texas, where I live, I currently invest in one of them (Texas Alliance for Life [texasallianceforlife.org]).

3. There may be other effective national organizations of which I am not aware. If you know of any you would like me to evaluate, please contact me through the contact form on my website at BrettAttebery.com.

Here are my top ten "supply side" Pro-Life Movement organizations, in order of priority:

1. SBA List

Website: sba-list.org

What It Does: SBA List helps elect pro-life legislators and holds them accountable to their campaign promises after the election. SBA List has grown in influence over the years to the extent that it can effectively exert influence over legislators to walk their talk when it comes to pro-life legislation.

Bottom Line: SBA List is the most important supply-side organization because it directly impacts the election of pro-life legislators who can pass pro-life laws.

Bonus Insights: For *Pro-Life Magazine*, I conducted an exclusive interview with Marjorie Danenfelser, who leads SBA List. You can find the transcript of the interview on my website at BrettAttebery.com, or on the *Pro-Life Magazine* website at ProLifeMagazine.org.

2. And Then There Were None

Website: attwn.org

What It Does: This organization has a successful track record of helping abortion workers leave the industry.

Bottom Line: From a business perspective, I love this organization because Planned Parenthood workers leaving the industry disrupts Planned Parenthood's ability to supply abortion services.

Bonus Insights: My colleague Karen Garnett did an exclusive interview with Abby Johnson in *Pro-Life Magazine* about And Then There Were None. You can find the transcript of the interview on my website at BrettAttebery.com, or on the *Pro-Life Magazine* website at ProLifeMagazine.org.

3. Live Action

Website: liveaction.org

What It Does: This organization offers convincing information about the nefarious workings of Planned Parenthood.

Bottom Line: The content on Live Action's website motivates pro-lifers to take action by showing them, with evidence, that Planned Parenthood's business pursues evil purposes.

4. Students for Life of America

Website: sfla.org

What It Does: This organization brings the pro-life message to our young generation, particularly students, and equips them to share the pro-life message in a convincing way with their fellow students.

Bottom Line: Young folks are our future leaders and lawmakers. Convincing them of the correctness of the pro-life message while they are young increases the likelihood that their beliefs will impact society in a positive way when they take positions of influence in the future.

5. 40 Days for Life

Website: 40daysforlife.org

What It Does: Conducts coordinated prayer vigils in front of abortion facilities nationwide.

Bottom Line: This organization has many years of data proving that the constant presence of pro-lifers standing and praying in front of abortion facilities turns abortion-seeking women away from going in to the facilities, and oftentimes leads to them seek life-giving alternatives instead.

6. March for Life

Website: marchforlife.org

What It Does: Conducts the National March for Life in Washington, DC, every year, an event that draws hundreds of thousands of participants from across the nation.

Bottom Line: There is power in numbers. The March for Life event not only motivates pro-lifers to continue fighting against pro-abortion forces but also reminds legislators how many Americans oppose *Roe v. Wade*.

Bonus Insights: For *Pro-Life Magazine*, I conducted an exclusive interview with Jeanne Mancini, who leads March for Life. You can find the transcript of the interview on my website at BrettAttebery.com, or on the *Pro-Life Magazine* website at ProLifeMagazine.org.

7. Support after Abortion

Website: supportafterabortion.org

What It Does: Helps women who have experienced abortion in the past to find healing.

Bottom Line: Repeat clients make up almost 40 percent of total abortions. If women find healing following their first abortion, they are much less likely to repeat abortion. This organization endeavors to connect women to healing to restore dignity and prevent repeat abortions.

Bonus Insights: My colleague Karen Garnett did an exclusive interview for *Pro-Life Magazine* with the founder of Support after Abortion, Janine Marrone. You can find the transcript of the interview on my website at BrettAttebery.com, or on the *Pro-Life Magazine* website at ProLifeMagazine.org.

8. Radiance Foundation

Website: radiancefoundation.org

What It Does: This organization promotes a powerful pro-life message by advocating for adoption as an alternative to abortion, as well as raising awareness of how abortion disproportionately affects the African-American community.

Bottom Line: According to the CDC, 35 percent of abortions in the United States are among African-Americans even though they make up just 14 percent of the total population of our country according to the 2020 census.

9. Equal Rights Institute (ERI)

Website: equalrightsinstitute.com

What It Does: Educates pro-lifers about the most effective ways to dialogue with pro-abortion supporters concerning pro-life beliefs.

Bottom Line: Equal Right Institute's practical approach to apologetics keeps its focus on dialogue techniques proven to convert pro-abortion supporters over to the pro-life side, particularly young folks.

Bonus Insights: For *Pro-Life Magazine*, I conducted an exclusive interview with Josh Brahm, who leads ERI. You can find the transcript of the interview on my website at BrettAttebery.com, or on the *Pro-Life Magazine* website at ProLifeMagazine.org.

10. Priests for Life

Website: priestsforlife.org

What It Does: Father Frank Pavone has led this organization for decades, aggressively pursuing a multifaceted approach to building a culture of life.

Bottom Line: Priests for Life offers extensive content on how to build a culture of life in your community, including how to motivate more pro-lifers to actively engage in impactful pro-life activities.

So there are my current top ten. I update my supply-side investment list from time to time based on new information, as well as my own analysis of the impact of these organizations. To see my most recent list, as well as the breakdown of my investment percentages on both the supply side and the demand side, please visit my website at BrettAttebery.com.

As you will notice on my website, I embrace an investment portfolio approach to my pro-life investments, and I encourage you to do the same. An investment portfolio mentality shifts your mindset to an expectation of ROI, a mindset that is key to winning, and something I discuss extensively in the coming chapters. For my personal investment of pro-life 3T assets, I commit 100 percent of my time and talent to the demand side of the business equation. That's why I can write this book!

But even for my investments of treasure, I commit the majority of it, 80 percent, to pro-life organizations focused on the demand side, and 20 percent to pro-life organizations focused on the supply side. My 20 percent of supply-side investment is committed to the organizations on the list just presented, along with a small investment in one pro-life organization in Texas focused on state-level pro-life issues. Why do I commit so much of my pro-life investment capital to the demand side of the business equation? Because I believe that, to shut down Planned Parenthood, the greatest potential impact lies on the demand side of the business equation. I turn to the reasons why in the next chapter.

Chapter Four BOTTOM LINE

You should continue investing (time, talent, treasure) in organizations leading the Pro-Life Movement because they impact Planned Parenthood's ability to supply abortion services—what I call the supply side of the business equation. However, you can achieve greater ROI by concentrating your investment capital (time, talent, treasure) on the demand side of the business equation.

CHAPTER FIVE: PLANNED PARENTHOOD'S *POTENTIAL* WORST NIGHTMARE

The purpose of a business is to create a customer. Peter Drucker

In business, competition is never as healthy as total domination. Peter Lynch

I would like you to do something for me. For just a moment, I would like you to forget the fact that Planned Parenthood's abortion business is the most abominably immoral business on the face of the planet—and it is. The reason I want you to briefly suspend judgment on Planned Parenthood's business is because I think Planned Parenthood's leaders are actually happy if they can keep the attention of most pro-lifers focused on the moral issue of abortion rather than on the measurable overwhelming success of Planned Parenthood's abortion business.

A Fly on the Wall at Planned Parenthood

Imagine you were invited to observe a strategy meeting of Planned Parenthood's top leadership at its national headquarters. Certainly, Planned Parenthood's leadership would spend some of the time in their strategy meeting discussing how to counteract the human rights advocacy activities of the Pro-Life Movement. They know that to the extent the Pro-Life Movement succeeds, Planned Parenthood's ability to supply abortion services decreases. And that would not be good for business.

But then, suddenly, in the middle of the discussions about the impact of the Pro-Life Movement on its abortion business, one of the Planned Parenthood leaders at the table asks, "If *Roe v. Wade* is overturned, in terms of our abortion numbers, what's the worst-case scenario?"

Planned Parenthood's director in charge of national operations answers, "About a 13 percent reduction in the number of our total abortions."

A significant reduction? Yes. Think about your business and ask if you would be happy about a 13 percent drop in sales. Of course you wouldn't. But would a 13 percent drop in sales be an existential threat to your business? It depends on what type of business you're in, but for most businesses, probably not. So returning to the Planned Parenthood strategy meeting, you're not surprised when the leadership team decides not to spend too much time on this topic and instead moves on to other business. After all, the supply-side issue about the impact of overturning *Roe v. Wade* was a worst-case scenario, not a likely one.

News from the Field about a New Competitor!

Next on the Planned Parenthood strategic planning agenda: a regional director from Planned Parenthood's Los Angeles operation has requested a hearing with Planned Parenthood's national leadership team to talk about an alarming development in the Los Angeles market—Planned Parenthood's largest market in terms of number of abortions. The Los Angeles regional director begins her presentation by recounting how, just twelve months earlier, a new business opened one location in central Los Angeles, and in that time frame had already succeeded in taking 2 percent of Planned Parenthood Los Angeles's abortion-seeking clients. That raises eyebrows and causes a few coffee spills.

Then the Los Angeles regional director grabs everyone's attention by revealing that the new competitor recently opened two new locations in high-abortion-incidence neighborhoods in Los Angeles, and she forecasts that over the next twelve months this new business, with its three locations, will take an additional 5–10 percent of Planned Parenthood's clients. More coffee spilled!

Now a question for you. From your vantage point as a meeting observer and as a successful business professional yourself, how do you think Planned Parenthood's national leadership team would react to this news from the Los Angeles regional director? I think you would agree with me that there would be a "fire alarms going off all hands on deck we had better solve this problem ASAP" reaction by Planned Parenthood's leadership. But why such a strong reaction? Because the new business is successfully taking Planned Parenthood's abortion-seeking clients, taking *market share*, from Planned Parenthood's Los Angeles business.

And if the new business can take customers from Planned Parenthood in Los Angeles, then it may have a business model that can be replicated, enabling it to also take customers from Planned Parenthood in other markets. I can assure you, when that realization kicked in among Planned Parenthood's leadership team, there would be a lot of heartburn around the table.

But Wait. There's More...

Then the Los Angeles regional director delivers an unexpected shocker. The new business taking Planned Parenthood's market share in Los Angeles is not a competing abortion facility. It's a pro-life pregnancy center! Jaws drop. Blood pressures rise. Heads explode. Get the outrageously expensive strategy consulting firm on the phone! Now!

Truth Is Stranger Than Fiction

You're probably thinking, "That's great to dream about. But in reality, is there any pro-life pregnancy center that has ever taken it to Planned Parenthood like that?" I am happy to tell you that the answer is a resounding **YES**! Not long ago, one pro-life pregnancy center truly became Planned Parenthood's worst nightmare, and I share that case study with you later in this book.

Don't Skip to the Best Part Yet!

I know you'll now be tempted to jump right over to the case study chapter that concludes Part II of this book. You want to know the answer. I completely understand, but I ask that you hold off. The reason? Before you see how one pro-life pregnancy center won that battle, it's important that you first understand why most centers do not operate based on the concepts of competing and winning against Planned Parenthood. I will show you some important historical reasons for why that is the case, and remember, we should salute those who work in pro-life pregnancy centers, both past and present. They are pro-life warriors worthy of our gratitude and admiration, and most of the centers they work for offer a valuable service to women facing the fear of an unexpected pregnancy.

However, when you read about the resounding success one pro-life pregnancy help center has achieved in its battle against Planned Parenthood, I believe you will come to understand that there is a new and significantly more effective way for a pro-life pregnancy center to beat Planned Parenthood. The measurable performance gap in terms of lives saved from abortion between this one successful center and most other centers is frankly enormous. But the exceedingly great news is those performance gaps *can* be overcome!

How do I know? The pro-life pregnancy center profiled in the case study chapter used to operate using the traditional approach most other centers still use. But not anymore. What did the leadership team of this one center change to launch themselves on a trajectory of winning the battle against Planned Parenthood? They decided to engage Planned Parenthood on a different battlefield—*the battlefield of business*.

Be All You Can Be!

I emphasized *the battlefield of business* for a reason. Unlike the center in our upcoming case study chapter, in general, the leadership teams (including boards of directors and executive staff) of most of the pro-life pregnancy centers in the country do not operate with a mindset that they are *competing* against Planned Parenthood for the same clients.

I go into the reasons for this in more detail later, but first I want to make something very clear. My purpose in this book is not to denigrate the people who work tirelessly full-time or on a volunteer basis in either the Pro-Life Movement or in the PLBI, nor the philanthropists who support them. I'm sure you would agree that someone giving fully of their time, talent, and treasure for the cause of life is highly admirable, a holy pursuit. That said, throughout the book, I evaluate both the Pro-Life Movement and the PLBI from the perspective of *measurable impact*.

The measurable data I present to you in many chapters reveal that neither the Pro-Life Movement nor the PLBI are achieving the level of measurable success at saving lives from abortion that all of us pro-lifers desire, and when I point out the reasons for those measurable shortcomings, my tone will usually be critical. That does not mean that I am criticizing the people, only that *I am criticizing the strategies* both the Pro-Life Movement and the PLBI have pursued historically. My claim is that those strategies probably made perfect sense at the time they were hatched following *Roe v. Wade* almost half a century ago.

However, the pro-life world has learned much over those fifty years, and *I believe there is strong evidence to indicate a business strategy based on a strong consumer marketing program can have a much greater measurable impact on ending abortion than the pro-life strategies the Pro-Life*

Movement and the PLBI have traditionally pursued. That is the central claim of this book in a nutshell.

As it currently stands, extremely rare is the pro-life pregnancy center leadership team that views the interaction with an abortion-determined woman from the perspective of consumer marketing: that the woman is now "in the market" as a prospective client to "buy" a service. What can she "buy"? She has only two options: abortion services or choose life services. Those are the two services that battle for the attention of an abortion-determined woman's mind. Currently, in the vast majority of cases of women in the market for these two services, abortion services easily win the battle of the mind.

It Takes a Business to Beat a Business

The successful pro-life pregnancy center profiled in the upcoming case study learned that the way to beat Planned Parenthood was to compete against it *like a business*. I hope you are encouraged by the fact that this one pro-life pregnancy center succeeded against Planned Parenthood, because as a successful business professional, you know successful business models can be *replicated* to win in other markets. So I want you to have hope. That said, I think it is important you understand the current reality on the ground for the vast majority of pro-life pregnancy centers.

So here goes. I know of a pro-life pregnancy center in a large, heavily populated market that is situated next door to an abortion facility. On average, the pro-life pregnancy center wins about one hundred abortion-seeking clients over a twelve-month period, compared to the abortion facility winning about ten thousand abortion-seeking clients over the same period. That's not a typo. You read that correctly. That's only a 1 percent market share for the pro-life pregnancy center: for every one hundred prospective clients, Planned Parenthood wins ninety-nine for its abortion services, and the pro-life pregnancy center wins one for its choose life services. And in case you're wondering, in my experience these kinds of 1 percent market share numbers are the rule for pro-life pregnancy centers in other markets as well, not the exception.

Let's Do This!

The 1 percent market share number probably has you thinking, "How do pro-life pregnancy centers develop a mindset of competing to win?" First and foremost, in the same way our case study pro-life pregnancy center did, other centers need to adopt fundamental competitive business practices proven to help an organization win in the market.

And that's where *you* come in. As a skilled, experienced business professional, you possess valuable assets that you can bring to the table. Pro-life pregnancy centers need *your* pro-life 3T assets in order to start making serious competitive headway against Planned Parenthood, and to eventually win a total victory over it. I am convinced that when you, and thousands of other successful business professionals like you, invest your 3T assets in a way that turns pro-life pregnancy centers into competitive organizations, then, eventually, total victory over Planned Parenthood is assured. Can you imagine that day? I can!

Plan Your Work and Work Your Plan

But in the excitement of seeing Planned Parenthood fall at some time in the future, we're getting a little ahead of ourselves. We need a plan to get there. As a successful business professional, you already know you can't help a pro-life pregnancy center win against a strong competitor like Planned Parenthood without a plan. And before you can put together a winning plan, you first need to analyze and understand the competitive landscape.

I can help you with that, so that's exactly where we're going in Part II. We will dive deep into analyzing the status quo of the competitive landscape between Planned Parenthood and pro-life pregnancy centers, starting with a macro-level industry view, and then working our way down to the level of pro-life pregnancy centers as individual nonprofit organizations. You will finish Part II with a clear understanding of the battlefield.

That understanding will equip you with the foundation you need before I address in Part III exactly how you can start using your 3T assets to help pro-life pregnancy centers take down Planned Parenthood on the battlefield of business. With your help, no longer will pro-life pregnancy centers settle for a score of ninety-nine wins for Planned Parenthood, and only one win for pro-life pregnancy centers. Instead, pro-life pregnancy centers will energetically purse missions of completely flipping that score on its head. And when they do, we will collectively have put an end to Planned Parenthood and the abortion industry!

Chapter Five BOTTOM LINE

Pro-life pregnancy centers have the *potential* to beat Planned Parenthood at business, but currently lose the vast majority of prospective clients to Planned Parenthood. The cause for this massive underperformance is that the typical pro-life pregnancy center does not compete against Planned Parenthood as a business.

PART II: THE BUSINESS OF CHOOSING LIFE

As you have undoubtedly experienced in your professional career, consistently winning at business over the long term is hard. A host of market forces can suddenly shift, causing your product or service to fall out of favor. Sales suffer, market share falls, profits evaporate. Not fun.

But imagine for a second what your business results would be in the areas of sales, market share, and profits if your business *completely ignored* those fundamental business metrics. You likely would not be in business for long. That brings us to the *business* of choosing life, in other words, the pro-life pregnancy centers that compete against companies involved in the *business* of choosing abortion—Planned Parenthood and the abortion industry.

In Part II, I first offer you my assessment of the current landscape of the companies involved in the business of choosing life. As we survey that competitive landscape together, I anticipate you will feel some distress, perhaps even some anger, about what you discover. It will be eye-opening for you, I'm sure, but we will keep in mind Benjamin Franklin's famous quote, "There are no gains without pains." What gains? The current problems obstructing the competitiveness of pro-life pregnancy centers *can be fixed*.

I discuss some of the business fundamentals pro-life pregnancy centers can implement to fix their lack of competitiveness. Finally, you are likely curious if any pro-life pregnancy centers exist that have embraced business fundamentals, and as a result, have substantially improved their competitiveness, as measured by market share, against Planned Parenthood and the abortion industry. The answer is YES! In the final chapter of Part II, I present a case study of an actual pro-life pregnancy center that is winning the market share battle against Planned Parenthood. There is real-world proof that we can win the battle against Planned Parenthood and the abortion industry!

CHAPTER SIX: THE PRO-LIFE BUSINESS INDUSTRY: AN OVERVIEW

We do not realize how deeply our starting assumptions affect the way we go about looking for and interpreting the data we collect. Sue Savage-Rumbaugh

Worldviews seem real but they aren't real. Our worldviews tend to guide our thinking about everything. And then our assumptions come out of those worldviews. Petros Scientia

As I said in Chapter 5, it takes a business to beat a business. I'll take it a step further: It takes a *strong* business to beat a *strong* business. And make no mistake—Planned Parenthood is a strong, well-run business operation. It has the market share numbers to prove it—as I revealed to you at the end of the last chapter, a local Planned Parenthood abortion facility often wins ninety-nine abortion-seeking clients for every one abortion-seeking client a competing pro-life pregnancy center wins. As a business professional, you know if your business is at 1 percent market share versus your local competitor, you've got some serious work to do. And pro-life pregnancy centers, as competitive organizations, have some serious work to do.

We've Got Superior Numbers, but…

Let's take the discussion of a local pro-life pregnancy center competing against a local Planned Parenthood abortion facility up one level, from an individual business perspective to an industry perspective. Let's start with the abortion industry, for which Planned Parenthood serves as the vanguard. I define the abortion industry as all of the facilities in aggregate that conduct abortions in any way, surgical or medication abortions, plus any and all organizations that support those facilities. Easy enough to understand.

But you may be wondering if there is an industry that competes against the abortion industry? Indeed there is! It is the industry that consists of all of the pro-life pregnancy centers in aggregate that offer women life-giving alternatives to abortion, plus any and all organizations that support those centers. I call this industry the Pro-Life Business Industry (PLBI).

The PLBI competes against the abortion industry for the same clients: women seeking an abortion because they are experiencing profound fear due to an unexpected pregnancy. Now for a statistic that, on its surface, seems like good news for the PLBI: in the United States, pro-life pregnancy centers outnumber abortion facilities by at least two to one! There are between three thousand and four thousand pro-life pregnancy centers in the United States, compared to approximately fifteen hundred abortion facilities (Planned Parenthood operates between six hundred and seven hundred of these).

Advantage PLBI, right? Well, no. Why not? Because the market share number of ninety-nine client wins for the typical abortion facility for every one client win for the typical pro-life pregnancy center does not equal winning for the PLBI. Does it really matter if the organizations representing your industry boast twice as many locations when the organizations in the industry you're competing against have a 99 percent market share advantage?

Born of the Pro-Life Movement

You're probably wondering how a typical pro-life pregnancy center could so vastly underperform its local abortion facility competitor in terms of market share. I too puzzled over this in the early days of my involvement in the PLBI. Having been deeply involved in full-time work within the PLBI for more than seven years now, I believe I have a solid grasp on the primary reasons why.

As I touched on at the end of Part I, it boils down to the simple fact that very few nonprofit pro-life pregnancy centers compete in the same way for-profit businesses do. But let's take it a step further. Why don't they? There are very good reasons, actually. First, it is essential to understand this. *Back in the 1970s, the first pro-life leaders to start pregnancy centers came from within the ranks of the Pro-Life Movement*. Now your reaction to that may be, "so what?" The answer is this: the first pro-life pregnancy centers were established based on the same foundational principles as the Pro-Life Movement—the right to life of preborn human beings. Over time, as the number of pro-life pregnancy centers proliferated across the country, the motivations of those who started new centers were the same as those of the early pro-life pioneers who built the first centers: the focus, the raison d'être, for establishing and operating pro-life pregnancy centers was, and continues to be for most of them to this day, about fighting for the right to life of preborn human beings.

And again, thank God for all of those pro-life warriors who, over many decades since *Roe v. Wade*, have answered the call to work on the front lines in pro-life pregnancy centers. But I want to ask you to change your perspective for just a second. I want to challenge you to view the abortion issue from a different angle by taking off your human rights hat and replacing it with your consumer marketing hat.

Do you have your consumer marketing hat on? Good. A question for you: do you think a woman experiencing the fear of an unexpected pregnancy and thinking about getting an abortion would seriously consider becoming a client of a business that is focused more on the needs of the preborn human growing in her womb than on her own? I invite you to ponder that question deeply from a consumer marketing perspective, not from a human rights perspective.

What's Wrong with This Picture?

The human rights–centered, right-to-life worldview among pro-life pregnancy center founders was established at the outset of the pro-life pregnancy center movement, and that worldview persists to this day. Rarely are the assumptions of that worldview questioned. But question those assumptions we will!

Now that you are becoming more aware that the PLBI has a fundamental systemic problem in terms of its competitiveness versus the abortion industry, I think the following quote, a favorite of mine, will ring true: "If you always do what you've always done, you always get what you've always gotten" (Jessie Potter).

Even so, you are a business professional, so I don't expect you to just take my word for it that the PLBI continues to massively underperform year after year due to a fundamental systemic problem. You want evidence. I hear you. So get ready, because I offer you an abundance of proof in the chapters that follow.

Chapter Six BOTTOM LINE

The fact that pro-life pregnancy centers significantly outnumber abortion facilities isn't very meaningful from a business perspective because the typical abortion facility has a dominant market share versus the typical pro-life pregnancy center. Pro-life pregnancy centers in general, from the first locations established in the 1970s to new centers built recently, were not established based on business principles of serving clients and competing to win clients away from abortion facilities. Instead, pro-life pregnancy centers operate principally on the same fundamentals that motivate the Pro-Life Movement: the right to life for preborn human beings.

CHAPTER SEVEN: THE PRO-LIFE BUSINESS INDUSTRY IS LOSING BADLY

Good guys don't always win, especially when they are divided and less determined than their adversaries. Madeleine K. Albright

Never change a winning game; always change a losing one. Bill Tilden

Again, as I have done so far in this book, it's important to distinguish clearly between the Pro-Life Movement, a human rights movement focused on the right to life for preborn human beings, and the PLBI, an industry made up of pro-life pregnancy centers that compete to win clients away from Planned Parenthood and the abortion industry. Yes, the Pro-Life Movement and the PLBI are closely related.

But they are playing different games. The Pro-Life Movement could claim that, through the programs of many pro-life organizations, legislation and cultural changes (from culture of death to culture of life) have resulted in fewer women getting abortions. As I covered in Chapter 4, that very well may be the case, and it is certainly valuable. However, it is incredibly difficult to measure exactly how many women did not get an abortion because of the efforts of the Pro-Life Movement. Why?

Because those pro-life programs tend to impact women's consciences and beliefs *before* they become pregnant. So when they do become pregnant and choose life for their preborn babies, unless they specifically tell someone, "I would have aborted my baby if not for such and such pro-life program I saw five years ago that changed me," then we don't know. I don't think there is any doubt that the Pro-Life Movement has had an impact, but it's difficult to know exactly how to quantify it.

Winning = Highest Market Share

The same quantification issue does not exist for the PLBI. The PLBI as a whole, as well as each pro-life pregnancy center that operates within the PLBI, can measure success based on the number of client "wins" it achieves compared to its competition—Planned Parenthood and the abortion industry. A pro-life pregnancy center tallies a "win" when a pregnant woman who is actively seeking an abortion becomes a client of the pro-life pregnancy center and through her interaction with the center changes her mind about abortion and instead chooses life for the preborn human growing in her womb.

How do we determine which industry is winning? Simple. Add up the total client wins by all of the PLBI's pro-life pregnancy centers (total number of abortion-seeking clients who went to pro-life pregnancy centers and ended up choosing life), and compare that number to all the client wins by all the abortion industry's abortion facilities (total number of abortion-seeking clients who went to abortion facilities and ended up getting an abortion).

The "winner" is the industry that has the largest number of client wins relative to the total number of available clients, also known as market share. "Winning" in the PLBI in its competition against the abortion industry should be measured in terms of market share. Market share is the primary Key Performance Indicator (KPI) that indicates who is winning. Unfortunately, the PLBI doesn't have an industry body that keeps track of market share numbers, but because of the work I do with pro-life pregnancy centers around the country, I have access to the "client chose life" numbers of many centers as well as the abortion numbers of competing abortion facilities when published. Based on those data, I can assure you the PLBI is NOT winning in its battle against the abortion industry, especially against Planned Parenthood. As a matter of fact, it's not even a contest.

What Do the Numbers Say?

Remember that in 2019, Planned Parenthood accounted for 354,871 of the abortion industry's estimated total number of approximately 850,000 abortions. Let's do a quick thought experiment. To make the math easy, let's say in 2019 there were 1,000,000 pregnant women actively seeking an abortion. The women will either choose abortion, which would be a client win for the abortion industry, or will choose life, which would be a client win for the PLBI. Add up the total client wins of both the abortion industry and the PLBI and you have what marketers call the TAM (Total Available Market). A simple graphical representation would look like this:

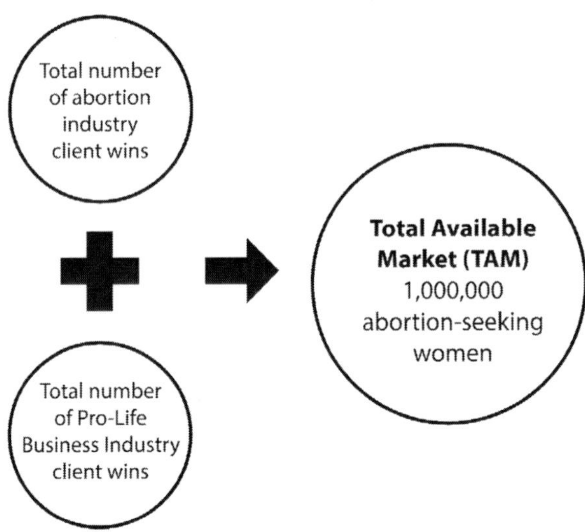

An industry's market share is simply its total number of client wins divided by the TAM. So, for example, if the abortion industry had 850,000 client wins for its abortion services out of a total of 1,000,000 potential abortion-seeking clients, it could claim an industry market share of 85 percent. If the abortion industry won 850,000 of the 1,000,000 potential clients, then that leaves the competing PLBI with 150,000 client wins (1,000,000 minus 850,000 = 150,000). So the PLBI's market share would be 15 percent (150,000 divided by 1,000,000), meaning 150,000 women who actively sought an abortion became clients of pro-life pregnancy centers in the PLBI, changed their minds about abortion, and chose life for their preborn babies.

You may not think 15 percent industry market share is all that great, and I would agree with you, but oh how I wish 15 percent was the PLBI's market share! In my experience working at Heroic Media (which I discuss in both the prologue and Chapter 16), I interact directly with pro-life pregnancy centers across the country, and metrics from those centers reveal that a market share of 5 percent or less is common. If we extrapolate 5 percent market share to the PLBI as a whole, I don't know about you, but I wouldn't call that winning. I'd call it losing, and losing badly.

But That's Not What I Heard!

This information may come as a shock to you, especially if you are a pro-lifer who follows the daily news put out by various pro-life news services. My claim that the PLBI is losing badly may cause you a lot of consternation and confusion because it contradicts what you have read in many pro-life articles. You may have read, for example, an article like the one posted on LifeNews.com on December 11, 2019, with the following headline: "One-Third of All Abortion Clinics Have Closed in the Last 5 Years, Saving Babies from Abortions."

Does the Conclusion Follow?

I have to admit that is an impressive headline! It sure sounds like winning. However, if you have studied philosophy and covered logic as part of your studies, I would remind you that if the conclusion does not follow from the premises (that is, the premises could be true, yet the conclusion false), the argument is invalid. I bring this up because there is a strong belief in the Pro-Life Movement that goes like this: "When an abortion facility closes, babies' lives are saved from abortion." Premise: Abortion facility closes. Conclusion: Babies' lives are saved.

If this were true, then couldn't I say something like, "When my local liquor shop closed, people stopped drinking"? Do you see the problem here? Just because one location that supplies a product or service no longer supplies that product or service, it doesn't necessarily follow that customers for that product or service are choosing the competing product or service. In other words, just because an abortion facility closes, it does not necessarily follow that women experiencing unexpected pregnancies choose life for their babies. They could just go to a different abortion facility to get an abortion.

Granted, it might be more inconvenient for them, and in some cases, women may have to travel hundreds of miles to procure an abortion, but a reduction in access to the local supply of abortion services does not necessarily mean an increase in client wins for the competing alternative: choose life services (aka "babies saved"). If the demand for a product or service is very strong, then a consumer will go to great lengths to find the supply of that product or service.

Does an Abortion Facility Closing Mean It Failed?

Put on your business strategy hat and consider the following question. Is it plausible that when Planned Parenthood closes one of its abortion facilities in a small town, it's doing that as part of a strategic plàn to open larger abortion facilities in urban areas, with the expectation that women will travel from small towns to those urban facilities? I think you will agree, of course, that's plausible.

Why might Planned Parenthood do this? Perhaps it knows demand for abortion is so strong that women will go to the trouble of traveling far distances to get an abortion. Do you think Planned Parenthood studied this issue in depth before it made the strategic move to close smaller abortion facilities? Of course it did.

So why does the Pro-Life Movement consider the closing of an abortion facility a win? I think the reason the Pro-Life Movement shouts with joy about abortion facilities closing is because it supports the narrative that the Pro-Life Movement is winning. An abortion facility closing is indeed a win in one sense. It is a moral victory, for sure, because no more preborn human beings will be killed at that particular abortion facility.

However, an abortion facility closing doesn't necessarily mean it's a business victory that will lead to an increase in market share for the PLBI. To draw the conclusion that the closing of an abortion facility is a competitive win in a business context, you would have to show evidence that the potential clients of the closed abortion facility then availed themselves of "choose life services" *because of* the closing of that abortion facility.

I think you would agree it would be difficult to make that case when we consider that Planned Parenthood's total number of abortions has continued to increase year after year, despite numerous closings of its smaller abortion facilities. My objective in presenting these market share data is not to depress you, but to simply make you aware that the PLBI is not winning from a business perspective. I hope that has you asking, "Brett, then how do we start winning?" That's the right question!

There is not a single answer, but the good news is, there definitely are answers! In the next chapter, I present you with one of the answers—a key mindset shift that if a pro-life pregnancy center gets right dramatically improves its chances of increasing its market share against its local Planned Parenthood abortion facility.

Chapter Seven BOTTOM LINE

In a certain sense, the Pro-Life Movement can claim it is winning because abortion numbers have dropped by about half in the past thirty years. But total annual abortion numbers are still almost a million, so it's probably more accurate to say the Pro-Life Movement is not losing as badly as in the past. The conclusion for the PLBI, on the other hand, is clear. The PLBI is losing badly as measured by market share. The PLBI must stay focused on one key KPI: market share—measured by how many women who wanted an abortion choose the services of a pro-life pregnancy center versus how many women choose the abortion services of a facility like Planned Parenthood.

CHAPTER EIGHT: THE FIRST STEP TO BECOMING A "WINNING" PRO-LIFE PREGNANCY CENTER

Nothing happens until a sale is made. Thomas Watson Sr. of IBM

Have you ever heard of a philosophical principle called "Hanlon's Razor"? Hanlon's Razor says you should "never attribute to malice that which is adequately explained by incompetence." Said another way, Hanlon's Razor encourages us to not assume an action occurred due to someone's ill intentions, if it's possible that the action occurred due to incompetence instead. I begin this chapter discussing Hanlon's Razor because I do not attribute the failure of the PLBI—failure in this case defined as having extremely low market share versus the abortion industry—to the ill intentions of any leaders and team members of pro-life pregnancy centers.

I am personal friends with many leaders of pro-life pregnancy centers, and they are some of the most amazing human beings I have ever met. Their motives are honorable—to save the lives of preborn human beings. Many are hired specifically because of their demonstrated passion to help save lives from abortion. However, rarely, if ever, does anyone ask those leaders before hiring them if they can provide proof from their work history that they possess the demonstrated competence required to measurably achieve breakthrough results at saving lives from abortion.

Passion for the pro-life cause may inspire those leaders to work full-time in the PLBI, but it's demonstrated competence that will determine whether their actions will help their centers gain market share against Planned Parenthood. The question is, what is the required demonstrated competence that will increase the chances of winning market share against Planned Parenthood?

How Many Points Can Your Team Score?

I believe the general answer to that question is as follows: if your business wants to win the market share battle against your competitor, then you need demonstrated competence at successfully encouraging clients to choose your product or service instead of your competitor's. For a pro-life pregnancy center specifically, this means hiring team members with the skills to effectively encourage women who want an abortion at a local abortion facility to instead become clients of the pro-life pregnancy center, and then choose life instead of abortion.

In the business world, this skill is known as *sales*. As Thomas Watson Sr. of IBM fame once said, "Nothing happens until a sale is made." You, through your own experience as a successful business professional, likely understand Mr. Watson's statement in the core of your being. However, please believe me when I tell you few things evoke a stronger negative emotional reaction from the leaders of many pro-life pregnancy centers than to suggest to them that, like any successful business, they have to be highly skilled at sales.

They will assure you sales is NOT what they do. *Ministry* is what they do! Doesn't "ministry" sound so much nicer than "sales?" Be that as it may, I would argue that "ministry" and "sales" have much more in common than most people think. In a certain sense, I believe the two words are interchangeable.

Radically "Other-Oriented"

Why do so many people gives sales such a bad rap? I believe it's because they harbor a belief that sales is about *manipulating* people into transactions they don't really want to enter into. I'm sure we all have stories about manipulative salespeople who pushed us into getting something we didn't really want or need, and then we experienced buyer's remorse. However, if you ask those same folks who cringe when they hear the word "sales" to share any experiences they've had about salespeople who sold them products or services that made their lives measurably better in some way, they will surely be able to share those "good" sales stories with you as well. Those good stories demonstrate how I define sales.

Sales is the process of asking people to buy products or services that make their lives measurably better. Sales, done like it is supposed to be done, seeks a transaction between two parties only if it measurably improves the well-being of the buyer. In other words, sales done correctly is radically *"other-oriented."*

Wait a second. What other vocation is radically "other-oriented?" That's right. Ministry! So if I claim that the PLBI is losing badly, as measured by market share, because of poor sales performance, and "sales" and "ministry" are interchangeable, does that mean I think the PLBI is losing because of poor "ministry" performance? Indeed it does. Wait. What? How could I claim these amazing individuals who work at pro-life pregnancy centers are poor at ministry?

Who Are You Ministering To?

It comes down to confusion about *who* a pro-life pregnancy center is ministering to exactly. Let me explain what I mean by borrowing from something written by one of my favorite entrepreneurs, Jason Leister. Jason writes daily for his blog called *Incomparable Expert*. Here's an excerpt from one of his posts discussing a challenge he experienced with one of his consulting clients. "I had skipped over what is really question

NUMERO UNO for any business owner hoping to do anything but struggle: What problem do you solve and for whom do you solve it? A clear answer to that question can tell you a lot of things about your chances."

When I first read that piece of business wisdom from Jason, it was music to my ears. Notice Jason doesn't say "an answer" to that question, but "a *clear* answer" to that question will be a strong indicator of your chances for success. So let's pose that question to a typical executive director of a pro-life pregnancy center, and I will give you what I believe would be the typical answer:

Question Part 1: What problem do you solve? Answer: "Ending abortion."

Question Part 2: And for whom do you solve it? Answer: "Ummm ... " (confused look on her face).

I think most executive directors would give the answer to Question Part 1 with great enthusiasm! After all, are there many things more personally and professionally fulfilling than working full-time at ending abortion, the greatest human rights violation in the history of humanity?

Why the Confusion?

But what about the answer to the second part of the question: "And for whom do you solve it?" Remember. We're looking for a *clear* answer, not just an answer. The reason I think a typical executive director of a pro-life pregnancy center would struggle to immediately answer the second part of the question is because she knows the "for whom?" part of the question involves two people—the preborn baby and the pregnant woman.

So, after some thought, the executive director will probably answer something along these lines: "Well, we help *both* the woman *and* her preborn baby. We help save the life of the preborn baby from abortion, and save the woman from the pain and regret of having aborted her baby."

This kind of response is very common from those who work in the PLBI. It is a laudable response, for sure, from a *moral* perspective.

But here's the problem: from a *sales* perspective, "we help both the woman and her preborn baby" is not a *clear* answer. Why? To succeed at sales, we need to know who is making the decision to choose our services instead of our competitor's services. Who makes the "buying" decision?

The First Step to Making a Comeback for the Win!

To gain market share against Planned Parenthood and the abortion industry, and then eventually win the market share battle, pro-life pregnancy centers in the PLBI must be clear that they are solving a problem for the one person who will make the decision to choose abortion or choose life—the pregnant woman. In the past few years, a number of pro-life pregnancy center executive directors have asked me what they should do to save more lives from abortion.

Note already in that question the focus is on the preborn baby, not the pregnant woman who will make the decision about getting an abortion or choosing life. When the leaders of centers ask me that question, I think they are expecting me to offer some fancy marketing tactics that have proven effective at putting a smackdown on Planned Parenthood. Instead, I advise them to learn from Planned Parenthood. That raises eyebrows!

What do I mean by learning from Planned Parenthood? Simply this. One of the keys to Planned Parenthood's market share success against pro-life pregnancy centers is that Planned Parenthood has zero ambiguity about whom it serves. Planned Parenthood's answer to the "for whom?" question is crystal clear: Planned Parenthood serves women facing unexpected pregnancies who want an abortion. Yes, I realize Planned Parenthood talks about other things related to "women's health," but those are just tactics designed to brand Planned Parenthood as a "caring" organization in the minds of women—tactics used with the ultimate aim of eventually winning as many clients as possible for the organization's real moneymaker: abortion services. From a sales perspective, Planned Parenthood's very clear answer to the "for whom?" question gives it an enormous competitive advantage over typical pro-life pregnancy centers that divide their attention between thinking about *both* preborn babies *and* pregnant women.

I conclude this chapter with a statement I believe is true: The first step pro-life pregnancy centers in the PLBI must take to eventually achieve significant market share gains against Planned Parenthood is to focus solely on solving problems for pregnant women who want an abortion. Remember: The pregnant mother, not the preborn baby, is the one who will decide either to get an abortion or to choose life.

Chapter Eight BOTTOM LINE

To win the market share battle against Planned Parenthood and the abortion industry, pro-life pregnancy centers must hire team members who are effective at selling—meaning successfully encouraging women who want an abortion to instead become clients of a pro-life pregnancy center, and then choose life instead of abortion. One of the main reasons typical pro-life pregnancy centers suffer from low market share is because they are not clear about who they actually serve. In answering the question "What problem do you solve and for whom do you solve it?" they will answer that they serve both the preborn baby and the pregnant woman. The first step pro-life pregnancy centers in the PLBI must take to eventually achieve significant market share gains against Planned Parenthood and the abortion industry is to focus solely on solving problems for pregnant women who want an abortion.

CHAPTER NINE:
WHO IS THE CLIENT?

If you are not taking care of your customer, your competitor will. Bob Hooey

In 2018, Jeff Bezos of Amazon.com fame established the Bezos Day One Fund. The $2 billion fund seeks to help homeless people as well as improve children's access to education in poor areas. In terms of the "improve children's access to education in poor areas" aspect, note the principles the Bezos Day One Fund uses to determine its funding priorities. From the fund's website: "The Fund uses the same set of principles that have driven Amazon. Most important among those will be genuine, intense customer obsession. The child will be the customer." Did you catch that? *"...genuine, intense customer obsession. The child will be the customer."* That provides a very clear answer to the "for whom?" part of the question we discussed in the last chapter.

Who Is the Client?

It is my hope that, one day, pro-life pregnancy centers in the PLBI will demonstrate the same clear understanding of *who* their client is in their daily battles against Planned Parenthood and the abortion industry. A pro-life pregnancy center's client **IS NOT** the preborn human being. A pro-life pregnancy center's client **IS** the woman who experiences fear because of an unexpected pregnancy and then seeks to abort her preborn baby. Rare is the pro-life pregnancy center that can offer measurable proof of an "intense client obsession" toward serving women who seek to abort their preborn babies.

If you doubt me on this, I invite you to "mystery call," or have someone mystery call, any of the pro-life pregnancy centers operating in your local community. During your mystery call, act as if you just discovered you are pregnant, that your unexpected pregnancy causes you great fear, and that because of that fear you want an abortion. If the pro-life pregnancy centers you call are founded on the principle of an intense client obsession to serve abortion-seeking women, your call will be answered by highly trained and skilled professionals who understand they are engaging you in a *sales call.*

Giving You What You Truly Need

In other words, they understand you are in the market for a service, and what they have to offer you—choose life services—is what you truly *need*, but not necessarily what you think you *want* at the present moment. With that understanding, the pro-life pregnancy center sales professional you have on the line will be well versed in how to gently guide you toward making an appointment with their center with the aim of eventually helping you see what is truly best for you: choosing life for the preborn human growing in your womb.

If you have a business background, especially in marketing and sales, this sales approach will likely seem rather obvious. But if you mystery call pro-life pregnancy centers, this is not what you will encounter for the vast majority (I would say more than 90 percent) of your calls. For most of the calls, you will be appalled by what you hear.

What will you likely hear from those answering the phones at the pro-life pregnancy centers? Here's a typical response many centers will give to a woman who says she wants an abortion. "We neither perform nor refer for abortions."

In an upcoming chapter, I go into more detail about this type of response by pro-life pregnancy centers, but as I like to say to centers who believe that is a good response, "By saying that to the woman, do you realize you actually just did refer her for an abortion? When she hangs up, who do you think she is going to call next? She will call Planned Parenthood." How could so many pro-life pregnancy centers get this wrong?

For business professionals who don't have much knowledge about the PLBI, a response like "We neither perform nor refer for abortions" may appear to be an incredibly amateurish sales error. But it's not quite so simple. I'm not going to completely let pro-life pregnancy centers off the hook here, but I do understand why so many continue to make this fundamental sales error, and why leaders of pro-life pregnancy centers can also be quite stubborn in defending such an approach.

Here's what's happening. Recall from previous chapters that the people who work at pro-life pregnancy centers are primarily motivated by the mission of the Pro-Life Movement: the right to life of the preborn human being. Therefore, the majority of individuals on the teams of pro-life pregnancy centers are overly focused on the moral issue of abortion, instead of focusing on the decision maker, the pregnant woman. "We neither perform nor refer for abortions" is a *moral* statement focused on the needs of the preborn human being. It is not a sales statement that offers to measurably improve in some way the life of the abortion-seeking pregnant woman on the other end of the telephone line.

A New Devotion

Most pro-life pregnancy centers are devoted to the moral issue of saving preborn humans from abortion. That devotion manifests itself in some obvious ways. As one example, I encourage you to survey the business names of the pro-life pregnancy centers in your local area. You will discover that some of them actually use baby-centric business names. Your business sense should tell you that such names are not going to win over many clients who want to abort their preborn babies.

While holding on to their conviction that abortion is morally repugnant, the pro-life warriors who work at pro-life pregnancy centers should put on a different hat when they show up for work at the center. They should devote themselves completely and obsessively to serving and empowering the pregnant women who will decide between the options of getting an abortion, or choosing life. Interestingly, as you will see in the case study presented in the last chapter of this part of the book, making that shift can dramatically increase the results of exactly what a center wanted most in the first place: more preborn babies' lives saved from abortion!

What's in It For Me?

Now let's assume a typical pro-life pregnancy center that has historically been primarily devoted to the moral issue of abortion decides to make this mental shift. How does a center effectively do that? I propose the center take a deep dive into the heart and mind of the pregnant woman. What is going on inside of her heart and her head? In her heart, the answer to what is going on is almost always the same: fear.

Yet in the face of that intense fear she must choose. She must decide. And that's where the head comes in. And when it comes to making a decision, at a fundamental level, the pregnant woman consciously or subconsciously uses the same filter you and I use in our decision-making. The filter is called WIIFM: "**W**hat's **I**n **I**t **F**or **M**e?"

I know what you might be thinking. "I don't make decisions that way!" Sorry, but yes, you do. If you don't believe it's true, I invite you to investigate the published research on this topic. Research shows that it's true, even for those who appear to be the most saintly and other-oriented. But you may have had a negative reaction to WIIFM because it sounds selfish and self-centered. Rather than thinking of WIIFM as selfish, I invite you to consider that what it really means is, "How does this make my life better?" Or even a level deeper, "Is the thing being proposed here a winning proposition *for me*, or a losing proposition *for me*?"

Posed this way, you are simply saying you want to engage in things that improve your life. You want to win at the game of life, and the more wins, the better! I don't think that's selfish. I think that's smart!

Is Choosing Life the Best Choice for Me?

Back to the pregnant woman and the question of WIIFM. One of the questions going through a woman's mind, *at least subconsciously*, when facing an unexpected pregnancy is, "What would preserving the baby's life mean *for me*?" Stated another way, "How does preserving this baby's life help *me* win at the game of life?" I have been assisting pro-life pregnancy centers with their marketing efforts since 2015, and I have yet to hear any center formulate an answer to that question in a compelling way such that the woman would say, "Oh, now I get it! Yes, I can see how choosing to preserve my baby's life would make *my* life better. I can see and feel clearly what's in it *for me* if I choose that option."

My point is that in order to have increased success—as measured by market share—against Planned Parenthood, a pro-life pregnancy center should singularly and obsessively focus the development of its choose life services, as well as its marketing and sales efforts, on answering that woman's question in a way that leads her to say, "Now I see that what you're offering is the best option *for me*." In my opinion, if the PLBI had been focused the past fifty years on working tirelessly to improve the attractiveness, *from the pregnant woman's perspective*, of the "choose life" product vis-à-vis the abortion services product, the PLBI would have had Planned Parenthood running scared long ago, and would already be winning the market share battle. But as they say, better late than never. What can pro-life pregnancy centers do to make their choose life services more attractive to pregnant women seeking an abortion? I turn to that question in the next chapter.

Chapter Nine BOTTOM LINE

A pro-life pregnancy center's client **IS NOT** the preborn human being. A pro-life pregnancy center's client **IS** the woman who experiences fear because of an unexpected pregnancy and then seeks to abort her preborn baby. The majority of individuals on the teams of pro-life pregnancy centers are overly focused on the moral issue of abortion. In order to have increased success—as measured by market share—against Planned Parenthood and the abortion industry, a pro-life pregnancy center should singularly and obsessively focus its marketing and sales efforts on answering a woman's WIIFM question in a way that leads her to say, "Now I see what you're offering me is the best choice *for me*."

CHAPTER TEN: WHO OFFERS THE BETTER PRODUCT?

Don't find customers for your products, find products for your customers. Seth Godin

Planned Parenthood and other abortion facilities offer pregnant women who want an abortion a product called "abortion services." Pro-life pregnancy centers offer pregnant women who want an abortion a product called "choose life services." Which of those two product options do you believe is more attractive to pregnant abortion-seeking women?

My question to you is a bit of a trick question in this sense: it doesn't really matter which product you or I think is more attractive. We are not the prospective clients. The pregnant woman who wants an abortion is the prospective client. At the end of the last chapter, I made the claim that if the PLBI had focused the past fifty years on working tirelessly to improve the attractiveness of the choose life services product vis-à-vis the abortion services product, we would have already had Planned Parenthood running scared, and we would be winning the market share battle.

No doubt my claim will likely anger many leaders of pro-life pregnancy centers. My response to them would simply be this number: 354,871. As you recall, that's the number of abortions Planned Parenthood conducted in 2019: 972 abortions every single day on average. Of course, the choose life services product is winning some clients, but the abortion services product is dominating the market share battle.

Let's Ask Mr. Maslow What He Thinks

Evaluating product attractiveness from the perspective of a pregnant woman seeking an abortion, which of the two offerings is more appealing, choose life services or abortion services? A useful framework to help us answer that question is Maslow's hierarchy of needs. If you haven't heard of this, please do an internet search and familiarize yourself with it. Here's a graphical representation of Maslow's hierarchy of needs.

This is a bit of an oversimplification of the hierarchy, but it basically says a person's sense of fulfillment increases as she moves up the hierarchy from her most basic needs being met at the bottom of the hierarchy—physiological needs—to the ultimate sense of fulfillment at the top of the hierarchy—self-actualization. Maslow's hierarchy posits that every human being, subconsciously at least, strives for self-actualization. We are wired for it.

However, Maslow also said you can't achieve fulfillment at a higher level on the hierarchy unless and until your needs have been met at the levels below. For example, Maslow would say you can't reach your highest capacity at being creative (an aspect of self-actualization at the top level of the hierarchy) if you have no money and are worried about where your next meal will come from (an aspect of physiological needs at the bottom). I would submit to you that Planned Parenthood's abortion services product is very attractive to many women facing unexpected pregnancies because they fear—sometimes consciously, sometimes subconsciously—that their pregnancies threaten their needs on ALL five levels of Maslow's hierarchy.

Mr. Maslow Meets *Groundhog Day*

How so? Let me use an example from the world of Hollywood. Do you remember the movie *Groundhog Day* starring Bill Murray? Bill Murray's character keeps reliving the same day over and over, but each "new" day, he remembers what happened and the mistakes he made each day. This gives him the opportunity to correct course and change things that didn't turn out how he would have liked. He gets a seemingly endless string of do-overs. Finally, after so many days of do-overs, he lives the perfect day that he always wanted to live.

From the perspective of Maslow's hierarchy, Bill Murray's character finally achieved perfect self-actualization. Now I would like you to think about all the things that have occurred in your life, or if that's a bit too much to think about, then think about the things you did in just this past year. Would you like a do-over for some of those things? Yes, me too!

Imagine if someone offered you a "Groundhog Day" product for the past year, where you could "undo" things that didn't turn out like you had hoped, and try, try again until everything happened just as you wanted. I think you would agree with me that any company that could develop such a product would make a pretty penny!

Well, consider this. In a sense, Planned Parenthood offers a type of "Groundhog Day" product for a woman experiencing the fear of an unexpected pregnancy. What do these women actually want? They want to rewind the clock. They believe if they can get back to being "un-pregnant," then their fears will disappear. Planned Parenthood's product, abortion services, is so attractive to women because ***it gives them exactly what they think they want****: to return to the way things were before they became pregnant*. Planned Parenthood offers a woman the opportunity to rewind the clock, so to speak. An abortion can serve as a kind of time machine for the woman, returning her to the state she was in before she became pregnant.

The cornerstone of Planned Parenthood's marketing, at the subconscious level, is that abortion services provide a woman a way to "undo" the past, a way for her to get back on the path of pursuing self-actualization by removing an obstacle to that pursuit—the preborn human growing in her womb. Make no mistake, products and services that offer to take someone back to the way things were—what I call "time machine" services, in the sense of going back in time—have very compelling value propositions.

Abortion services fall in that category, and as such, are very tough to compete against. If Planned Parenthood's abortion services, by taking a woman back to the way things were before her unexpected pregnancy, promise to empower her by opening a path for her to achieve self-actualization, you may be wondering how pro-life pregnancy centers are countering that. Are pro-life pregnancy centers promising to empower women by opening a path for them to reach self-actualization by way of choosing life for their preborn babies? For the most part, no, they aren't.

Defense Is Not the Best Offense

Why not? Recall again that pro-lifers are primarily oriented toward the *defense* of life of preborn human beings. Pro-lifers want to *defend* preborn humans from abortion, and naturally, pro-lifers also believe the women carrying preborn humans in their wombs should want to defend those lives as well.

This defensive orientation is on full display at most pro-life pregnancy centers. Leaders of pro-life pregnancy centers talk a lot about "protecting" women—protecting them from Planned Parenthood, from bad fathers, from the culture of death, etc. Protection is about defense. An orientation toward protection leads pro-life pregnancy centers to focus primarily on the bottom two tiers of Maslow's hierarchy: physiological and safety needs. On the other hand, an orientation toward empowerment covers not only physiological and safety needs, but all five levels on Maslow's hierarchy.

Empowerment is about *offense*. Just from the perspective of Maslow's hierarchy of needs, I think you can see why the abortion services product is more attractive to women than the choose life services product. The choose life services product attends to a woman's basic needs, whereas the abortion services product promises to open a path for a woman to reach self-actualization. Granted, objectively speaking, the promise offered by the abortion services product is a lie, but women want to believe that promise is true.

Bring the Offense on to the Field

Pro-life pregnancy centers and the philanthropists who support them believe that a woman facing an unexpected pregnancy should **want** to choose life for the preborn human being growing in her womb. From a ***moral*** perspective, they are absolutely right. **However, from the perspective of developing a product offering that is more attractive than**

Planned Parenthood's, most pro-life pregnancy centers are completely missing the point.

A key reason Planned Parenthood's abortion services product wins in the market, as measured by market share, is because it clearly answers the question on a woman's mind: **What does getting an abortion mean for** *me*? **How can pro-life pregnancy centers go on offense and offer a choose life services product that effectively counters** *Planned Parenthood's abortion services product*? It starts with answering, in a very compelling way, the competing question that is on the woman's mind: **What does choosing life for this baby mean for *me***?

Offering a choose life services product that gives a woman an attractive answer to that question moves a pro-life pregnancy center from a marketing and sales approach that is defensive in orientation to an offensive orientation that seeks to empower women. What might such an empowering choose life services product look like? I answer that question in the case study found in the concluding chapter of this part of the book. But for now, think of it this way. Creating a successful business is a simple two-step process:

1. Find out what your customers want.

2. Give it to them.

Most businesspeople read that simple two-step formula and say, "Duh!" But if it's so simple, ask those same businesspeople to **prove** that their companies are actually doing this, and you'll find them saying they have to run because they're late for a meeting, and they'll get back to you on that. You likely **won't** hear back.

Product marketers, yours truly included, have a tendency to create what they think their customers *should* want, not what they actually *do* want.

Some Very Good News

Here's what I believe is very good news for pro-life pregnancy centers. From the perspective of Maslow's hierarchy of needs, even though the choose life services product offered by pro-life pregnancy centers face a huge competitive disadvantage versus the abortion services product offered by Planned Parenthood, pro-life pregnancy centers still win some clients away from Planned Parenthood. I have read hundreds of stories revealing how women changed their minds about getting an abortion after going to pro-life pregnancy centers. I think there is a fundamental reason why many women change their minds: they know the life growing in their wombs is a human being.

Currently, the subconscious drive for self-actualization may play to the advantage of Planned Parenthood, but the conscious drive to "do no evil" plays to the advantage of pro-life pregnancy centers. Simply, deep down, many if not most women, do not want to end the lives of their own children. However, with the desire to achieve self-actualization ever present in their subconscious minds, many women need from pro-life pregnancy centers more than a product that meets their physiological and safety needs.

Therefore, I believe the product improvement path for pro-life pregnancy centers to pursue is clear. Pro-life pregnancy centers in the PLBI will win more battles against Planned Parenthood to the extent they can offer and then deliver on the promise that a woman choosing life for her preborn baby will meet not only her physiological and safety needs, *but also* her needs for love and belonging, esteem, and self-actualization. Within the environment of our current culture of death, I don't underestimate the monumental undertaking required to successfully brand choosing life as the more empowering choice compared to choosing abortion.

Such a marketing campaign would be an expensive, long, and hard-fought war fraught with failures, relentless attacks from the abortion industry, and numerous starts and stops, with no guarantee of success.

However, unless the PLBI as a whole goes on offense by repositioning in the minds of young women that choosing life results in greater empowerment for women than choosing abortion, I believe pro-life pregnancy centers will gain little ground in their market share battle against Planned Parenthood and the abortion industry. In business, "repositioning" your product or service in the minds of your clients is all about marketing, which I turn to in the next chapter.

Chapter Ten BOTTOM LINE

Planned Parenthood's product, abortion services, is so attractive to women because **it gives them exactly what they think they want**: to return to the way things were before they became pregnant. One of the reasons Planned Parenthood's abortion product wins in the market, as measured by market share, is because on a subconscious level, it clearly answers the question on the woman's mind: **What does getting an abortion mean for** *me*? **Pro-life pregnancy centers can counter that by** answering, in a compelling way, the competing question that is on the woman's mind: **What does choosing life for this baby mean for** *me*? Offering a choose life product that gives an attractive answer to that question moves a pro-life pregnancy center from having a marketing and sales approach that is defensive in orientation to putting an offense on the field that seeks to empower women. Pro-life pregnancy centers in the PLBI will win more battles against Planned Parenthood to the extent they can reposition choose life services as not only meeting a woman's physiological and safety needs *but also* empowering her by meeting her needs for love and belonging, esteem, and self-actualization.

CHAPTER ELEVEN: MARKETING IS EVERYTHING

Marketing is not a function; it is the whole business seen from the customer's point of view. Peter Drucker

I ended the previous chapter with a bold claim: the PLBI must go on offense by repositioning in the minds of young women that choosing life results in greater empowerment than choosing abortion. Repositioning falls within the business practice known as *marketing*. In the case study presented in the next chapter, you will learn how one pro-life pregnancy center successfully achieved such a repositioning. What the center in our case study accomplished in terms of winning the market share battle against Planned Parenthood was the fruit of marketing done exceedingly well and consistently over a long period of time.

I want to be very clear what I mean by "marketing" because even among business professionals there is a lot of confusion. Many think marketing just means getting the message out to your target clients about the value of your product or service and inviting them to buy it. Of course that is critically important for business success, but it's only one aspect of marketing.

My definition of marketing is much more comprehensive, where essentially, as famed management guru Peter Drucker put it, "Marketing ... is the whole business seen from the customer's point of view." So what does a customer see in the "whole business"? She sees the product, the price of the product, and where she can buy the product (where the product is placed), and she learns about those three things when the business promotes them to her in some way, usually through some form of advertising.

Those four fundamental elements of marketing are known as the 4 Ps: Product, Price, Placement (i.e. distribution), and Promotion. Of course developing a compelling product is the most important P of the 4 Ps. Without a product or service to offer a customer or client, no other function in a business really matters, does it?

The PLBI Already Has a Great Product! But ...

Here is some exceedingly good news! As you will see in the next chapter, the pro-life pregnancy center profiled in our case study has already proven it is possible to win against Planned Parenthood (as measured by market share). To achieve that, the center obviously offers a winning product to its clients! So consider this. That winning product can be modeled and used by other pro-life pregnancy centers!

But wait. There's even more good news on that front. All pro-life pregnancy centers in the PLBI are already excellent at one of the other 4 Ps, and that's price. Most centers offer their choose life product to prospective clients at the best price there is: FREE! And to keep the good news going, there are also many pro-life pregnancy centers that excel at placement (distribution), with brick-and-mortar locations in major populated areas, sometimes situated right next to or across the street from a Planned Parenthood abortion facility.

Think about that. The PLBI already has a winning formula in three of the 4 Ps of marketing! Pro-life pregnancy centers could follow the winning product blueprint of the pro-life pregnancy center profiled in the upcoming case study chapter, and many centers already have a winning formula for price and placement. With those three Ps in place, surely the PLBI will be able to shut down Planned Parenthood and the abortion industry, right?

Unfortunately, I don't think so. Even with very competitive product, price, and placement, I am not optimistic that the majority of pro-life pregnancy centers would gain much in market share versus Planned Parenthood. Why don't I think they would succeed? Because if you want to win the market share battle against your competitor, especially when your competitor already has a dominant market share, you've got to be excellent at all four of the 4 Ps. The 4 Ps are a package deal. Your business can be great at three of the Ps, but if it is seriously deficient at just one of them, that can sink the whole ship.

Currently, I don't believe it is in the operating DNA of most pro-life pregnancy centers to commit to excellence at all of the 4 Ps of marketing. In my experience, centers are far too enamored with their product as it currently is (our product saves lives!) and believe that will carry the day for them. Market share data say otherwise. To be fair to pro-life pregnancy centers, the "product is so good it sells itself" mentality is very common in many organizations, not just in the PLBI. Let me share with you a story from my own experience that demonstrates why just having the best product is not a formula for winning the market share battle against your competitor.

A Bad Case of "It's So Good It Sells Itself"

About fifteen years ago, my wife, our kids, and I trained at a local karate dojo. My wife was born and grew up in Japan, and we raised our kids to be bilingual and bicultural, so karate for us was about more than just self-defense. It was another way for us to connect to Japanese culture. Anyways, this karate business had one master karate trainer at one location. The karate master offered standard beginning karate classes to anyone (he even took me!), but the core product he was known for was that he successfully developed champions who won international karate competitions. He had achieved this success consistently over several decades.

His product was top of the class in terms of generating championship-level karate skills. Yet he had only one location in a strip mall (placement), underpriced his offering relative to the quality provided (price), and brought in customers by word of mouth only (promotion). His business struggled mightily to stay afloat. He had to move locations often (couldn't afford rent increases), and had myriad other business operations challenges. Yet no one denied that he offered the best karate product. He built champions!

In contrast to this, his nearest geographic competitor, a business called Tiger Schulmann's Martial Arts, didn't have quite as good a product in the sense that he didn't turn out karate experts who won international competitions. However, Tiger Schulmann's TV ads (promotion) showed normal, everyday folks training hard, dressed in cool-looking karate clothes (*gi*). You may not actually become a karate tournament champion with Tiger's training, but Tiger made you look and feel like one. He also offered a number of convenient locations all around the city (placement), as well as attractive "starter packages" (price) to entice you to try out his training. You could say that Tiger's product, karate training, was not the top of the class, but it was still very good, and importantly, his business also excelled at the other three Ps of marketing. I think you can probably figure out which karate business was more financially successful and created more perceived value for more clients.

If You Build It, Will They Come?

In my work with pro-life pregnancy centers, I often run in to the same mentality my karate master suffered from: the curse of "our product is so good it sells itself." As you will see in the next chapter, the case study pro-life pregnancy center certainly has an amazing product, but it doesn't stake its success only on its product. On the contrary, it commits to being excellent at ALL of the 4 Ps of marketing. Which brings us to the major flaw in the marketing strategies of most pro-life pregnancy centers in the PLBI: promotion.

Most pro-life pregnancy centers' attitudes about promotion remind me of the 1989 movie *Field of Dreams* where the character played by Kevin Costner keeps hearing the whisper "If you build it, they will come." In the movie, after ignoring the whispered message for a time, he finally builds a baseball field in his cornfield in Iowa, and many ghosts of past professional baseball players show up to play ball again. Listening to that message and finally acting on it worked out well for him in the end.

In business, however, "If you build it, they will come" is not a sound marketing strategy. You have to tell people what you built and what problem it will solve for them, and then invite them to take action. The template is something like, "Hey you! Come to my place of business because when you do, our business has a product/service that will solve a problem/frustration you are experiencing in this particular area of your life." Telling prospective customers what you've got for them and inviting them to take advantage of it is called promotion. You can never fall into the trap of thinking your product somehow sells itself. Even Apple, the company that has probably the most "sells itself" product imaginable, the iPhone, promotes the iPhone constantly, exhaustingly, without ceasing. If you live in the United States, you would have to practically shut yourself in a room 24/7 to avoid being exposed to some kind of advertising about the iPhone.

Pro-life pregnancy centers in the PLBI come up woefully short in promoting their organizations to their prospective clients. From a marketing perspective, this is particularly devastating when you consider that research (see Charlotte Lozier Institutes study titled "Turning Hearts toward Life II: New Market Research for Pregnancy Help Centers") reveals that more than 90 percent of young women in the United States know the brand name of Planned Parenthood, the primary competitor of most pro-life pregnancy centers. As I often say to leaders of pro-life pregnancy centers, if women don't know about your center *before* they face an unexpected pregnancy, then they will not go to your center *when* they face an unexpected pregnancy. You've got to promote your choose life services aggressively, *all the time*.

But Promoting Our Services is So Expensive!

Even when I've been successful convincing leaders of pro-life pregnancy centers how critically important promotion is, they predictably offer an objection: advertising is so expensive! They'll say something like, "We want to get the word out about our services, but we just don't have the available funds to do so." In other words, investments in advertising are not a priority, just something the center might do if there are a few extra dollars lying around. Most leaders of pro-life pregnancy centers view advertising as an expense, not an investment. They prioritize available funds to flow to servicing the needs of women, in other words, funding the "product" the center offers to its clients.

To illustrate this, let me share with you what happened at a meeting I attended not long ago with the leadership team and board of directors of a pro-life pregnancy center operating in a large city. As we discussed the dollars needed to execute an effective long-term advertising program, one of the board members said something to the effect of "It's so expensive. If possible, I would rather use that money to buy more things to give for free to the women coming to our center." There you have it in a nutshell—the view that advertising and promotion is a cost, and not an investment.

To be fair, it is not uncommon at all to hear this type of statement by leaders of nonprofits, and believe it or not, by leaders of some for-profits as well. It's remarkable how many get so caught up in the wonderful benefits of their product that they just don't see how critical it is to promote it to target clients.

Invite Them to the Party

To emphasize how critical promotion is to business success, here's an example I used recently when speaking with a board member of a pro-life pregnancy center to try to get him to "step out" of the overly excessive focus on the product and understand that women won't know about the center's choose life services unless the center advertises it. I said to him, "Imagine you plan to have a party at your house. You have already acquired all the basics you need to make sure your guests have a good time at the party. Let's say you have about $1,000 remaining in your party budget. But at this point, the guests you want to come to your party are just 'prospective' guests, because they don't yet know that you're having a party. Therefore, it seems logical that you should 'invest' your remaining $1,000 to send out invitations that contain a very attractive message so that your prospective guests think, 'No way am I going to miss that party!' That $1,000 is an investment, not an expense, because if you don't send invitations, no one will come to your party, and the 'return' (outcomes, impact, results, etc.) on your party will be **ZERO**. If instead of sending invitations to prospective guests, you decide to spend your remaining $1,000 on even fancier food and drink so that your party will be even more awesome, what will happen? You will end up having a party with a lot of great food and drink, perhaps even worthy of an article in the local newspaper it looks so awesome, and no one will come to your party to enjoy it. As the party time arrives, and you stand there all alone, surveying your exquisitely prepared party environment that no one is there to enjoy, you may think to yourself, 'Man, look at this great party! Those people don't know what they're missing!' You're probably right about the great party part, but those people won't be 'missing' it, emotionally at least, because they don't even know about it. You've just fallen into the trap that most pro-life pregnancy centers fall into: treating advertising and promotion as an expense, an afterthought really, instead of treating it as an investment."

The board member's reaction to my story? "Brett, I understand, but advertising is just so *expensive*." Sigh....

It's a Nonnegotiable

I'm sure you've experienced times when you didn't have the words to say to someone, and then later on when you've had time to think about it, you think to yourself, "I wish I had said that." Here's what I wish I had replied to that board member after his comment about advertising being so expensive: "You think advertising is expensive because you view it as an *option*, not as a necessity. If you viewed advertising about your center to be as necessary to your 'success' as you view having an ultrasound machine and a skilled ultrasound technician to be necessary, then you would simply look at advertising not as a 'nice to have' for your business, but as a 'must have'—a nonnegotiable."

"If you viewed promotion of your center that way, when the executive director of your center presented her plans to the board of directors, you would defend the promotion budget line item as fiercely as you defend the budget line items for an ultrasound machine and a skilled ultrasound technician."

"The reason you don't do that is because you don't view your center as a business that competes against Planned Parenthood where 'success' is defined by winning the market share battle, not by just developing and offering a great product."

I realize that last paragraph may seem like a harsh assessment on my part. But in my experience working with many pro-life pregnancy centers, it's true for the most part that they don't consider significant investment in promotion a nonnegotiable necessity.

Put Promotion at the Front of the Line

If I had a team that was starting a new pro-life pregnancy center tomorrow, I would *not* begin with the product strategy. It is reasonably well known how to create an attractive pro-life pregnancy center product. There are already several product models to choose from that we could quickly replicate or model.

Instead, I would begin with a robust promotion strategy backed by a substantial, nonnegotiable advertising budget. I would only bring on board members who bought in to that strategy. And what would happen once our center had been up and operating about six months, the whole time relentlessly promoting our services to prospective clients? I believe our center would quickly pass other local pro-life pregnancy centers in terms of client volume, even centers that had been operating for years with a great choose life product.

More important than outshining other local pro-life pregnancy centers, however, would be that our new center's ever-expanding client volume would slowly and continually increase our market share versus our real competitor, Planned Parenthood. This is exactly how the pro-life pregnancy center in our case study won the market share war against Planned Parenthood in a large city. The center essentially drove the local Planned Parenthood abortion facility out of business. In the next chapter, I take a deep dive into how they did it.

Chapter Eleven BOTTOM LINE

To gain market share against Planned Parenthood and the abortion industry, pro-life pregnancy centers in the PLBI need to excel at the four fundamental elements of marketing known as the 4 Ps: Product, Price, Placement (i.e., distribution), and Promotion.

Currently, most centers don't commit to excellence at all of the 4 Ps of marketing, believing that the attractiveness of their choose life services will make them successful. Pro-life pregnancy centers fail to promote because they typically consider advertising an unnecessary expense instead of a nonnegotiable investment.

CHAPTER TWELVE: PROOF IT IS POSSIBLE TO BEAT PLANNED PARENTHOOD: A CASE STUDY

> *Our advantages over Planned Parenthood are infinite because we have Christ. So we're always going to be better than Planned Parenthood. We're going to look better, smell better, and be better, because we love these girls who come to us. Planned Parenthood could care less about them.* Bridget VanMeans

This is the payoff chapter in this book. It is a book within a book. In this chapter I share with you proof it is possible for a pro-life pregnancy center to win the market share battle against Planned Parenthood. And consider this: if it's possible for one pro-life pregnancy center to win, then shouldn't it also be possible for other pro-life pregnancy centers to win? And if many pro-life pregnancy centers across the country win, then isn't it plausible that the PLBI could shut down Planned Parenthood and the abortion industry? I think the answer to that question is a resounding YES! Think about it. If you add up enough wins in local market share *battles* around the country, eventually you win the market share *war* against abortion on a national level.

Before we dive into the case study of the pro-life pregnancy center that actually won the market share battle against Planned Parenthood, effectively driving it out of business, let me repeat for you the quote by Bridget VanMeans that begins this chapter: "Our advantages over Planned Parenthood are infinite because we have Christ. So we're always going to be better than Planned Parenthood. We're going to look better, smell better, and be better, because we love these girls who come to us. Planned Parenthood could care less about them."

That quote captures the essence of how one pro-life pregnancy center beat Planned Parenthood on the battlefield of business. Bridget VanMeans leads ThriVe Express Women's Healthcare, and she was the visionary behind the strategy that effectively drove Planned Parenthood out of business in St. Louis, Missouri. I had the honor of visiting ThriVe (yes, the V is capitalized) in St. Louis twice, as well as conducting two in-depth interviews with Bridget. Those interactions helped me better understand exactly how the ThriVe team won.

I want to share those insights with you in this chapter. As we proceed, I'll let Bridget do most of the talking, sharing with you in her own words how ThriVe accomplished such a remarkable feat. As we go along, I will add my own analysis here and there, but if I had to summarize in my own words how ThriVe beat Planned Parenthood, I would say ThriVe is excellent at marketing—meaning *all* the 4 Ps of marketing we discussed in the previous chapter. And remember, *marketing is everything*.

However, there is something much greater at ThriVe than excellent marketing. In my view, excellent marketing is ThriVe's business foundation, but that foundation is built on another foundation—the foundation of the foundation, if you will. What is that foundation of the foundation?

It is this: ThriVe is first and foremost centered on Christ, and from that orientation flows excellent, effective marketing, because ThriVe truly seeks to do the Father's will in all things, and from that emanates an authentic passion in the hearts of ThriVe's team members to love its clients as Christ loves them.

Prove It: Part 1

I hope you are excited to learn more about ThriVe, but I also bet the business professional part of your mind is a bit skeptical that one pro-life pregnancy center could outcompete Planned Parenthood, especially in a large city. I'm sure you want to conduct a little due diligence, because as our Lord tells us, "By their fruits you will know them" (Matthew 7:16). So before we hear from Bridget about the detailed inner workings of ThriVe's strategy that beat Planned Parenthood in St. Louis, let's set the stage by first verifying the "fruit." After all, if my claim about ThriVe's success can't be measured with real data, then why trust that ThriVe is really on to something special? So here we go with some "fruit."

ThriVe operates in St. Louis, the largest city in the state of Missouri. So let's first take a look at the number of abortions in the state of Missouri for the years 2009 through 2020.

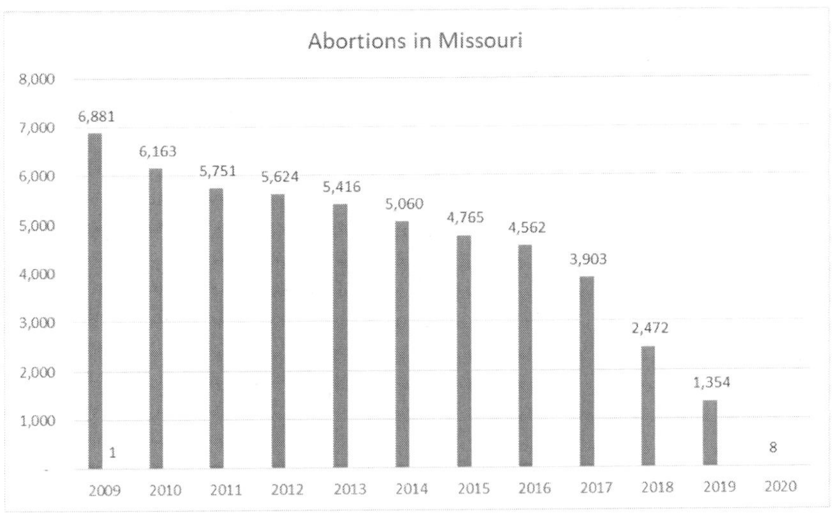

As you can see, abortions in Missouri were declining gradually year after year, and in 2018, declined suddenly and dramatically, then repeated another dramatic decline in 2019, and then essentially went to near zero in 2020, making Missouri for all intents and purposes our country's first abortion-free state. We should all praise God for that!

So was that momentous achievement all because of the work of ThriVe? Of course not, and Bridget would never make that claim. Bridget would tell you that winning the war against Planned Parenthood and the abortion industry requires a highly coordinated strategic campaign on both the demand side (decrease demand for abortion services while increasing demand for choose life services) and the supply side (decrease supply of abortion services while increasing supply of choose life services).

In other words, becoming an abortion-free city, and then an abortion-free state, and then an abortion-free nation requires the combined efforts of pro-life organizations succeeding on the demand side (the PLBI!) and on the supply side (pro-life legislators and advocacy groups)—the achievements of both groups made possible by pro-life philanthropists like you investing their 3T assets. So can we quantify ThriVe's specific impact as Missouri progressed toward becoming an abortion-free state? Yes, we can.

Prove It: Part 2

We can show quantitatively that ThriVe won its marketing battle against Planned Parenthood in St. Louis. Again, remember that marketing from our perspective means the 4 Ps. Excellence in all of the 4 Ps is critical for success. Without excellent marketing, ThriVe, or any other pro-life pregnancy center, would have fewer opportunities to make "sales"—sales in this case defined as the client's final decision to "buy" choose life services instead of abortion services. Think of marketing as the 4 Ps working together to attract clients, and sales as successfully encouraging the clients to buy.

From the perspective of a pro-life pregnancy center like ThriVe, marketing means what ThriVe offers resonates with young women. Sales means that once the women arrive at ThriVe, they discover that everything ThriVe offers them is in fact congruent with what attracted them to ThriVe in the first place, and because of that, the women are more open to being encouraged to select ThriVe's choose life product instead of the abortion services product offered by Planned Parenthood. So using measurable data, how effective has ThriVe been at marketing? Take a look at the graph that follows.

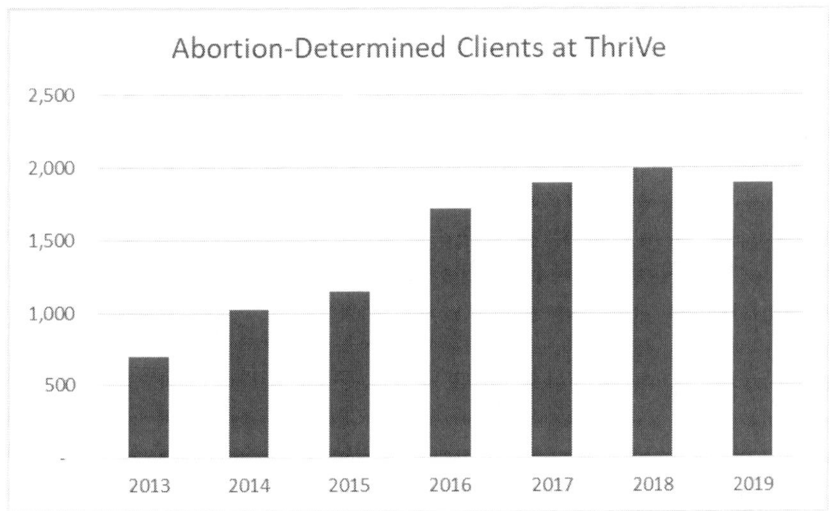

The graph shows how many pregnant abortion-determined women came through the doors at ThriVe's St. Louis locations each year from 2013 through 2019. Now we can take these data and combine them with the Missouri state-level abortion data to understand ThriVe's specific impact. Here's what we see when we show Missouri state-level abortion data as bars, and ThriVe's number of abortion-determined clients as a line.

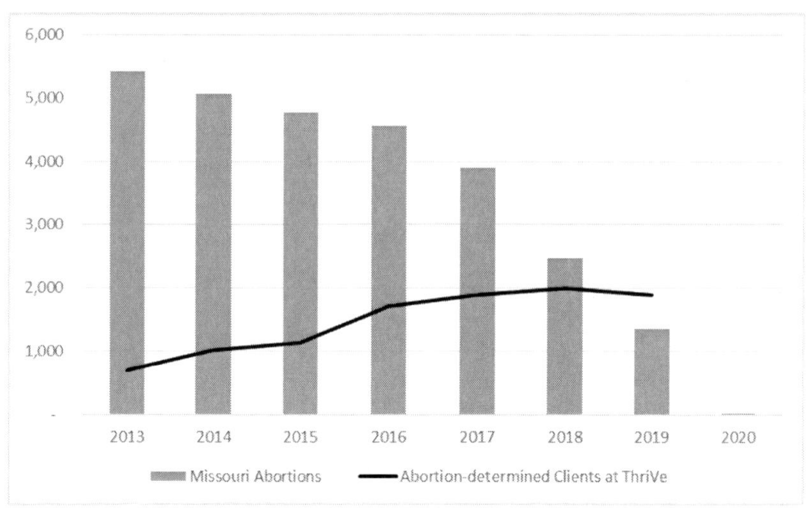

Note in the graph that as the cumulative effect of ThriVe's marketing programs in St. Louis began to kick in significantly in 2016, Missouri's abortion numbers began to drop rapidly in 2017. Now that's what I call winning the marketing battle! You as a business professional can imagine how great it would feel to show this kind of graph to those who invested in your particular business—a graph revealing your sales increasing year after year while your main competitor's sales drop in lockstep with your sales increases.

Your investors see that, year after year, an increasing percentage of all available clients came to your business instead of going to your main competitor. Exciting, yes!? How did you achieve those market share gains against your competitor? You did it the same way ThriVe did—by serving your clients with a product that had more perceived value than your competitor's, and by doing an excellent job of marketing it to your prospective clients. Winning feels great, doesn't it?

Let's get back to ThriVe. I would like you to picture in your mind that same chart showing ThriVe's impact on abortion numbers in Missouri, but now go through a list of the largest cities in the United States and imagine that same thing coming true in each of those cities. I hope that image gets you excited! ThriVe has proven that winning the market share battle against Planned Parenthood is not wishful thinking. It can be done. ThriVe's success in St. Louis proves a pro-life pregnancy center, by implementing a market-share-winning business model, can shut down Planned Parenthood inside of a decade. From a business perspective, again, it's all about excellent marketing and the operational excellence built into ThriVe's "product."

In The Beginning ...

I hope the data, the proof of impact, the measurable "fruit" ThriVe achieved in St. Louis has you eager to learn more details about how the ThriVe team did it. Let's dive into that now. But a word of caution. Please understand that ThriVe's success did not happen overnight. At this point, it is good to recall what Bill Gates of Microsoft fame once said: "We always overestimate the change that will occur in the next two years and underestimate the change that will occur in the next ten."

In fact, before Bridget arrived a little over ten years ago at the pro-life pregnancy center that would eventually evolve into ThriVe, the center she took over was fairly typical of other pro-life pregnancy centers around the country. It had been founded years earlier by someone who was passionate about the Pro-Life Movement and wanted to do something hands-on to help more women who were experiencing unexpected pregnancies. The center was relatively successful for many years, but then suddenly fell on hard times financially and was on the verge of shutting down, when in a last-ditch effort, the board of directors of the center took a chance on someone who did not come from the ranks of the Pro-Life Movement. And that someone was Bridget VanMeans.

> Bridget shares:
>
> When I decided to join the center that would later become ThriVe, they were spiraling down, less than thirty days away from bankruptcy. So when I drove into St. Louis with my daughter (I'm a single mom) and my two dogs, the center had twenty-one days left. The organization was living off of a line of credit on a credit card. There was no money in the bank. They had laid off people, and the donors were staying away by the thousands. So when I hit the ground, we had twenty-one days to turn things around, or everybody went home. Because ThriVe was rapidly spiraling down, I acted. If the organization had been doing well, I would have been tempted to adopt their existing ways of doing things. But because it was less than thirty days away from bankruptcy, I couldn't afford to adopt their existing ways. I don't think the Lord wanted me to think about this challenge like a religious person. In order to fully engage me, He didn't want me to think like the other pro-life pregnancy centers think. What that did was engage in me the business turnaround methodology I already knew so well from my business experience.

Already, I hope you can see in ThriVe something you rarely see in other pro-life pregnancy centers—the bold decision by the board of directors to turn the keys of the organization over to someone committed to running the organization *like a business*. That in itself was groundbreaking, but it wouldn't have meant much if Bridget hadn't brought with her strong business qualifications. What were her qualifications?

> Bridget explains:
>
> I professionally modeled throughout all of my childhood years and my teen years, and as I was modeling, I was interacting with some very successful businessmen in the fashion

industry. They thought I had business acumen, and one of them gave me an opportunity. And so it turned out that I had a natural gift for leadership, and I ended up making a transition from modeling into sales, and that opened some pretty incredible doors for me.

The most notable portion of my career, before I met the Lord, was that I became the senior regional manager for Nutrisystem in Chicago. I was very young at that time, only twenty-four years old. My peers were all in their forties. That opportunity led to my running about twenty-five Nutrisystem centers in the greater Chicago area. About 350 employees, $35 million in revenue. But even more importantly, I got to see the company grow from about a $50 million company to a $1.3 billion company, and we did that over a period of only four years.

My mentors at Nutrisystem were some of the best business operators out there. Nutrisystem would recruit from Texaco, IBM, GE, those kinds of companies. The president I reported to had been one of the top Texaco executives. Nutrisystem would hire these people called "Turnaround Kings." These are guys who are able to walk into a failing business, and within about a year, turn it around. And so I received this priceless education in terms of leadership and mentoring teams. In fact, when I joined the center that would become ThriVe, I went back to those mentors. I sent them the spreadsheets. I shared with them exactly what I was getting into. And some of my mentors, who had blueprinted that turnaround method I had learned, were great Catholic men. They said these principles will work, whether faith-based or not faith-based. These are principles that God will honor. These are basic business principles, in any situation.

Nutrisystem is different now, but when we had our brick-and-mortar locations, it was a medical model. So I was managing physicians, nurses, behavior modification specialists who were psychologists, and a sales force. The other thing that was very unique about it was that Nutrisystem was a female-oriented business model. Ninety-five percent of our patients were women. Only God could plant me in something like that, where I could gain experience that would prepare me to replicate a powerful business model in the women's pregnancy care movement. The skills and experiences I acquired married perfectly to what God had intended for the center.

Therefore, I came into the center like a businessperson. And we really broke almost every paradigm. We tried to hold onto the sacred nature of the pro-life movement, but we were probably breaking most of the day-to-day operational perspectives and paradigms that pro-life pregnancy centers typically follow. It turned out that the core business muscle that God had taught me had a worthy place in this work. That strong, almost military-like discipline in very aggressive, demanding environments made me quite confident and fearless. I felt like I could do it. I wasn't afraid. I believed in the principles. I believed in myself. And I believed in God. I think that was an important ingredient.

I think like a competitor. When I was at Nutrisystem, we had a competitor. Her name was Jenny Craig. Nutrisystem made a couple of critical strategic mistakes, and Jenny Craig was poised and ready to take advantage of those mistakes. So I learned that just as quickly as an organization could grow, it could also fall. That experience taught me that we could compete against—and beat—Planned Parenthood. Nutrisystem, at our peak, did $1.3 billion revenue. When I took over the

> center that would become ThriVe, Planned Parenthood was at about $1.1 billion revenue. So I didn't want to hear anybody say, "They're too big," because I knew they could be beaten. In addition, I was confident that Planned Parenthood had far less inspired leadership than Nutrisystem did, and I also knew that God was opposed to them. So let that inspire us to work harder! Let that passion drive us, but let it drive us to use ruthless business methodology!
>
> Let us remember that these young women are consumers, and that Planned Parenthood is a business. And like any business, they can be beaten. No business is too big to fail. I have experienced that, and it can actually happen quickly. So the Lord dropped me into St. Louis to turn around the center, and we started hitting some home runs.

As you can see, Bridget was certainly *not* cut from the mold of the Pro-Life Movement. From day one, she was thinking like a competitor, bringing a business mindset into the center, acknowledging that Planned Parenthood is a business, and understanding that the young women the center served were consumers. Bridget's words are not the human rights language of the Pro-Life Movement. Her words are the consumer-oriented language of the PLBI.

Whom Do We Serve?

Even though Bridget brought the language of business to the center, she knew that turning around the center and making it successful would require it to evolve into a fundamentally different kind of business. Different in what way? Then, as now, Bridget and her team knew the Lord was actually the source of the center's successful turnaround. As Jesus tells us, "I am the vine, you are the branches. Whoever remains in me and I in him will bear much fruit, because without me you can do nothing" (John 15:5).

Bridget again explains:

ThriVe has very strong business disciplines, but those disciplines will lay empty if they're not proven out and legitimized through Scripture, if they're not fueled by prayer, and if they're not granted by the Father. So if you were to sit down with my staff and they were to order our priorities, they would say that God, prayer, and the Word of God are first and foremost. And then they would get right to strategy, and then they would get right to outcomes.

So in other words, you can have a business model all you want, but you have to have a team who has caught the heart of God. The weapons of our warfare are not carnal, so even though we're highly strategic—using the language of smart business such as strategies and outcome measurements and KPIs—what has really moved us forward is the focus on God, and people actually seeing Him do miraculous things that they know transcend what's possible just through human effort.

So that is critical, the combination of the two (God and business model). We've seen what happens when other pro-life pregnancy centers implement business strategies, but leave God out. You'll hear them say such things as, "Well, we incorporated a medical model, and it didn't change anything." Or, "We bought a mobile unit and we couldn't get the girls to come." Or, "We put a mobile unit outside of the abortion clinic, and it hasn't made a big difference."

So the business strategies are important, but we believe our strategies are God-given, which is part of why they're so successful. We've not had one epic fail yet, although we have given ourselves permission to do so, but it's really God that gives that power. We want God to get all the credit. And we try to stay humble because we've seen enough cautionary

> tales out there with other centers. So that's also one of our prayers, is we ask the Lord for humility, because we've seen so many great works come off the tracks through man getting in the way of God.

Whom Does God Want Us to Serve?

I'm sure there are pro-life pregnancy center leaders, or philanthropists who support them, who upon learning about ThriVe's success would say, "Okay, we too hired a great leader with a business background, and we too serve God first. But we still aren't experiencing the success against Planned Parenthood ThriVe has achieved. Why aren't we winning the market share battle against Planned Parenthood? What are we missing?" You're about to hear Bridget answer that question. It comes down to this: ThriVe is crystal clear about who its client is and what its client wants. I believe that zeroes in on why ThriVe has been so successful in its competition against Planned Parenthood, and why so many other pro-life pregnancy centers have not been successful.

> We think about the young woman as a consumer. What is she buying? People think she's buying an abortion, but she's not. She's buying a future. She sees her unexpected pregnancy as the end of hope and the end of a future. She's also feeling like she's buying a medical solution because Planned Parenthood and the abortion movement brainwashed her into thinking that this was a medical choice—not an ethical choice, not even a parenting choice, but a medical choice that simply requires a medical solution. One of the things I constantly remind my partners about is this: The girl walking into our center, pregnant, is the single most pro-abortion consumer in the world at that moment.
>
> For these young women, we've lost the moral argument. If we could win the moral argument, the young woman

> wouldn't already be scheduled for an abortion appointment at Planned Parenthood. Seventy percent of our girls already have made an appointment at Planned Parenthood when they come to us. Whatever she wanted to hear about morally, she already knows. She's justified it. We have girls who'll look at us and say, "Well, we already know God forgives. So He's going to forgive me." Or, "I believe in Heaven, and Heaven's better for the baby than here." Pro-life pregnancy centers, for the most part, market themselves as a moral solution or as a care solution. They are not marketing themselves as a medical solution, and they are not marketing themselves as a solution that provides hope and a future for the woman.

In that statement, Bridget gets right to the crux of the matter. Let's start with her statement that "we've lost the moral argument." Before the Pro-Life Movement part of your brain reflexively reacts to Bridget's statement with something along the lines of, "But abortion is the most significant human rights issue of our lifetime! It *is* a moral battle!" I want you to understand that Bridget would wholeheartedly agree with you on that point. And while I make this next statement, which will likely irritate many pro-lifers, I want you to keep in mind ThriVe's market share results against Planned Parenthood that I covered earlier.

From the perspective of a pro-life pregnancy center winning the market share battle against Planned Parenthood, the undeniable truth that abortion is the most significant human rights issue of our lifetime is *completely irrelevant*. Why would I say such a thing? Because, as Bridget pointed out, the moral issue of abortion does not matter to the young pregnant women who seek an abortion. As Bridget said, the young women have already morally justified their decisions. Please take a second to read that again and let it sink in: *the young women have already morally justified their decisions*.

I understand why Bridget's claim can be very difficult for pro-life people to acknowledge, but for those who work in pro-life pregnancy centers in any capacity, it is critical to accept. Why? Because if a team member of a pro-life pregnancy center does not acknowledge this uncomfortable truth, it can lead to her slipping the immorality of abortion, sometimes subtly, sometimes quite overtly, into her initial interactions with young abortion-seeking women.

The result when that happens? The center team member's words can be perceived by the young women as completely incongruent with what is going on in their minds and therefore they will reject any words that contain moral undertones of judgment. That's right. Young women perceive such messages as judgmental.

She's Buying a Future

How to avoid coming off as judgmental? A center must effectively match its marketing to a young woman's mindset in a way that achieves a high level of congruency with what the young woman currently believes—to borrow a common phrase, "meeting her where she is." So if moral marketing is incongruent with a young woman's mindset, then what type of marketing is congruent with a young woman's mindset?

Bridget gave us the two essential elements that describe the mindset of a young woman: (1) "She's buying a future." (2) "She's buying a medical solution." Recall the discussion about Maslow's hierarchy of needs in Chapter 10. Remember that all people—you, me, everyone—ultimately pursue the top of Maslow's hierarchy: self-actualization. "She's buying a future" is about a woman seeking self-actualization.

As I discussed in Chapter 9, the woman either consciously, but more likely subconsciously, is thinking to herself, "What's In It For Me?" aka WIIFM. In other words, when choosing between alternatives—abortion services versus choose life services—for a young woman, WIIFM means "How does the option I'm considering make my life better? Which alternative, abortion services or choose life services, best empowers me to reach self-actualization in my life?" The business that gives a woman the most convincing answer to that question will win the most clients over time.

She's Buying a Medical Solution

Did Bridget's statement about young women "buying a medical solution" surprise you? Here are Bridget's words again: "She's also feeling like she's buying a medical solution, because Planned Parenthood and the abortion movement brainwashed her into thinking that this was a medical choice—not an ethical choice, not even a parenting choice, but a medical choice that simply requires a medical solution."

For pro-life people caught up in the language of the Pro-Life Movement, Bridget's statement can be hard to accept. Understandably, the Pro-Life Movement despises the fact that Planned Parenthood and the abortion industry position abortion in women's minds as a medical solution because pro-life people correctly perceive that making such a claim is deeply deceitful and intentionally hides the reality from young women that abortion, as a so-called medical solution, is in fact nothing but a license to abort a preborn human being. And pro-life people are 100 percent correct that Planned Parenthood is deceiving women. Nonetheless, Planned Parenthood, backed by significant financial resources, has been very effective at convincing millions of women over many decades that abortion is a medical solution. It requires humility to admit that Planned Parenthood and the abortion industry have already won the market positioning battle in women's minds.

Please note that I am not claiming the long-term market positioning war is over. Pro-life organizations can and will continue to work to influence young women to believe that choosing life is the best option for an unexpected pregnancy. However, in any industry, marketers on the front lines must deal with the reality of the here and now in order to win more clients than their competitors. And the current state of affairs in the PLBI is that Planned Parenthood and the abortion industry have won the positioning battle in women's minds, meaning most young women view abortion as a medical solution. Once an industry or a competitor has won the battle of positioning in a target client's mind, it is very difficult to reposition her mind. Does that mean a pro-life pregnancy center can't compete against Planned Parenthood? Not necessarily.

Practice Marketing Aikido

How can a pro-life pregnancy center compete and win at marketing when Planned Parenthood and the abortion industry have already won the battle of market positioning? An effective approach is to accept the reality that your competitor has won the market positioning battle, but then use your competitor's strengths to your advantage. In other words, even if your competitor has invested multimillions of dollars over many years to win the market positioning battle in the client prospect's mind, you can still turn your competitor's strength to your advantage.

How does one turn a business competitor's marketing strengths against him? Certainly not by yelling at the target clients, "Their product is terrible! Ours is better!" Your clients already believe your competitor's product is exactly what they are looking for, so yelling at them that they are wrong will resound like a clanging gong.

Instead, practice marketing aikido. Aikido is a Japanese martial art whereby one turns an attacker's strength and momentum against the attacker. I believe marketing aikido is exactly what ThriVe is skillfully practicing when it includes "Women's Healthcare" in the client-facing brand name of their business: ThriVe Express Women's Healthcare. If your competitor has successfully conditioned women to believe the choice of what to do about an unexpected pregnancy is a medical one, then don't waste your time and money pushing back against that positioning. Instead, be congruent with your prospective client's current belief system. Position your competing services in a way that aligns with what women already believe—brand your services as a medical choice: Women's Healthcare. That is smart marketing.

What Does Our Client Want?

Let's now go a little deeper into the 4 Ps of ThriVe's marketing.

The First P: PRODUCT

Let's start with PRODUCT. Bridget explains:

> We designed this Trojan horse of a superior business model that we could take into the marketplace that did not have on it the outward trappings of a pro-life or spiritual brand, but extremely turbo-charged spiritually from the heart. We decided that we must shake off the care and moral brand that so many pregnancy resource or pregnancy help centers put forward. The fact is that the girls want to be un-pregnant. So we focus on the young woman as a consumer. She's buying a product that's different than what most pro-life pregnancy centers think she's buying. We sell her that product.
>
> At our ThriVe center, she doesn't know we are pro-life because the model is medically driven. The only way she's going to know we're Christians is if she wants to know because we ask permission. So the way we approach it is we say, "Many of our patients prefer a holistic approach to their crisis. Are you open to hearing a little bit more about the spiritual dynamic?" If she says yes, then we move toward that. If she says no, it's strictly a medical visit. She definitely doesn't think she's encountered pro-life people. Still, prayer is key because that girl was made in God's image. She's already been prayed for, before she even walks in to our center.

There is a lot packed into Bridget's statements that is meaningful in terms of ThriVe's product, but I want to focus on two parts: "At our ThriVe center, she doesn't know we are pro-life because the model is medically driven," and "She definitely doesn't think she's encountered pro-life people." This is a key success factor: ThriVe positions its product toward young women based on the reality that those young women already believe abortion is not a moral issue, but a medical one.

Again, when those young women are at the point where they are actively seeking an abortion, do not push back against their strongly held beliefs. Meet them where they are. Accept the reality that they believe abortion is a medical issue. Invite them into your orbit where, through offering them authentic LOVE, you can start developing a relationship with them based on trust, which can become the seed that eventually leads them to choose the medical solution that is *always* the best option for them: carrying their pregnancies to term. ThriVe boldly expresses authentic love for young women right from the initial interaction.

> When a young woman walks in at ThriVe, she is going to feel something different. She's going to engage with wonderful people who also understand cultural relevance. We know how to wear our hair, our scrubs, the gear that we have on in the center. We outfit ourselves in a way where we have the greatest opportunity to position great medical services. We have her in an environment that screams of abundance, so when we tell her that we're going to help her, she feels, "Oh yeah, I guess these people really could help me. This place is awesome. It looks like a million-dollar place!" It's not a million-dollar place, but it looks like one.
>
> God talks about the dimly burning wick. We believe that motherhood is a dimly burning wick in every woman. It's written in women's spirits to be mothers! We all have motherhood written on our spirits. We need to speak to that in a

> way that clears away the fear—which allows that true hidden desire to come through! We want to neutralize the fear that almost always involves material things and a future. We speak to her of a bright future with confidence and love. We affirm her vision for college and career and all the things that she thinks have been derailed. We show her that none of those things have to be derailed and that we want those things for her as well.

There's Maslow again! These young women seek whatever will help them eventually get to the top tier of Maslow's hierarchy: self-actualization. The product ThriVe offers a young woman does exactly that. Think about Maslow's hierarchy of needs as you consider what the team at ThriVe does to show each young woman how much they love her: neutralizing fear about material things (safety and security—the first and second levels of Maslow's hierarchy), speaking to her of a bright future (love/belonging and esteem—the third and fourth levels of Maslow's hierarchy), and affirming her vision for college and career (self-actualization—the highest level of Maslow's hierarchy).

<u>The Second P: PLACEMENT (aka DISTRIBUTION)</u>

Next, let's consider PLACEMENT, commonly known in marketing as DISTRIBUTION. A couple of things to note about placement. As you read Bridget's comments about ThriVe's product, think about the importance of the visual environment to a young woman when she walks into the ThriVe center for her appointment.

Recall Bridget's statement. "We have her in an environment that screams of abundance, so when we tell her that we're going to help her, she feels, 'Oh yeah, I guess these people really could help me. This place is awesome. It looks like a million-dollar place!' It's not a million-dollar place, but it looks like one." I would like you to imagine how a young woman would react if upon arrival at ThriVe's center, the visual environment in the center expressed not abundance, but poverty. The woman, consumed with fear by her unexpected pregnancy, is already experiencing emotional and spiritual poverty, so if the visual environment at ThriVe also expresses poverty, how open do you think the woman would be to listening to the words of ThriVe's team members? Not very.

The reason this ties closely to placement (distribution) is that a physical location, in this case a pro-life pregnancy center facility, is essential for success. It would be much more difficult to create an empowering, neurologically triggering visual environment through virtual communication only. But there is a second reason the physical location is essential: the ultrasound machine. As Bridget explains concerning the ultrasound: "We show her an image of her baby, show her that heartbeat, and do it in a professional, non-manipulative way. We have the best ultrasound images that money can buy because we want that image to be as clear as possible."

Seeing an ultrasound of her baby enables a woman to come face to face with the reality of the life growing in her womb. The ultrasound is an essential piece of the puzzle to help a woman seeking an abortion to change her mind and choose life instead.

The Third P: PRICE

What's your favorite price for the goods and services you value? That's right: FREE! From the perspective of price, a major competitive advantage pro-life pregnancy centers have over abortion facilities is that pro-life centers typically offer their services at the best price there is: free. Abortion facilities charge a significant amount for their services, typically starting at more than $500. As Bridget says about ThriVe's services, "And then it's all at no cost to her. It's all free."

Of course, as a skilled business professional, you know nothing is actually free. So who is actually covering the costs of the services ThriVe offers its clients? The answer is pro-life philanthropists are paying for those services by way of their financial investments in ThriVe. For pro-life philanthropists, a willingness to cover the cost of those services is a sacrifice, an expression of the philanthropist's Christlike love for the young women. Remember Jesus saying in the sermon on the plain, "and lend expecting nothing back; then your reward will be great and you will be children of the Most High" (Luke 6:35).

That expression of love extends beyond the initial services ThriVe provides to young women free of charge. Remember that deep in a young woman's subconsciousness, what she truly desires more than anything is self-actualization. Bridget explains: "We love these girls so we offer full mentoring and discipleship through our Parent University, which is a minimum of an eighteen-month follow-up, and all of the supplies and everything that she gets, the life coaching, the job prep."

"Full mentoring and discipleship" for a minimum eighteen-month period is an expression of authentic love, of walking the talk, of earning credibility in young women's minds, of proving to them you really do love them. And what's more, to close out our discussion on price, these mentoring services are also offered to the women at the best price possible: free. The costs are covered by generous philanthropists who follow the Lord's command to "lend expecting nothing back."

The Fourth P: PROMOTION

And that brings us to the fourth P, and the one that is the major obstacle for so many pro-life pregnancy centers: PROMOTION. Pro-life pregnancy centers face two fundamental challenges concerning promotion. The first challenge is simply a question of whether a pro-life pregnancy center invests in promotion. Does the center's leadership make investments in promotion a nonnegotiable and then raise the necessary funds to run advertising campaigns? Or, as is the default for the vast majority of pro-life pregnancy centers, does the center leadership decide not to make promotion a priority?

Unfortunately, most centers invest little to nothing in promotion. But why is promotion essential for success? Remember what I already covered. If women don't know about pro-life pregnancy centers *before* they face an unexpected pregnancy, then women won't go to pro-life pregnancy centers *when* they face an unexpected pregnancy. From that viewpoint, promotion is not an expense. It's an investment.

But even if we assume a pro-life pregnancy center does decide to make investing in promotion a top priority, it's not out of the woods yet. Why not? Because bad promotion can be worse than no promotion at all. In other words, the center now faces the challenge of how to make the center's promotions actually work, how to make them effective. After all, if you invest in promotion and it doesn't bring any new clients through your door, you've basically wasted the valuable funds the pro-life philanthropists invested in your center.

So what are the keys to successful promotion for a pro-life pregnancy center? The essential key to success will be how well the center's promotional messages resonate with young women. A definition of the word "resonate" will be useful here. Here are two definitions from dictionary.com:

1. In electronics, to reinforce oscillations because *the natural frequency of the device is the same as the frequency of the source.*

2. To produce a positive feeling, emotional response, or opinion.

I love both definitions, but especially that first electronics definition! Let's try a little word play with that definition. Change the word "device" to "pro-life pregnancy center" and the word "source" to "young woman," and you have the following definition for resonate: "to reinforce oscillations because *the natural frequency of the pro-life pregnancy center is the same as the frequency of the young woman*." In other words, we can say the pro-life pregnancy center and the young woman are on the same wavelength.

And if the pro-life pregnancy center and the young woman are on the same wavelength, then there is a much higher likelihood of the center's promotional messages resonating with the young woman, resulting in the second definition of resonate: to "produce a positive feeling, emotional response, or opinion." And when that happens, there is a greater likelihood of a young woman trusting the source of the message and becoming a client of the pro-life pregnancy center.

Let's talk about the elements of a center's promotional messages that, if done well, increase the likelihood of those messages resonating with a young woman. As you will see, again, ThriVe is a model of success in this area.

What's in a Name?

Let's start with something very basic: a pro-life pregnancy center's name. Names, using just one word or several words, can be very important vehicles for conveying meaning to someone. This is especially so in the world of client-oriented businesses. If an eye doctor puts the word "dentist" on his sign, well, he will likely not attract many clients who need help with their vision. That probably sounds very obvious to you, but pro-life pregnancy centers make the fundamental mistake all the time of not using words in their business names that resonate with young women.

For example, in their business names, pro-life pregnancy centers will use words that focus on the preborn human being—words like "birth," "life," and even "baby." These are "clanging gong" words to young women who, as Bridget explains, think of abortion as a medical issue: "If you have a name that is pro-life or aspirational or spiritual, that name has to go. Girls are looking for a medical solution to a medical problem. She's been told her whole life that this is a medical decision and she wants to make a medical decision."

Words in a pro-life pregnancy center's business name that don't resonate with "abortion as a medical decision" will not be effective. So what did ThriVe do? First, instead of assuming they already knew what young women believed about abortion, or even worse, developing a business name expressing what they thought young women *should* believe about abortion, Bridget and her team invested in research to find out what young women *actually did believe* about abortion. Bridget explains: "We spent a quarter of a million dollars doing brand research to decide on our ThriVe Women's Express Medical Center name. We actually believe it has a spirit of supernatural unction on it. We believe it's God-breathed."

So the ThriVe name resonates with young women. But there's more.

<u>Look and Feel</u>

Being on the same wavelength with young women goes much deeper than just a business name that resonates. The look and feel of your pro-life pregnancy center has to resonate as well. Bridget explains: "The other thing that we thought would be important was branding, because these kids are all addicted to branding. They only buy branded clothes. They only drink branded drinks. If you don't have a brand, you are not relevant to them. We thought it would be pretty easy to come up with a magnificent aesthetic look for the ThriVe centers. We decided to develop a highly stylized aesthetic and a very strong brand so that young women could start identifying with us as being kind of the hip, in-fashion, on-trend brand."

Note how ThriVe's approach leverages branding approaches already used successfully by other industries toward the same prospective clients—young women. What process did ThriVe use to develop a "highly stylized aesthetic" it believed would resonate with young women? Again, ThriVe turned to research. Here is Bridget's explanation of their research process:

We observed these brilliant people who spent millions of dollars figuring out how to market to young people. We went to New York City and spent four days encompassing Thanksgiving and Black Friday so we could see how the top retailers in the world sell something to nineteen-to-twenty-nine-year-olds. We had a scientific way of evaluating the various retail stores. We took young people with us to see how they acted, where they had to go, where they had to stay, where were they willing to stand in line because they had to buy something. We took thousands of pictures. By the end of that four days, we had a really solid model that we knew would trigger those kids from nineteen to twenty-nine. And so everything is branded: our signage, our center, our social media.

So the three-legged stool that matters to Gen Ys and Gen Zs is Technology, Entertainment, and Design (the TED Talk model). I certainly see that with my kid and her friends. And so we've really pressed into that as the aesthetic, so very technologically savvy, very entertainment-focused, and really high design appeal. So when you walk into our centers, they are going to be slicker and more neurologically triggering than maybe even a lot of the fancy plastic surgery places, or some kind of fancy spa. So when the girls walk in, it's just like, "Whoa, what is this?"

And then they interact with the ThriVe team—these beautiful, poised, loving, patient, gorgeous women, which I always joke that I don't hire for looks but it does seem to happen. So just healthy living and loving God. Just full of life, and beautifully groomed, and matching. We have great gear so that the teams are all outfitted in really gorgeous-looking scrubs and shirts. So when the young women walk in, it's a really strong brand. And then God's presence is there. So what does all this

> do? It gives ThriVe credibility with these girls. It shouldn't, but it does, because that's just how these young women are.

Bridget continues about branding:

> From a branding perspective, we're really just modeling what Steve Jobs at Apple did so successfully with young people. How did he sell computers to them? He took the hardware and stuffed it into a really slick-looking computer. It was all about the colors and the shape of that module. That's how he took the market, with aesthetics. He had a great platform that didn't break down as much, but he knew that if he was going to sell it successfully to these young people, he had to put it in a hip little capsule.
>
> Then what does he do next? He drags it into an iPod, because he knows if he brands it with entertainment, he owns the kids. Then what does he do after that? He opens up iTunes. Then after that he's got the iPhone. He's got it all condensed down now, and he owns every child in the United States. They will not have anything but an iPhone.

<u>They're Into What I'm Into</u>

But ThriVe goes even deeper still. ThriVe wants to talk with young women about other things the young women are interested in, what they're into if you will, and do it in a way that resonates authentically. Bridget explains:

> You know, we're impressed with the Kardashians. No, they're not teaching us how to live life, but you know what they are teaching us how to do? How to have more followers than any other individual in human history. I want to know, what's Kim doing? Oh, she uses this color a lot or she's talking about this subject. Now we're not going to do anything that's irreligious or offensive, but we're going to get wise about the

> things they're doing that we can replicate. You'll see in our social media, we have health days where we look like a health desk. We have fitness days where models are talking about fitness and health. We have some days where the outreach is all fashion-oriented. You would think it came out of *Vogue* magazine.

And all of this flows into ThriVe's advertising strategy as well.

> And then our advertising. We have dominated the airwaves with not just the frequency, through the ad buys themselves, but the content of the ads just exploded on the scene. And we basically chased Planned Parenthood off radio, and we chased them off TV.

There are two key points here about ThriVe's advertising. First, Bridget mentions *frequency*. For ThriVe, that means running advertisements constantly. ThriVe *invests* in consistent, ongoing outreach to its clients through advertising. But advertising for advertising's sake is a waste of money if your message doesn't resonate with prospective clients. And the second key point Bridget mentions is the *content of the ads*. ThriVe's ads express the same elements already discussed in this section about promotion: medical solution, a business name that resonates with empowerment, a hip brand.

Let's close this section about promotion by letting Bridget summarize how all the elements of the marketing 4 Ps come together to result in ThriVe winning more clients than Planned Parenthood: "Love never fails. The abortion clinics will never be able to compete with us pound for pound. We're always going to smell better, look better, be nicer. The people that work in those abortion clinics aren't very nice and their clinics are never very nice. Their advertising is never going to be as clever and appealing as ours. **They don't have the relationships with the girls that**

we have, where we can be with them and listen to them and ask them questions, and they get caught up in the quest too."

In that last sentence that I bolded, I hope you see again Maslow's highest level on the hierarchy of needs: self-actualization. The abortion industry promises women self-actualization, but then doesn't deliver, whereas ThriVe promises women self-actualization and then keeps its promise. That is why ThriVe wins.

What Beating Planned Parenthood Looks Like

At the beginning of this chapter, we looked at data showing how the number of abortions effectively reached zero in the state of Missouri. ThriVe's business model played a key role in that momentous achievement. I don't believe it is possible to eradicate the scourge of abortion from your local community unless there is a pro-life pregnancy center like ThriVe that can outcompete Planned Parenthood.

Bridget recounts the story of ThriVe's victory over Planned Parenthood:

> They [Planned Parenthood] never had anyone rise up and give them a black eye and move them. There have been small abortion clinic locations that have closed, but there hasn't ever been a situation where a whole market got shut down. And we told Planned Parenthood early on we were going to drive them out. It was a little bit of a David moment. "Who are you, Planned Parenthood? This uncircumcised Philistine that's calling out the children of God. Today I will cut off your head and feed it to the birds." We basically told them that. And then they start seeing it happening. So we were all in their head because we made them run; we made them run across the bridge. And not through violence, but through a superior business model.

Let me repeat what Bridget said there at the end: "through a superior business model." What ThriVe achieved reminds me of something I once heard on a podcast about marketing. "Marketing is about connecting the dots for people. They don't know they need it [your product or service]. But *because you have their best interests at heart*, you help them see that they need it." I italicized "because you have their best interests at heart" since I believe the foundation of ThriVe's success is that it genuinely and authentically has young women's best interests at heart.

I hope you have seen so far in this chapter how everything ThriVe does is intensely focused on the needs of the young women facing unexpected pregnancies. And as more and more young women every year chose ThriVe's choose life product instead of Planned Parenthood's abortion product, ThriVe eventually drove Planned Parenthood out of business in St. Louis.

Bridget summarizes exactly how that happened: "That's always been our target, that we would eat into Planned Parenthood's market share by 50 percent. We hit that number in 2018. It sent them cascading exactly as planned. It was surgically precise, military-like execution. In 2019, they started spiraling, and October 21st, 2019, is when the last abortion clinic in Missouri pulled up their tent pegs and went running across the bridge to Illinois, literally stating that it was just too difficult to do business in Missouri. And so we had this mighty victory and became the first abortion-free state in the nation."

Upon reading that last sentence, I hope you will join me in a loud "Praise God!"

Return on Investment

A question for you. Would you agree with me that ThriVe's client wins in its competition against Planned Parenthood have a much deeper meaning than client wins in most industries? Client wins for ThriVe mean a woman changed her mind about getting an abortion and chose life. A client win for ThriVe means a preborn human life was saved from abortion at the hands of an abortionist.

How do you put a value on that? Have you ever thought about what a human being's life is worth? Believe it or not, there are economists who calculate such values, denominated in dollars. But when you look deeper at what those economists are talking about, they're just calculating what the average person will produce, economically speaking, over the average human life span. Of course, that can be useful to know.

But as faith-based people, when we ask what a human being's life is worth, we have something different in mind, don't we? We are asking what a human being's life is worth *from God's perspective*. And when we contemplate Christ on the cross, we all know the answer: each human being, made in the image and likeness of God, has *infinite* value. Yet, here on earth, the resources of time, talent, and treasure God has gifted to each one of us are not infinite. So we have to make choices: you, me, all of us have to choose where to invest the gifts God has given us.

And concerning an issue as emotional as abortion, it's easy to get caught up in our feelings and invest based only on emotions. There is nothing wrong with appealing to your emotions per se, unless pro-life organizations who appeal to your emotions aren't actually achieving any measurable successes at battling against Planned Parenthood and the abortion industry.

With that in mind, I encourage you to carefully investigate any pro-life organizations you currently support or are considering supporting. You will discover that a large number of those organizations have little real evidence of impact. And an investor who is satisfied investing in a pro-life organization that the investor knows can show no evidence of real impact is an investor engaging in "feelgoodism," not an investor engaging in actual impact philanthropy.

So if you were a prospective investor in pro-life programs, and you were seeking proven impact, what would you discover concerning ThriVe if you conducted thorough due diligence? Well, as you have gotten to know Bridget quite well in this chapter, you probably won't be surprised to hear her say that it is of paramount importance to Thrive to show its investors hard evidence of cost-effective impact and ROI. Remember that Bridget and her team run ThriVe like a business, so you will probably not be surprised to learn that ThriVe carefully tracks and measures the quantitative impact of the strategies it pursues.

Bridget explains:

> First of all, we're very evidence-based, because all good businesses are. When I was at Nutrisystem, we turned our numbers in every four hours. So I had twenty-five centers reporting in every four hours. That gives you an idea of the metric disciplines that I came out of. At ThriVe, we're very outcomes oriented. We are proud to say that we know we have reduced Planned Parenthood's numbers. And this is something I've never heard another pregnancy center be able to articulate. When we started the ThriVe model, our Planned Parenthood competitor clinic was doing about eight thousand abortions a year. In 2018, they did twenty-four hundred. So we've helped drop their business by close to 70 percent.

And then Bridget explains how ThriVe focuses specifically on ROI for its investors: "We're here to save a baby that would have been aborted if we weren't here. That's our metric." Naturally, saving babies from abortion is what pro-life philanthropists want. When they invest their treasure in pro-life pregnancy help centers, the ROI they seek is as many preborn babies' lives saved from abortion as possible. From a business perspective, the very good news is a pro-life pregnancy center's success or failure at achieving that ROI can be measured.

How does ThriVe measure up on this metric? For the answer, we can look at the report card ThriVe sends its investors every year. In ThriVe's

2019 report card for the St. Louis market, we see that ThriVe saved 1,692 preborn human lives from abortion. Unless you already have a fairly deep understanding of the work of pro-life pregnancy centers, you may be asking yourself, "How do I know that's a good number since I don't have any reference to compare it to?"

Excellent question. Let me demonstrate for you what a staggering achievement ThriVe's saved lives number is by comparing it to the saved lives results of another successful pro-life pregnancy center I am very familiar with. I will refer to the other pro-life pregnancy center as the "comparison center." Among pro-life pregnancy centers across the country, I would rate this comparison center a top-class competitor against Planned Parenthood. First, remember that ThriVe achieved the 1,692 lives saved number as a single pro-life pregnancy center business consisting of two physical brick-and-mortar facilities and several mobile bus units (clinics on wheels). Also remember that ThriVe achieved that number in the city of St. Louis, which has a population of about 2.2 million in its greater metro area.

Holding those facts in mind, how does that compare with the comparison center? Like ThriVe, our comparison center operates a single pro-life pregnancy center business consisting of two brick-and-mortar facilities. The comparison center operates in one of the top five most populated cities in the country, with a population in the greater metro area of 5.8 million, nearly three times the population of St. Louis.

While I admit there are other operating factors to consider, a simple comparison would lead us to estimate that with a population 2.64 times as large as St. Louis, if our comparison center's marketing was as effective as ThriVe's, then it should achieve 2.64 times more lives saved from abortion annually than ThriVe achieves. If we use that 2.64 calculation, taking ThriVe's 2019 saves number of 1,692 and multiplying it by 2.64, that would equate to our comparison center saving 4,467 preborn human lives from abortion in one year.

But actually, our comparison center achieves about 500 lives saved from abortion per year on average, *only 30 percent the number of lives saved from abortion* that ThriVe achieves even though the number of prospective clients for our comparison center is 2.64 times larger. Conclusion: ThriVe's lives saved numbers, adjusted for city population size, are unparalleled among pro-life pregnancy centers across our country.

But at What Cost?

As momentous as ThriVe's achievement is, I hope the business professional in you is thinking, "That is a fantastic result, but a result achieved *at what cost*?" In other words, ThriVe's lives saved numbers show that its marketing is extremely effective, but is it *cost-effective*? Bridget anticipates the question:

> But someone might say, "Well, doing all of that sounds expensive." However, ThriVe is in the top 1 percent in cost efficiencies per baby saved. It costs us about $1,200 per saved baby. So at $1,200 per baby saved, on the one hand I'm saying it's expensive, but it's actually wildly efficient. The national average for pro-life pregnancy centers is going to be somewhere between $5,000 and $10,000 per baby saved. Most pro-life centers don't even track it, but if they do, it's not unusual to find a metric of $30,000 per baby saved. Is that baby worth 30,000? Yes. But if you could save twenty-five babies for that same amount of money, then clearly that's a better Kingdom mindset.

I want to confirm a few things in Bridget's statement, based on my extensive experience working directly with pro-life pregnancy centers across the country. First, many centers do not even measure what it costs them to save a preborn baby's life from abortion. My question for you as you consider investing any of your valuable 3T assets in a pro-life pregnancy center is, "Why would you invest in a center that doesn't even bother to measure its own effectiveness?"

Second, for those pro-life pregnancy centers that do measure cost per baby saved, the $5,000, $10,000, or even $30,000 metric Bridget mentions results primarily from a center's unwillingness—specifically the leadership team's unwillingness—to embrace a philosophy of running a pro-life pregnancy center like a competitive business that seeks to win the market share battle against Planned Parenthood.

Third, no matter what "cost per baby saved" metric a center publicizes, you *must* be skeptical of the number and conduct your own due diligence. Why? Because if your definition of a life saved from abortion means that unless the pro-life center had intervened a woman almost certainly would have had an abortion, you will discover that is not necessarily how the pro-life pregnancy center will define a life saved from abortion. Many centers significantly expand the definition of a life saved to include *any* woman who walks through their doors and then ends up carrying her pregnancy to term—even if the woman wasn't seeking an abortion in the first place.

Your question to the center that demands a clear answer is simple. Would the woman have been almost certain to have ended up getting an abortion if not for the intervention of the pro-life pregnancy center? If the center's answer to that question is yes, then you know the center has achieved a genuine life saved from abortion. So before you invest your time, talent, or treasure in a pro-life pregnancy center, make sure you ask very detailed questions about the center's definition of what it means by a life saved from abortion.

In addition, for your past or even current investments in pro-life organizations, if you made those investments without expectation of results, my hope is that by this point in the book you are strongly considering changing your approach and becoming more demanding—meaning from now on you will demand pro-life organizations you invest in demonstrate proof of results. When you demand proof of results, many pro-life organizations, and I will venture to say most pro-life organizations, will not be able to give you that proof. From an investment perspective, the likelihood of an ROI in such organizations is extremely low. In other words, for every dollar you invest, the reward in terms of expected return (lives saved from abortion) is close to zero. Admittedly, there may be a return on your own feelgoodism, but not on actual measurable impact at ending abortion.

So why do pro-life philanthropists continue to invest in these types of zero-impact pro-life organizations and programs? I think pro-life philanthropists either haven't thought about investing with a mindset of demanding proof of results, or even if they have such a mindset, they aren't aware of any pro-life organizations that offer proof of impact in terms of measurable results. So pro-life philanthropists just go ahead and invest and hope for the best.

If this describes how you have approached your investments in pro-life organizations to date, I would like you to carefully read the following comments from Bridget, and consider if the hard-earned dollars you allocate to pro-life philanthropy could be invested in pro-life organizations and programs that offer a much higher expected ROI than you are currently achieving. Bridget says the following about ROI in pro-life organizations:

> Not that we're openly competing with other pro-life organizations, but I'm about stewardship. And a lot of people have given a whole lot of money in good faith. Don't get me wrong about this. I know that everybody who's in this movement is in it for the right reasons. But the bottom line is that there has been a lot of money given that has not produced outcome. It's not uncommon for a market to have five thousand to twenty thousand abortions annually, and the total number of babies rescued is under one hundred. And yet you'll see that a lot of money is being invested by pro-life people

> in those markets. Nothing against the pregnancy centers, because I know that their hearts are in the right spot. But the donors deserve good outcomes for what they invest in. We actually call our donors stakeholders. And twice a year, we sit in front of them if they've given more than $5,000, and we present an investment portfolio where we report the return on their investment. It shows every dollar they've invested and how many babies they've rescued.

Question for you: How many pro-life organizations that you currently invest in directly connect your investments with the exact return you desired from those investments—preborn human lives saved from abortion? As you can see in the case of ThriVe, it *is* possible for pro-life organizations to track results for their investors.

If a pro-life organization can't show you the ROI on your investment or is unwilling to do the work to show you the ROI on your investment, I would ask, why are you investing in that organization? If your answer is "because I haven't been able to find any other pro-life organizations that will show me my ROI," my reply would be "I just showed you one."

Winning at Scale

At this point in this chapter, if you believe the ThriVe business model is a serious competitive threat to Planned Parenthood and the abortion industry, and you also have experience in your professional career of expanding a successful business, I wager the thought has occurred to you something along the lines of, "How can Bridget and the ThriVe team expand their model into other cities?" After all, winning the market share battle against Planned Parenthood and the abortion industry in St. Louis is one thing, but replicating that success in multiple cities is quite another.

Well, I have good news for you! When Bridget and the ThriVe team discovered they were on to something big, they designed the ThriVe business model to be scalable. Bridget explains:

> Our business model has been painstakingly developed to be easily replicated. If it's something that's unique only to the St. Louis market, or something only I could do, that would mean those "special sauce" things have been stripped from the model. We have a model that we've tested in Orlando, Florida, and Savannah, Georgia, with stunning results. That's proof the model can be replicated. But what we've actually done now is we've identified the top five of the top fifteen states in the nation that make up the majority of abortions. Fifty percent of the abortions are performed in five states: New York, California, Texas, Illinois, and Florida. That's strategically very attractive, right? In other words, if we could do a blitz in five states, we could bring abortion down to its knees.

Bridget brings up a point here that I don't believe many pro-life people think about enough—the fact that abortion numbers are concentrated geographically. Yes, abortion is a nationwide tragedy, but taken one woman's decision at a time, the vast majority of abortion decisions take place in a relatively small geographic area if you add up the square mileage of all the large cities that account for the vast majority of abortions. Understanding this brings to light the realization that the ThriVe business model does not have to be replicated in every city in the nation in order to have a major impact on reducing abortion numbers.

If the PLBI replicated the ThriVe business model in all of the major cities in the states of New York, California, Texas, Illinois, and Florida, and over time in each of those cities eventually won the market share battle against Planned Parenthood and the abortion industry, I believe it would turn the tide of the war against abortion and set the PLBI on an almost certain path of eventual victory over Planned Parenthood and the abortion industry—*even if* Roe v. Wade *was never overturned.*

Maximizing Return on Investment

Okay, so I threw in that last statement about overturning *Roe v. Wade* to shake you up again. As I covered earlier in the book, yes, *Roe v. Wade* was a gravely immoral legal decision by the Supreme Court. And yes, all people of goodwill should work diligently to try to overturn it. But again, pragmatically speaking, as I covered in Chapter 2, remember that overturning *Roe v. Wade* would result in a reduction of abortions nationwide of only 13 percent.

True, the overturning of *Roe v. Wade* would be by far the greatest victory over pro-abortion forces in the history of the Pro-Life Movement to date. However, the overturning of *Roe v. Wade* would be winning a key *battle*, not winning the *war*, against the abortion industry. And consider that last statement from the perspective of pro-life philanthropy. To this day, much pro-life philanthropy continues to flow into programs that have as their ultimate aim the overturning of *Roe v. Wade*. (If you're curious about exact dollar figures, no one tracks them at a macro level. I'm just speaking from my experience interacting with many pro-life philanthropists.)

In my view, going all in investing your pro-life philanthropy funds with an expected return of overturning *Roe v. Wade* is *not* a prudent investment. Why not? Because I think the risk/reward ratio on that investment is very poor. In the for-profit world, if you invested in a new company that was developing a product with the potential to fundamentally transform an entire industry, but the incumbent companies in the industry were powerful and determined to defend their turf, you would know that your investment in the new company carried significant risk of low return, or perhaps even zero return.

Therefore, in exchange for you taking that risk, you would expect the return on your investment in the new company to be much higher (aka "risk premium"). Keep that example in mind as you think about the risk/reward ratio of investments in pro-life organizations that seek to overturn *Roe v. Wade*. Over many decades now, cumulatively, hundreds of millions of dollars (possibly billions) of pro-life philanthropy funds have been invested in organizations that seek through different means to overturn *Roe v. Wade*. So far, the return on the philanthropy funds invested in the "overturn *Roe v. Wade* project" has been exceedingly disappointing for investors.

But let's say for argument's sake that next week, the Supreme Court of the United States strikes down *Roe v. Wade*. Certainly, that action by the Supreme Court would cause the ROI for pro-life investors to increase. How? Recall from the analysis in Chapter 2 that overturning *Roe v. Wade* would lead to a 13 percent reduction in the number of abortions annually, which would equate to one hundred thousand lives saved *per year*. An enormous blessing, no doubt.

But I don't think pro-life philanthropists would be at all satisfied with that ROI. Why? Because there would still be seven hundred and fifty thousand abortions per year on average, and pro-life philanthropists want to win the war against abortion, ending it once and for all, not just win pitched battles here and there. From a national perspective, even after the overturning of *Roe v. Wade*, the enemy—Planned Parenthood and the abortion industry—would still rule in many of the key geographic areas where the majority of abortions take place.

If that's the case, if you were one of the philanthropists who contributed capital that led to the overturning of *Roe v. Wade*, you would still have to ask yourself whether you successfully maximized your ROI in terms of pro-life philanthropy. I believe the answer to that question is no. I believe there are pro-life investments that offer significantly higher ROI than "overturn *Roe v. Wade* projects," and also offer substantially better risk/reward ratios.

Consider the ThriVe business model. From the perspective of maximizing ROI on your philanthropic investment at a favorable risk/reward ratio, think about this. Even without *Roe v. Wade* being overturned,

ThriVe played a key role in shutting down Planned Parenthood's business in St. Louis. In other words, even though *Roe v. Wade* is still in force in St. Louis, ThriVe was able to beat Planned Parenthood on the battlefield of business, successfully encouraging more women to choose their services than the abortion services offered by Planned Parenthood.

From an ROI perspective, pro-life philanthropists who invested in ThriVe earned a very high reward relative to the risk. Their ROI is exceedingly high at both the micro level—$1,200 per baby saved—and the macro level—Planned Parenthood closed its abortion business in St. Louis. ThriVe's investors won the war at the local level in St. Louis. *They maximized their investments*. Now think about your own city where you live, or the largest city near where you live. Which of these two investments makes more sense to you?

1. An investment that has the potential to win a battle, but not the war, and carries a very poor risk/reward ratio (e.g., an overturn *Roe v. Wade* project), or
2. An investment that has the potential to win the war and carries a very favorable risk/reward ratio (e.g., a competitive business model project like ThriVe)?

I realize you may have never looked at your pro-life philanthropy in this way before, but I believe if all pro-life philanthropists evaluated their pro-life investments this way, it would not be long before Planned Parenthood would be closing down its abortion businesses in cities across the nation. I believe that changing your mindset with a view of maximizing the ROI on the investment of your pro-life 3T assets is so critical that in the next and final part of this book I propose a plan for how you can do exactly that.

Chapter Twelve BOTTOM LINE

ThriVe Women's Express Healthcare, a pro-life pregnancy center in St. Louis, Missouri, has proven it is possible to compete against and beat Planned Parenthood, *even without* Roe v. Wade *being overturned*. The foundation of ThriVe's success is excellent marketing—all 4 Ps of ThriVe's marketing are congruent with a young woman's mindset that abortion is a medical choice, not a moral one. The foundation of the foundation of ThriVe's excellent marketing is authentic empowering Christ-centered LOVE offered to young women who become ThriVe clients. ThriVe offers its investors a superior ROI in both *effectiveness* and *cost-effectiveness*. In 2019, for example, ThriVe saved 1,692 babies from abortion at a cost of $1,200 per life saved. ThriVe's business model is designed to be easily expanded to other cities.

PART III: HOW *YOU* CAN SHUT DOWN PLANNED PARENTHOOD

After reading Parts I and II of this book, I hope you are excited to have discovered that there is an answer for how to shut down Planned Parenthood and the abortion industry, and that answer is not based in theory. As you saw in our case study in Chapter 12, a real pro-life pregnancy center actually made it happen in a large city. The question now is, what can *you* do specifically to put your 3T assets to work to send Planned Parenthood packing from your local community? That's what I cover in Part III.

CHAPTER THIRTEEN: ALL THE RIGHT STUFF: TEAM!

> *We have met the enemy and he is us.* Walt Kelly in his comic strip *Pogo*, April 22, 1970

In the hands of the wrong team, even with a Planned Parenthood–beating strategy like ThriVe's, a pro-life pregnancy center will very likely achieve mediocre results at best. That is why I am starting the final section of this book with a chapter about how important it is to invest only in centers that have the right team members in place. My assumption is you want to invest your 3T assets in a pro-life pregnancy center team that is *great at marketing* (the 4 Ps of marketing) or has the potential to become great at marketing.

Before we discuss how to identify a team with "all the right stuff," I want to emphasize again that I do not question the passion of the vast majority of team members who currently work at the thousands of pro-life pregnancy centers across the country. Heart matters a lot and we all owe a great debt of gratitude to these frontline pro-life warriors. But if passion for the pro-life mission is not married with a very high level of marketing skill, I do not believe it is possible for a center to win a large number of abortion-determined clients away from Planned Parenthood. As proof of my claim, I simply look at the results of pro-life pregnancy centers currently in operation across the country. Extremely rare are centers that can show strong market share numbers versus their local Planned Parenthood abortion businesses.

Who Do Pro-life Pregnancy Centers Work For?

As a matter of fact, few pro-life pregnancy centers even think about measuring their market share relative to Planned Parenthood. It seems strange, doesn't it? After all, in my experience, if you ask philanthropists who invest in pro-life centers what they want the centers to achieve, the responses are overwhelmingly something along the lines of, "We want the center to save as many babies' lives from abortion as possible." That answer is very direct and clear, with zero ambiguity. So it should provide great clarity to the board of directors of a pro-life pregnancy center about the strategic direction the center should pursue.

Yet in the PLBI, a complete lack of accountability for measurable performance gains persists industry wide. It should make investors in pro-life pregnancy centers very unhappy that their desires are completely ignored for the most part. But imagine a scenario where the investors in a particular center banded together and informed the center's board of directors and leadership team that they would make no further investments in the center unless it achieved verifiable market share gains against Planned Parenthood. What do you think would happen? Do you think the center's leadership team would go back to the drawing board and soon emerge with a new marketing plan that would have the local Planned Parenthood shaking in its boots?

Do you know what I think would happen? I think the center's directors and operations leaders would hand in their resignations. The reason? Because they were hired due to their passion for the Pro-Life Movement, *not* for their demonstrated marketing skills at winning market share battles against tough business competitors.

To demonstrate using a sports analogy, it's like you as an investor decide to invest in a football team that you want to win the Super Bowl.

However, you discover that the players on your team aren't football players, but baseball players—skilled baseball players, for sure, but not skilled at what it takes to win football games. In the same way, pro-life pregnancy centers, with few exceptions, are not staffed with people who have the right skills and experience to win market share battles against Planned Parenthood.

Why are centers not hiring people with the skill sets required to achieve their investors' desired outcome? I believe the primary reason is because pro-life philanthropists who invest in the centers aren't sending the right signals about what they actually want the centers to achieve. Philanthropists are not acting like owners, demanding measurable performance and a return on their investments. In other words, if you ask leaders of the center who they are working for, whose interests they are trying to serve, they won't say, "we're working for our investors."

Investor Revolt?

What to do? First, a good quote to keep in mind: "If you always do what you've always done, you'll always get what you've always got" (Henry Ford).

If investors in a pro-life pregnancy center are satisfied with its results and continue to fund it year after year, why would a center change its strategy? Should investors be satisfied with a pro-life pregnancy center's 1 percent market share versus Planned Parenthood's 99 percent share? I don't think so. I strongly believe the investors in the center are the ones who must force the issue in order for any significant change to take place at a center. Not until the board of directors of the center embraces a mindset that the center works for the interests of its investors will the center's leadership begin to focus on doing what it takes to win the market share battle against Planned Parenthood. If the board of directors refuses to do that, then the investors should cease investing in that center and instead find a center led by the right team, pursuing the right marketing plan to gain market share against Planned Parenthood.

Makeup of the Team

Let me begin by saying, if you are currently investing in a pro-life center that has very low market share against Planned Parenthood, and you decide to help them out by going to the board of directors and demanding accountability for results, your enthusiasm is likely to be met not with applause and thanks for opening their eyes, but more likely you will be met with "thank you for your concern" as they show you the door. You can then decide what to do next with your 3T assets. But on the off chance that the majority of the board of directors has also become frustrated with lackluster results and is looking for an answer, here's what I would recommend the board of directors do. Please keep in mind this is only a framework, and there could be many variations on this approach.

First, the board of directors must change their thinking and begin treating their investors (benefactors/philanthropists) like owners. With that change, the board of directors should be focused on one question: "What do our owners want?" Fortunately, the answer is simple: The "owners" want the center to save as many babies' lives from abortion as possible. (Quick note: Yes, I realize that legally no person can own a non-profit. This is about mindset, not technicalities.)

With that answer in hand about what the "owners" of the pro-life pregnancy center want, the board's core strategic planning questions become very clear: (1) How do we save as many babies' lives from abortion as possible? (2) How do we measure success concerning question 1? I believe all other strategic questions are of secondary importance.

What I find interesting is that both of those strategic planning questions are marketing questions. "How do we save as many babies' lives from abortion as possible?" asks what is our 4 Ps strategy to attract prospective clients who are seeking an abortion, and "How do we measure success concerning question 1?" asks what our market share is relative to our center's competitors: Planned Parenthood and other abortion facilities in our geographic area. If I'm right about these questions, then it seems to me that the right team to lead this intense battle should be made up of savvy, experienced marketers.

Welcome to the Major Leagues

Again, please remember that I have worked with the leadership teams of many pro-life pregnancy centers across the country, so I can assure you that the vast majority of leadership teams—meaning the members of the board of directors and the executive director—are not made up of savvy, experienced marketers. Many center leadership teams do not have any marketers on the team at all. This fact goes a long way in explaining why so many women in the United States do not even know about the existence of pro-life pregnancy centers.

Again, marketing is everything. As long as the leadership team of a pro-life pregnancy center does not acknowledge that, they will not be able to successfully deliver what the "owners" of the centers want more than anything else: as many babies' lives saved from abortion as possible. The center will remain in the minor leagues when it could be playing in the majors.

Bring on the Coach's Coach

Now the difficult part. It's time for some "extreme ownership," as Navy Seals Jocko Willink and Leif Babin would put it. (I highly recommend reading their book *Extreme Ownership*.) Failure to achieve what the center's "owners" demand rests with the individuals tasked with holding the center accountable for results—the center's board of directors. Assuming members of the board of directors can conduct a humble self-assessment, both individually and as a group unit, based on facts (data!), not on feelings, then I think they would come to a conclusion along the lines of, "We're losing the market share battle. We don't have the right team (that means us!), and we don't have the right strategy to succeed in achieving what our benefactors expect us to achieve."

The question is, what should the board do? I think there are many good answers to that question, and those answers are as varied as are the personalities of all the board members of all the different pro-life pregnancy centers across the country. In other words, I don't think there is any set answer. However, let me propose one approach for you to think about. I think there could be multiple variations on this idea, so don't think of this approach as a concrete plan per se, but more as a framework and a guideline.

Let's say members of the board of a particular pro-life pregnancy center conclude that they should resign and let someone else take charge. While I understand that thinking, my question would be, "How do you know the person replacing you on the board is any more qualified?" Instead of jumping ship, I would propose that the board members receive mentoring or coaching to learn what to look for in terms of qualified candidates for the board. Turning to others for help and guidance is not unusual. Great leaders recognize that they also need mentors—a leader's leader, or a coach's coach, if you will. Those mentors bring both expertise and objectivity to the table because they are free to focus on the essentials needed to succeed.

So here's one potential approach. Instead of one mentor or coach, how about the board set up what I call a **Business Advisory Committee (BAC)**. The role of the BAC would be simple. Find prospective board members who bring the marketing expertise, based on real-world achievements, the pro-life pregnancy center needs in order to elevate its performance, as measured by market share, from minor league level to major league level. Relying on the wisdom of "it takes one to know one," the BAC members themselves could also be made up exclusively of those who bring marketing expertise and real-world success to the table.

Jack-of-All-Trades, Master of *One*

This brings up an interesting question. Should the board recruit for the BAC marketing generalists, specialists, or both? I believe it is best to recruit at least one specialist in each category of the **4 Ps**. Why? Let me demonstrate by example. Let's assume the board recruited just one well-known locally famous branding expert who was passionately pro-life. This marketing expert's career has been built on numerous successful branding campaigns for local businesses. So he is an expert at the promotion aspect of the 4 Ps of marketing. Therefore, over his career the expert has evolved to see marketing as "marketing = branding," and this just isn't true, no matter how much success the brand marketer has had. So if you don't have other marketers who are experts at product, price, and placement (distribution), the center's marketing strategy will likely get out of balance.

For example, if the center implements a robust branding campaign, but the center's product is not good, the center might see an initial bump in market share, but then over time the share increases will stagnate or even reverse course because the quality of the product doesn't match with the brand messaging. The BAC has to keep in mind that professional marketers tend to have a major strength in one of the 4 Ps.

My specialization as a marketer is product. Compared to my specific strengths in product, I would say I am a generalist at price, promotion, and placement (distribution). That doesn't mean that I don't know a lot about those three Ps. I do. It just means that if I was a candidate for a pro-life pregnancy center's BAC, the board members would slot me as a product specialist. In the same way, the board would look for BAC candidates who were proven specialists at price, promotion, and placement (distribution).

The Two Sides of Promotion

For the candidates who would fill the promotion slots on the BAC, the board could recruit two different types of promotion experts—one for direct response, and the other for brand marketing. Direct response marketers are experts at persuading prospective customers to *take action now*. Brand marketers are experts at creating for the organization an image that attracts new customers, and then maintaining and continually enhancing that image in the minds of the organization's existing customers so that they continue to purchase from the organization. I believe strong programs for both direct response marketing and brand marketing are essential for the success of a pro-life pregnancy center in its market share battle against Planned Parenthood.

Double the Impact

Once all of the specialists roles on the BAC are filled, those marketing experts can help the current board find new board members, possibly made up of some of the BAC members themselves, who understand that it will require an excellent marketing plan to win market share away from Planned Parenthood—meaning many more preborn babies' lives saved from abortion. The new board consisting of many marketing experts can then recruit an executive director who has the proven skills and experience to develop and execute a marketing plan that is very robust in all of the marketing 4 Ps. The executive director can then hire a frontline operations team that is qualified to execute the marketing plan.

Here's some additional good news for a board of directors that is creating a BAC. The marketing experts the BAC recruits for the new board can not only help the center massively increase its market share by making sure the new executive director implements highly effective marketing programs. Those same experts can also create a separate marketing plan that has as its goal attracting more pro-life philanthropists into financially supporting the center's new business strategy. The more success the center has at gaining market share against Planned Parenthood, the more likely additional funding from philanthropists will flow into the center to help fuel its market share growth. Again, please remember that this idea of establishing a BAC is only one of many possible approaches. Each center would need to understand its own unique situation to decide how best to proceed, but whatever the plan, the idea is to make sure that experienced successful marketers become the centerpiece of the center's leadership team.

Chapter Thirteen BOTTOM LINE

Most pro-life pregnancy centers are not staffed with team members who possess the marketing skills and experience necessary to win the market share battle against Planned Parenthood. To solve this problem, a center's board of directors should find team members skilled at marketing.

CHAPTER FOURTEEN: FOCUSING ON THE DECISION MAKER

> *Don't say things. What you are stands over you the while, and thunders so that I cannot hear what you say to the contrary.* Ralph Waldo Emerson

Have you heard of Simon Sinek? I recommend you find his short TED talk titled, "Start with Why?" In his talk, Sinek refers to what he calls the "Golden Circle," which is actually a group of concentric circles. In the middle circle is the question "Why?" The next circle is "How?" And the outside circle is "What?"

Sinek argues that most businesses describe themselves from the outside in, starting with *what* they do, then *how* they do it, and finally *why*. But Sinek's key insight is that most businesses don't even have a clear answer to the question "Why?" From Sinek's view, most businesses don't even know their true purpose—what they *believe*. "People don't buy *what* you do; they buy *why* you do it."

I begin this chapter with Sinek's insight because as an investor in pro-life pregnancy centers, you must carefully discern between centers whose why clearly indicates they are all in on empowering women experiencing unexpected pregnancies, versus centers that are so enamored with what they do that they can't even clearly articulate their why. How well you discern between the two types of centers, and then make your investment decisions based on your discernment, will determine whether your investment in a center will yield you a high or low ROI.

To maximize your chances of a high ROI, find the centers that have marketing programs (all 4 Ps!) focused on *empowering* women experiencing unexpected pregnancies. If you find such marketing programs at a center, you will know they have the right why. Such marketing programs will resonate with the clients who must ultimately decide whether to choose abortion, or to choose life: the young women.

New Trend in the Pro-Life Business Industry: Women's Healthcare

Unfortunately, many pro-life centers are more focused on the what than the why. For example, over the past ten years or so, the most important trend for pro-life pregnancy centers has been to "go medical," meaning the centers convert their operations from only providing young women with "resources," to providing them with comprehensive women's healthcare services. Overall, I think going medical has been a very positive trend for the PLBI. After all, recall what Bridget VanMeans said in Chapter 12: "Young women think of abortion as a medical decision."

Therefore, in principle, when a center offers comprehensive women's healthcare services, it should resonate with young women. However, from my experience speaking with the leaders of many of the centers who have converted their centers to medical, I don't expect they will achieve the breakout market share success against Planned Parenthood that ThriVe achieved in St. Louis. Why not? Because they tend to be extremely focused on the what (comprehensive women's healthcare) rather than the why (empowering women).

My Precious!

To be fair to the leaders of the centers, it is very common for marketers, no matter the industry, to fall in love with their products, *for the product's own sake*, rather than fall in love with the clients and their wants and needs. We marketers put in long hours over days, weeks, years, and sometimes decades, crafting our products, refining them over and over so that they shine. We gaze at their beauty and feel a sense of deep pride that we had the privilege of participating in the sculpting of such a beautiful work of art. It reminds me of the character Gollum in *The Lord of the Rings.* Remember how the ring becomes to Gollum "My Precious!" And as we constantly wax lyrical about the greatness of "My Precious," our clients and customers look at us and ask, "Hey, what about me?"

Your Precious!

Of course, I would agree that team members of companies do need to love their products in order to compete effectively. However, the correct orientation is to love the prospective clients through your products. In other words, your company's product is only a means to an end, not the end itself. It's your clients who are "Your Precious!" It's much easier to forget about your clients and love your product because you and your company are in control of creating your product, whereas you are most certainly not in control of your prospective clients. It is much more difficult to constantly seek to understand all of the seemingly ever-changing needs and wants—emotional, physical, spiritual—of your clients and bring that understanding back into your company's marketing processes to create products that will measurably improve your clients' lives.

But That's Different!

Let me give you an example of how this "love my product" problem affects pro-life pregnancy centers that have converted to medical. I once gave a talk about marketing at a conference that focuses specifically on pro-life pregnancy centers that have made the move to medical. During the Q&A discussion following my talk, I was not surprised to see the "My Precious!" tendency on full display. It was very clear to me during our discussion that leaders of centers wanted me to offer them a marketing strategy where they could push the wonderful features of their comprehensive women's healthcare services into the minds of young women. "Brett, help us develop marketing strategies that get women to accept the program!" I pointed out to them that pushing rarely works, and when it does, it usually only lasts for a short while as a fad. So instead, I offered them a real-world example of an alternative approach that uses a highly successful pull model: ThriVe in St. Louis.

I explained how ThriVe had done the groundwork to clearly define its why: to empower young women experiencing unexpected pregnancies. ThriVe then incorporated its why into its choose life product, resulting in many thousands of young women in St. Louis being attracted to ThriVe's business. After I talked about ThriVe, and the remarkable market share results ThriVe had achieved in St. Louis as a result of its pull model, the pushback from audience participants at the conference was, "Yes, but ThriVe's product is different than ours. We're *full* medical."

They might have been right that their centers offered a few additional women's healthcare services that ThriVe doesn't, but what's most interesting is their pushback wasn't focused on the needs and wants (remember Maslow!) of the young women experiencing unexpected pregnancies, but instead on their own centers' product features (the what)—a telltale sign of the "My Precious!" ailment.

But That's What Women Say They Want!

I pushed back on the audience, asking them why they thought offering an ever-expanding menu of healthcare services would matter to young women. The answer? "Because when we ask the women what they want, they say more healthcare services!" I was not surprised by this response because if you conduct market research and ask consumers if they would like a "comprehensive offering," most will reply "yes." It seems logical that more options are always a good thing, right? Therefore, based on such research, marketers in any industry have a tendency to "over-engineer" their products—meaning a tendency to try to develop a product that will be all things to all people.

What They Say, Mean, and Do

However, we human beings are complex, often saying one thing and then doing the exact opposite. What we say we would like to buy, and then what we actually do buy, are often very different—to the endless frustration of marketers around the globe. To illustrate: in his article "What Consumers Say vs. Mean vs. Do," consumer experience expert Colin Shaw said that Disney theme park vacationers and visitors often *say* they want salads and other healthy foods for themselves and their families, *but what they really want, and buy* are hot dogs and hamburgers. If Disney only followed the research of what consumers say they want, it would focus on offering salad, and this would diminish the overall park experience, potentially leading to churn. The Disney example is very insightful, but perhaps an example that might be closer to home for you is the rise of *specialist restaurants* versus *generalist restaurants*.

There are many examples, but to give just one that I am very familiar with (to the detriment of my expanding waistline!), the specialist restaurant Five Guys offers *one* primary food combination: a hamburger with fries. Of course you can also get a very nice hamburger-and-fries combination at a generalist restaurant like Applebee's, but Applebee's will also offer you many other food combinations. I would wager that in market research with the general population, if you asked a consumer, conceptually, if she would prefer the "only one combination" restaurant offering versus the "comprehensive selection" restaurant offering, most consumers would select the latter. Based on that research alone, an entrepreneur suggesting opening a restaurant like Five Guys would be considered crazy. But from what I can tell, Five Guys is quite successful.

Peeling Back the Layers of the Onion

Getting back to our pro-life pregnancy centers who have gone full medical, I think over-engineering of the product is on full display in many centers. The comprehensive healthcare model sounds great, but if not marketed based on a compelling why, I'm not convinced the model will succeed as a competitive counter to Planned Parenthood, even if "comprehensive women's healthcare" is what women say they want.

I don't doubt that's *what* women say they want, but the enormously important piece the centers are missing is not understanding the young woman's why that resonates psychologically and spiritually with what women really desire—freedom, happiness, success, self-actualization—the things at the top of Maslow's hierarchy of needs. If not marketed based on a compelling why that resonates with young women, then full medical is still stuck on the bottom two tiers of Maslow's hierarchy. Letting their why (empowering women) determine their what (their product) is what ThriVe in St. Louis gets right and what so many other pro-life pregnancy centers are still getting wrong.

Chapter Fourteen BOTTOM LINE

You must carefully discern between pro-life pregnancy centers whose why clearly indicates they are all in on empowering women experiencing unexpected pregnancies, versus centers that are so enamored with what they do, they can't even clearly articulate their why. Many pro-life pregnancy centers have gone medical, meaning the centers converted their operations from only providing young women with resources to providing them with comprehensive women's healthcare services. However, if not marketed based on a compelling why that resonates psychologically and spiritually with what young women really desire—the things at the top of Maslow's hierarchy of needs: freedom, happiness, success, self-actualization—it's unlikely the medical model will succeed as a competitive counter to Planned Parenthood.

CHAPTER FIFTEEN: BRAND MARKETING

A brand is the set of expectations, memories, stories and relationships that, taken together, account for a consumer's decision to choose one product or service over another. Seth Godin

I find the topic of brand marketing always revs up the emotions of business professionals—partly because they intuitively sense how important it is, and partly because they also sense how little they really understand about how brand marketing actually works. Folks who don't have deep experience, both successes and failures, with brand marketing tend to believe branding is about a company's logos, colors, fonts, and catchy memorable phrases and jingles. Companies create those things and then push them out into the market, hoping they attract target consumers.

Most of those branding campaigns end in failure. Why? Because human beings are not like cows. Wait. What? You're probably familiar with ranch hands branding cows to identify them as belonging to the ranch. The word "brand" originally meant using a hot instrument to burn a permanent mark into something. In the case of cows, branding with that hot instrument is a very one-sided affair with the cow having absolutely no say in the matter. It's a one way street for the poor cows. Unfortunately, this "one way street" mentality about branding is also how many companies think when they create their branding campaigns—"We'll push all these fancy graphics and clever jingles into our target consumers' minds, and they will accept the program." Not likely.

Can I Have a Say in This?

Prospective consumers *are not interested in what your company wants to push into their minds*. They *are* intensely interested in what they themselves actually want, not what your company thinks they should want. Effective brand marketing for humans is a two-way street whereby companies must bring the voice of the customer (VOC) into the brand creation process. If you don't position your company's products/services in a way that resonates with your prospective consumer's worldview, your branding program will hit them like a clanging gong.

Most companies aren't willing to do the hard work required to bring the worldview of their target customers into the branding process because, well, it's hard work. Additionally, the path to branding success is very uncertain because you are dealing with the complexities of human psychology, which can be very difficult to pin down. It's so much easier to just assume many things that you feel certain would resonate with your customers and get that branding campaign out there into the market ASAP!

What Kind of Thing Is It?

But even before your organization attempts to create its brand, there is an important condition that must already exist in order for your brand to have a chance at resonating with prospective consumers. Marketers often overlook this key prerequisite for successful brand marketing. It is simply that your prospective consumers must first know the kind of thing you offer and how that thing can improve their lives before your company has any chance of creating a successful brand. In other words, your product or service must fit into a product or service category your prospective consumer already knows and understands.

For example, the automobile is a well-known product category. An automobile offers both you and me the freedom to go where we want, when we want—both short distances, and very long distances. You and I recognize great personal benefits for being able to do that. But if we didn't already know about those benefits, in other words, if we had no idea what an automobile was, and then Ford, Toyota, Chevrolet, put out advertisements that assumed we already knew about the benefits of automobiles, their ad messages would fall on deaf ears, and they would have zero chance of creating successful brands.

So the first step in brand marketing is to educate your prospective clients about the benefits of the category in which your product/service fits, and then once your prospect consumers understand that, the next step is to work your brand marketing program to associate your company's particular brand name with the category. And if you're early to the game, your company's brand name can possibly become synonymous with the category itself: think about how Kleenex became synonymous with tissues.

You Can't Choose What You Don't Know

Unfortunately, millions of young women in our country don't even recognize the existence of the pro-life pregnancy center category. In other words, they don't even know what a pro-life pregnancy center is. Think about that from the perspective of the company where you currently work or a company where you worked in the past. Imagine if millions of your prospective clients had absolutely no idea about the concept or even the very existence of the kind of product or service your company offers. For example, you say, "We offer life insurance." And your prospect says, "What is insurance? I've never heard of such a thing." From a marketing perspective, your business is climbing a very steep hill if your prospects don't even recognize the existence of the kind of product you offer.

Yet, for now, that is the reality facing the pro-life pregnancy center category. The category is largely unknown by millions of young women in the United States. Unfortunately, the abortion facilities category does not face this problem—almost all young women know about abortion facilities like Planned Parenthood. The standard story line for the majority of women facing unexpected pregnancies is to turn to the category almost all of them know very well—abortion facilities, especially Planned Parenthood—not to the category so many women are largely unfamiliar with—pro-life pregnancy centers.

Let me share with you a quick story that demonstrates the reality of this standard story line. I spoke at a large event in early 2020, and during my talk, I invited a young woman up on stage to share a few words with the audience. She told the audience that in early 2019, she had become pregnant unexpectedly and was actively seeking an abortion when she encountered a well-placed advertisement that connected her to a very effective pro-life pregnancy center. She shared that the compassionate team at the center did an outstanding job ministering to her, and as a result, she changed her mind about getting an abortion and instead chose life for her preborn baby. In the next chapter on direct response advertising, I share more about the "well-placed advertisement" that connected this woman to the center, but for the purposes of this chapter I want to emphasize what she said next to those in attendance at the event. She said, "Please keep doing what you're doing because it saves lives! *So many women don't know about pro-life pregnancy centers*!" In other words, at the time she was seeking an abortion she had no idea that such a thing as a pro-life pregnancy center even existed. Ouch. Again, repetition is important for memorization so I'll say it once more: *If women don't know about pro-life pregnancy centers* before *they face an unexpected pregnancy, then women won't go to pro-life pregnancy centers* when *they face an unexpected pregnancy*.

One possible approach to help solve the problem of so many young women not knowing about pro-life pregnancy centers is to launch a generic category branding campaign. In my work at Heroic Media, in 2017 we launched just such a campaign in Oklahoma City placing thirty-second video ads on popular social media channels. The sole objective of these video ads was to raise awareness among young women aged eighteen to twenty-nine that pro-life pregnancy centers exist in their local communities, and to make them aware of this before they faced an unexpected pregnancy. Research by an independent firm shows that this advertising program has been effective at raising awareness about the existence of pro-life pregnancy centers, with aided recall among young women eighteen to twenty-nine years old of one of the video ads increasing from 13.4 percent in 2017 to 35.5 percent in early 2021.

As encouraging as this is, I believe there is an even more cost-effective approach to branding the pro-life pregnancy center category. I call it the "two birds with one stone" branding strategy. Think of it this way, while it's true that running video ads on social media helps increase awareness about the existence of the pro-life pregnancy center category, if a young woman who was made aware of the category actually needed the service, she would want to know the actual name of a local pro-life pregnancy center she could contact. So the good news is that as a result of our pro-life pregnancy center category branding program, the young woman knows about pro-life pregnancy centers, but the bad news is that she doesn't know the name of a center to contact.

As a marketer, in order for the young woman to know the name of a center to contact, I have to run advertising campaigns that brand a specific pro-life pregnancy center's business name. The result is that I have to invest in advertising twice. I have to run one set of advertising campaigns that build category awareness about pro-life pregnancy centers in general, and another set of advertising campaigns that build brand awareness about a specific pro-life pregnancy center business. The two birds with one stone branding approach eliminates the need to invest twice.

Here's how. If a viable national pro-life pregnancy center brand(s) emerged on the scene, they could run brand marketing campaigns for their centers that achieved both goals through one campaign: raising awareness about pro-life pregnancy centers and the women-empowering benefits they offer, and *at the same time* branding their names as organizations that provide the services that bring those benefits.

A Rising Tide Lifts All Boats

There is a fairly recent example in the for-profit world of a company that successfully pulled off the two birds with one stone branding strategy. The company educated consumers about a new product category that previously didn't exist, and then, at the same time, successfully tied its own brand name to that new product category. That company is Uber. The ridesharing category was relatively unknown to most consumers not that long ago. Uber changed that. Then other companies, particularly Lyft, rode on Uber's coattails, so to speak, benefiting from increasing awareness among consumers about the ridesharing category. I believe the emergence of a nationally recognized pro-life pregnancy center brand(s) would have the same effect on the pro-life pregnancy center category.

Chapter Fifteen BOTTOM LINE

Effective brand marketing for humans is a two-way street whereby companies must bring the VOC into the brand creation process. However, before creating your company's brand, your prospective client must first know the kind of thing you offer and how that thing can improve his or her life—in other words, your product or service must fit into a category that is known by your prospective client. Remember: If women don't know about pro-life pregnancy centers *before* they face an unexpected pregnancy, then women won't go to pro-life pregnancy centers *when* they face an unexpected pregnancy. If a viable national pro-life pregnancy center brand(s) emerged, they could run brand marketing campaigns for their centers that achieved two goals through one campaign:

raising awareness about the pro-life pregnancy center category and the women-empowering benefits centers offer, and at the same time branding their business names as the leading centers that actually provide the services—two birds with one stone.

CHAPTER SIXTEEN: DIRECT RESPONSE MARKETING

> *When I was twenty-five I took a correspondence course in direct-mail. I bought it out of my own pocket. Direct Response is my first love, and later it became my secret weapon.* David Ogilvy

I intentionally placed the brand marketing chapter ahead of this chapter about direct response marketing because an effective long-term brand marketing program is essential for winning the war against an industry-dominating behemoth like Planned Parenthood. It takes time, sometimes years, for a brand marketing program to begin to work its magic. The problem with waiting for years is that every day in the United States, on average two thousand to three thousand women choose abortion. While waiting for its brand marketing program to turn the tide in the war on abortion, what can a pro-life pregnancy center do *today, right now at this very moment,* to intervene and redirect abortion-seeking women away from Planned Parenthood and instead put them into the compassionate empowering care of a pro-life pregnancy center? In other words, what can the center do now to *win some daily individual battles* against Planned Parenthood? The answer is direct response marketing.

"I am looking for a clinic that handles abortions"

Recall from the previous chapter that the standard story line for women facing unexpected pregnancies is to turn to the category almost all women know well: abortion facilities. Many of those women already know where the local Planned Parenthood office is located and will make direct contact with them. When this happens, the story line for a woman will play out as it does thousands of times every day in the United States: the woman will make an abortion appointment and her preborn baby will die at the hands of an abortionist.

However, there are some women who, even though they may know about Planned Parenthood, still need to get more information in order to contact them. These women will turn to their cell phones to conduct an internet search for information about making an abortion appointment. It is at this point in the woman's internet search process that a pro-life pregnancy center has *a chance to intervene using direct response marketing*.

Let me illustrate how the process works by returning to the story in the previous chapter of the woman I invited up on to the stage. From the stage she shared a short version of her story, but I want to share with you here a longer version that I excerpted from an interview I did with the woman for *Pro-Life Magazine* (https://prolifemagazine.org) in its special edition covering the National Prayer Luncheon for Life (https://nationalprayerluncheonforlife.org). For clarity, I have edited some of the information in the original text of the interview. We pick up the woman's story at the point where she has just taken a home pregnancy test:

> "We're pregnant." My boyfriend was ecstatic, happy, and in tears. I still have a picture from that day, holding the pregnancy test.
>
> My mind is going in a million different directions. Part of me is excited. But then I'm also thinking to myself, "I can't have a baby right now! My career is at its peak! I'm doing wonderful!

My boyfriend is a new thing. My mom's going to kill me! My grandparents are probably going to have a heart attack!"

I started going through emotional roller coasters. I became devastated, and thought to myself, "We can't keep this baby. We're not ready to parent. We're just not ready for this life yet." We talked about it, and I said to my boyfriend, "I don't think that keeping this child is the right thing to do."

So I got on my cell phone and searched for information about getting an abortion. I responded to an ad that connected me to a women's clinic.

It was a Sunday, not normal business hours, but they had the option to send a text. So I texted: "I am looking for a clinic that handles abortions."

And just a minute or two later, I received a text response that said, "Hi! Is this for you? And, if so, have you taken a positive pregnancy test and an ultrasound yet?"

We kept texting back and forth, and then she told me that a positive pregnancy test only indicates a potential pregnancy, that one in four pregnancies end in miscarriage, and, therefore, that it was important to know for sure how many weeks along I was and if the pregnancy was viable. So I scheduled my appointment for the following Tuesday.

I went to the appointment and, sure enough, I was pregnant. I had a lengthy sit-down conversation with one of the counselors, and she shared her own story with me.

I then had an ultrasound and was told, "Well, it's definitely a viable pregnancy. However, you have some fluid here and, typically, if that gets worse, your body will naturally miscarry." And then she said, "You're only six-and a-half weeks along. Why don't you just sit tight for nine to fourteen days and see

> if your body even maintains the pregnancy? You can come back, we'll check, and if it's viable, you can make a decision from there."
>
> But in my mind, I'm still abortion-driven. I was thinking to myself, "I'm not keeping this child. It's early enough. I'm not going to feel guilty about it."
>
> And then the lady who did the ultrasound told me her story about when she faced an unexpected pregnancy, and I'm thinking to myself, "Okay, obviously I'm not the only person who's been through this. And if she can do it, maybe I can, too."

And thanks be to God, the woman did choose life. From a direct response marketing perspective, did you notice in the woman's story the point in time when the initial intervention took place? I bolded it for you to catch your attention. Here it is again: "**So I got on my cell phone and searched for information about getting an abortion. I responded to an ad that connected me to a women's clinic**." It is important to keep in mind that the woman *is not* searching for a pro-life pregnancy center. Remember, she doesn't even know that such a thing exists at this point in her story. In the process of searching for the abortion product, she responded to an advertisement that connected her to a completely different product—choose life services. The moment she responded to that ad, instead of the Planned Parenthood ad, the course of her life, as well as her baby's life, changed dramatically. Of course, it's a wonderful result that her baby is now alive because she responded to that ad, but since most young women have already been pre-sold on the abortion product, pro-life pregnancy centers must work hard using direct response marketing to sell their choose life services.

The Proof Is in the Pudding

You may be wondering at this point, how did I know for a fact that the direct response advertisement was responsible for connecting the woman to the pro-life pregnancy center? You're on your toes! After all, we always have to keep in mind the famous quote about advertising from John Wanamaker of Wanamaker's fame: "Half the money I spend on advertising is wasted; the trouble is, I don't know which half." A critical component of successful direct response advertising is to track results to make sure money is not wasted. We don't want to wonder, like John Wanamaker, if our direct response advertising dollars were wasted. We want to know with certainty that we earned a return on our advertising investment. Certainty is supremely important for our purposes because the ROI for our direct response advertising investment is a preborn human life saved from abortion.

The reason I know for a fact that the woman in the story I shared with you was connected to a pro-life pregnancy center by a direct response advertisement is because the advertising system that connected her, known as OAASYS™ (On-demand Alternatives to Abortion SYStem), pronounced "oasis," tracked every step in the process from the ad appearing on the woman's phone during her initial internet search, all the way to her final decision to choose life for her preborn baby. I developed OAASYS™ for Heroic Media (https://heroicmedia.org), an organization in the PLBI that offers pro-life philanthropists the opportunity to sponsor direct response internet ads that redirect abortion-seeking women away from Planned Parenthood, connecting them instead to highly skilled pro-life pregnancy centers. On a daily basis, I am privileged to witness the moving "save stories" of women who intended to get an abortion at Planned Parenthood, but instead were connected to local pro-life pregnancy centers by OAASYS™, and then after visiting the centers changed their minds about abortion and chose life for their preborn babies.

Here's a simple overview of how OAASYS™ works:

1. A woman facing the fear of an unexpected pregnancy decides she wants an abortion.

2. She uses her cell phone to conduct an internet search for information about getting an abortion.

3. Heroic Media's OAASYS™ inserts a direct response ad into the search results that appear on her phone.

4. The OAASYS™ direct response ad competes directly against a Planned Parenthood direct response ad.

5. When the woman responds to the OAASYS™ ad instead of the Planned Parenthood ad, she has the opportunity to connect with a pro-life pregnancy center that specializes in successfully encouraging abortion-seeking women to change their minds about abortion and choose life for their preborn babies. OAASYS™ provides objective proof that the PLBI can use direct response marketing to win daily battles in its competition against Planned Parenthood.

Chapter Sixteen BOTTOM LINE

Most young women have already been "pre-sold" on abortion services offered by Planned Parenthood and the abortion industry, but some women will still use their cell phones to search the internet for additional information about how to get an abortion. When they do, pro-life pregnancy centers can use direct response marketing to intervene and redirect abortion-seeking women away from Planned Parenthood and into the compassionate empowering care offered by the centers. The pro-life organization Heroic Media (https://heroicmedia.org) offers a direct response marketing service—OAASYS™ (On-demand Alternatives to Abortion SYStem)— that offers pro-life philanthropists the opportunity to sponsor direct response internet ads that redirect abortion-seeking women away from Planned Parenthood, connecting them instead to highly skilled pro-life pregnancy centers.

CHAPTER SEVENTEEN: BEST INTENTIONS VERSUS EARNED RESULTS

One of the great mistakes is to judge policies and programs by their intentions rather than their results.
Milton Friedman

Economist Milton Friedman once said in reference to governmental public policy programs, "One of the great mistakes is to judge policies and programs by their *intentions* rather than their *results*" (emphasis mine). I think Friedman's insight applies much more broadly than just to government programs. For example, think of professional sports. Recently, during a discussion with my youngest son, I used professional sports as an example to demonstrate the importance of measuring success using dispassionate metrics—dispassionate here meaning objective and unemotional. My son is a big fan of professional sports, especially the NFL, so I used the example of a famous football player to illustrate the point of how objective results-based measurements are the key to holding people (oneself or others) accountable to their intentions.

Tom Brady, likely the undisputed GOAT (Greatest Of All Time) NFL quarterback, changed to a new team in 2020, the Tampa Bay Buccaneers. Tom brought with him to Tampa an unprecedented resume of real-world success in professional football, as measured by objective, verifiable results—metrics like number of touchdown passes completed, number of games won, number of playoff games won, and, most important, number of Super Bowls won. His achievements on the field are unparalleled.

What Have You Done for Me Lately?

As excited as the Buccaneer franchise owners and fans were about Tom Brady quarterbacking their team, as soon as he took the field in the fall of 2020 in his new Tampa Bay uniform to receive his first snap from the center, *Buccaneer fans didn't care at all what Tom's past results were*. From the fans' perspective, Tom's results clock reset to zero. In addition, the fans didn't care what Tom Brady's intentions were for helping the Buccaneers win football games. The only thing the Buccaneer franchise owners and fans cared about was Tom's success on the field, as measured by touchdowns and wins, while wearing a Buccaneer's jersey.

Trying versus Succeeding

Professional sports is a brutal business when it comes to accountability to measurable results. The franchise owners and the team's fans don't care about how hard the players on the team try. They only care about measurable success—and that means winning games. Trying is about personal intentions, and is measured by emotional feelings. Succeeding is about measurable results, and is measured by objective data. And succeed Tom Brady did. In his first year in a Buccaneer's uniform, he led the team to a Super Bowl victory—the ultimate result in professional football.

Notice something interesting about professional sports leagues like the NFL—the extremely high level of accountability to measurable results, instead of to personal intentions, results in something remarkable: it forces athletes to continually raise the bar of what represents the standard of excellence in terms of performance. For example, if you put the Buccaneers team that won this year's Super Bowl on the field against the team that won the Super Bowl just twenty years ago, the Saint Louis

Rams, I guarantee you the Buccaneers would dominate the Rams at every position on the field. In other words, continual improvement in order to achieve desired results is contagious.

Our Emotions Draw Us In …

Imagine what would happen in the PLBI if all pro-life pregnancy centers across our country committed to continually raising the bar of their own performance, as measured by market share, to the level that ThriVe achieved in St. Louis. I believe it would transform the PLBI. But for now, what rules the day in the PLBI is "trying hard" and "having a passion for the cause." In other words, the leadership team's *intentions* seem to matter more than their *results*.

To be clear, it's not that I think intentions aren't important. I don't think I've met anyone who works full-time in pro-life who wasn't drawn into the work through some kind of powerful emotional experience that motivates them to try hard—including yours truly. For people of goodwill who believe in the right to life for all human beings, it is impossible not to have strong emotional feelings about the reality that, every day, many thousands of tiny human beings are aborted in their mothers' wombs. We feel deeply sorry for these tiny humans, and we desperately desire to stop the killing.

… But Then Our Emotions Betray Us

But do our strong intentions to stop the killing lead to strong results in actually stopping the killing? In the pro-life world, how often do we stop to ask the question, "What would strong measurable results in stopping the killing look like day to day?" In my experience, not often. On the contrary, we hand out praise for those who work full-time in pro-life based on how hard they try (intentions) to stop the killing, rather than how measurably successful (results) they are at actually stopping the killing.

Intentions rule the decisions made by the leadership teams at most centers. A center's board of directors, who themselves were very likely drawn into serving the center because of their own strong intentions to stop the killing, tend to evaluate the center's performance based on how hard the center's team members are *trying*, and how passionate and dedicated they are to the pro-life cause, rather than using objective analytical measurements such as market share that would reveal whether the team at the center is actually succeeding.

Getting the Facts Straight

But the trying (intentions) versus succeeding (results) problem affects not only the leadership teams at pro-life pregnancy centers but also the actions of pro-life philanthropists who invest in those centers. Think about it. If your local pro-life pregnancy center is typical, for every one hundred women seeking an abortion, ninety-nine of them will choose an abortion at Planned Parenthood and only one of them will choose life at the pro-life pregnancy center. Planned Parenthood market share: 99 percent. Pro-life pregnancy center market share: 1 percent.

Based solely on market share results, every pro-life philanthropist who invests in a pro-life pregnancy center should demand change at the center. But philanthropists generally don't demand change because they often subordinate facts to emotions. Admittedly, it's hard not to fall into the trap of subordinating facts to emotions when a pro-life pregnancy center shares with its investors emotionally powerful save stories of abortion-seeking women who changed their minds and chose life instead of abortion because of the efforts of the center. Could anything be more gratifying for a pro-life philanthropist than seeing a unique, one-of-a-kind, baby human being saved from abortion—a baby that would have died if not for the philanthropist's investment? But still, those feelings of emotional gratification do not change the facts on the ground: Planned Parenthood ninety-nine babies killed; pro-life pregnancy center one baby saved.

Into the Shark Tank

The antidote? I believe the competitiveness of pro-life pregnancy centers that make up the PLBI would increase dramatically if philanthropists who invest in the centers made their investment decisions based primarily on measurable data, not emotions. To understand what that might look like, let me offer an example from a popular TV series where you can witness this type of investment decision-making in action. If you are not familiar with the TV show called *Shark Tank*, I recommend that you watch it at least once. The way the show works is entrepreneurs present their product or service ideas to a group of five wealthy business investors, affectionately known as the sharks, and ask those sharks for investment funding to help grow the entrepreneurs' businesses. I think pro-life philanthropists and pro-life pregnancy center leadership teams can learn important lessons from *Shark Tank.*

Purchase Decisions Are Based on Emotions?

I think the most important lesson is how skilled the sharks are at evaluating investment opportunities based on "the numbers," not on emotions. When you observe the sharks' decision-making processes in action on *Shark Tank*, it's hard to conclude their emotions are driving their investment decisions. I can't emphasize enough how important the sharks' results-based decision-making process is because it appears to inoculate them from making decisions based purely on emotions.

When you watch *Shark Tank*, you will see the entrepreneurs walk in to the "shark tank" and present to the investors a "case for investment." Naturally, the entrepreneurs' presentations are very polished and designed to evoke an emotional response of, "Wow, that's awesome!" And very often, the sharks themselves have that reaction. After all, they're only human. But then...

Always, and I mean **ALWAYS**, the sharks quickly pivot from emotions to analysis by asking the entrepreneurs about the "numbers" that demonstrate proof of demand for their products, as well as the profitability potential of their businesses.

"And for that reason, I'm out!"

Turning from the excitement of emotions to analysis based on numbers often results in the sharks deciding to not invest in opportunities the entrepreneurs present. The famous line the sharks generally use when deciding not to invest is, "And for that *reason*, I'm out." Notice that "reason" implies analysis and thinking. The sharks' reasons for deciding not to invest generally come down to them either not finding the entrepreneur's business numbers attractive enough, or not believing the entrepreneur can plausibly grow the business profitably.

Shark Tank for Pro-Life Pregnancy Centers

I would like you to imagine the following scenario. You and a handful of other pro-life philanthropists have been invited to serve on an investor panel for a new show: *Shark Tank for Pro-Life Pregnancy Centers*! You and your fellow panelists want to invest in pro-life pregnancy centers that show the greatest potential to provide the ROI you desire most: the largest number of babies' lives saved at the lowest cost possible. Just like on the real *Shark Tank* show, the leaders of pro-life pregnancy centers that seek your investment present to you and your fellow panelists a case for support for their centers.

What do you think would be the primary content of those presentations? You can be sure that each center would present an emotionally moving story of a woman who was intent on getting an abortion, but after encountering the love and compassion of the staff at the pro-life pregnancy center, changed her mind about abortion and chose life for her baby. Each center would then show cute pictures of that baby taken after it had been born, and everyone present on the set of the show, including you and your fellow panelists, would know that an abortionist would have taken that baby's life if not for the intervention of the pro-life pregnancy center.

Of course, you and your fellow panelists would experience strong emotions after hearing each center's stories about babies' lives saved from abortion, and you would feel deeply grateful to the team at each of the centers for saving those babies' lives. And then...

Tell Us More about Your Sales Numbers

Just like on the real *Shark Tank* TV show, you and your fellow philanthropists would pivot from emotions to analysis. At the emotional level, you would very likely be interested in investing in each center because the stories of lives saved from abortion provide real evidence that each center offers a choose life product that at least one woman "purchased," so to speak. So there appears to be demand for each center's product. But of course you know one "sale" does not a successful business make. So you ask the presenting team for each center about their total "sales" numbers with the question, "How many babies' lives did your center save from abortion last year?"

What Is a Good Sales Number?

Many of the centers would report their total lives saved from abortion for the year were below one hundred. Now at this point, you don't know if that is a good or a bad result. Whether this is a good or bad sales number depends on what the total combined aggregate sales were both for a pro-life pregnancy center's choose life services and for the competing abortion facility's abortion services in the geographic market where the two compete. So you and your fellow panelists ask each center the combined aggregate sales for their market, calculated by adding a center's total lives saved from abortion plus the competing abortion facility's total number of abortions.

What kind of combined aggregate sales numbers would you see in most cases? To give one example of a pro-life pregnancy center I am very familiar with, in 2020 the center saved approximately one hundred babies' lives from abortion, and the abortion facility the center competed against did approximately ten thousand abortions. So the pro-life pregnancy center achieved a 1 percent market share in its competition against the abortion facility. Assuming you and your fellow philanthropists on our *Shark Tank for Pro-Life Pregnancy Centers* show heard each center present similar sales and market share numbers, the subsequent back-and-forth discussion with each center's leadership team could get tense very quickly.

"I'm Out, Until You Fix This"

After hearing each center tell you they achieved only a 1 percent market share against their local abortion facility competitor, would you and your fellow philanthropists be motivated to invest in each center? Probably not. It's more likely you would say, "I'm out, until you fix this."

Unfortunately for pro-life philanthropists, the vast majority of pro-life pregnancy centers cannot show any data that *prove* their center is competing successfully against Planned Parenthood, as measured by market share. In our imaginary *Shark Tank for Pro-Life Pregnancy Centers* scenario, I want to make clear I am not asking pro-life philanthropists to stop investing in pro-life pregnancy centers. On the contrary, the PLBI desperately needs *increased investment* in order to shut down Planned Parenthood and the abortion industry. But the PLBI needs philanthropists to invest in pro-life pregnancy centers that can win, as measured by market share, in their competition against Planned Parenthood.

All Hat, No Cattle

Instead of showing you data that prove success at gaining market share against Planned Parenthood, what do most pro-life pregnancy centers offer? Emotions! If you have ever attended a pro-life pregnancy center's fundraising gala, you will recall the presentation was filled with a lot of emotion, and likely zero analysis, before they asked you to invest in the center at the end of the event.

Do you see the problem here? Without any objective basis upon which to make your investment decision, you are likely to make a 100 percent emotionally based decision to invest in the center. As a result, it is possible that you are investing your hard-earned money in an organization that is more skilled at delivering style than delivering substance. As an investor, you want an objective, measurable ROI, not a feel-good story devoid of real substance. You don't want to *feel* like you're winning; you want to *know* you're winning.

Chapter Seventeen BOTTOM LINE

In general, pro-lifers praise those who work full-time in the pro-life movement based on how hard they try (intentions) to stop abortion, rather than how measurably successful (results) they are at actually stopping abortion. A pro-life pregnancy center's board of directors tend to evaluate the center's performance based on how hard the center's team members are trying rather than using objective analytical measurements such as market share that would reveal whether the team at the center is actually succeeding. The antidote to remedy investing based on intentions rather than results is for pro-life philanthropists to only invest in centers that show the most promising potential for saving the greatest number of babies' lives saved from abortion, at the lowest cost possible.

CHAPTER EIGHTEEN: ACCOUNTABILITY AND KEEPING SCORE

If winning is not everything, why do they keep score?
Vince Lombardi

By this point in the book, I hope I have persuaded you that you will save many more lives from abortion, and have much greater impact shutting down Planned Parenthood and the abortion industry, if you invest your 3T assets in a pro-life pregnancy center based on its results, as measured by market share, rather than investing based on your emotions. Before we move into the final three chapters where I specifically discuss investing your treasure in the PLBI, I think it is critical for you to first understand that the PLBI is not currently structured in a way that encourages pro-life pregnancy centers to be accountable for achieving measurable results.

To understand what I mean, a definition of "accountability" from Investopedia.com will be helpful: "Accountability is when an individual or department experiences consequences for their performance or actions. Accountability is essential for an organization and for a society. Without it, it is difficult to get people to assume ownership of their own actions because they believe they will not face any consequences." In general in the PLBI, do pro-life pregnancy center executive directors "assume ownership of their own actions" on behalf of their centers? Are there "consequences for their performance or actions"?

Given everything I've said so far in this book, you might be surprised to hear me say this, but I think the answer to both of those questions is "yes," in terms of how performance is currently defined by the board of directors of most pro-life pregnancy centers. As we learned in the previous chapter, in general, the board of directors of a typical pro-life pregnancy center defines performance as *trying hard* and *showing great passion for the pro-life cause*. The problem? Defining performance as trying hard and showing passion for the pro-life cause does not reveal to you, me, or anyone else whether a center is winning or losing in its competition against Planned Parenthood.

The only way to know whether a center is winning or losing is to compare over a given period of time how many client wins the center had versus how many client wins the local Planned Parenthood had. In other words, the only way to know if a center is winning is to keep score by calculating the center's market share versus Planned Parenthood.

The Great Divide

As a business professional, it may seem obvious to you that you have to keep score in business to know whether you are winning against your competition. But keeping score in this way is not obvious to most pro-life pregnancy centers operating in the PLBI. Why not? I think it is simply that all the stakeholders in a typical pro-life pregnancy center are not on the same page in terms of what the center's mission actually is.

You've likely experienced in life what it's like to not be on the same page with someone about something. Even in the world of public for-profit companies, I'm sure you've read stories about a company's investors not being on the same page as the company's executive leadership team when it comes to what the company's strategy should be. Unfortunately, I believe we have a similar problem in the PLBI. Currently, for the vast majority of pro-life pregnancy centers, there is not a clear common understanding between a center's leadership (the board of directors and executive team) and the center's investors (pro-life philanthropists) about how to measure a center's performance.

What is very interesting is that even though the center's investors wield tremendous influence over the center—after all, almost all of a typical center's revenue consists of funds given by philanthropists—rarely do the investors form a group to press the issue with the center's board of directors to demand the center's executive team be held accountable for performance, as measured by market share gains, against Planned Parenthood. Instead, the board of directors measures the center's performance based on how hard the center's team tries, and how passionate they are about the pro-life cause.

If we jump back to our Tom Brady example, can you imagine if "passion for football" and "trying hard" were the sole qualifications for the Buccaneers' quarterback position? If that were the case, one of the Buccaneers' overeager fans would likely be quarterbacking the team, also likely leading to the Buccaneers never winning a game during the football season. If center performance continues to be based almost solely on the center's leadership trying hard and their passion for the pro-life cause, then I think the PLBI will continue to gain very little ground in terms of market share in its competition against Planned Parenthood and the abortion industry.

Climbing the Wrong Wall

But let's say you currently invest in a pro-life pregnancy center in your local community, and you've decided to speak up and say something to the center's board of directors. You want the center's leadership team to pursue your interests as an investor. You want the center to achieve measurable market share gains against the local Planned Parenthood abortion facility. Of course, you appreciate the center's leadership team and how committed they are to the pro-life cause, but you now realize the team has spent years furiously climbing a ladder that is leaning against the wrong wall—the wall of intentions and trying hard.

You know that's the wrong wall because it has led to the center achieving only a 1 percent market share versus Planned Parenthood. So you want the center's leadership team to move the ladder to the right wall, the wall of results, of keeping score, as measured by increases in market share versus Planned Parenthood. As a business professional, that such a move would be the right one for the center probably seems so obvious to you, and you're confident the center's board members will see everything in a new light after you speak with them. Will the board members agree with you? I believe the board of directors will likely dismiss what you have to say. Not because *they* don't get it, but because they think *you* don't. What?

Let me explain by returning to the entrepreneurs that present their cases for investment on *Shark Tank.* From a psychology perspective, one of the most interesting aspects of the show is to listen to the reactions of entrepreneurs who did not secure funding from any of the sharks—in other words, a 100 percent rejection rate by all of the sharks. In the post-presentation interviews of these entrepreneurs, I've never heard one of them say something like, "You know, I think those sharks may be on to something with the points they made about *my* product not meeting *their* investment criteria. I think I'll go back to the drawing board and try to make my product more attractive *for them*." Instead, you often hear them say something like, "I know my product is going to be successful. The sharks just don't get it."

Arrogance? I don't think so. More likely is that the entrepreneurs have become so thoroughly emotionally invested in their products that they just can't see how those products won't be successful—*even when actual sales and profit numbers for the products don't indicate any likelihood of success*. I see the same dynamic at play in pro-life pregnancy centers. For the typical center, both the board of directors and the team operating the center are *deeply emotionally invested* in what the center has been doing for years—trying hard and being passionate for the pro-life cause—and can't see why that is not a sufficient case for investment by pro-life philanthropists. The leadership teams of most pro-life pregnancy centers aren't interested in your interests—measuring success by keeping score using market share metrics. I understand you may be skeptical about my claim, so I encourage you to test me on this by speaking with the board of directors of the pro-life pregnancy center you currently invest in.

There's Power in Numbers

Did you speak with them? Awesome! What happened? I'll wager they were nice to you, thanked you for your input, and told you they would take your ideas into consideration. I'll also wager the board will not implement any changes that could lead to the center being more competitive, as measured by market share. Remember, they think you're the one who doesn't get it.

So what can you do? First, keep this quote by Margaret Mead in mind: "Never doubt that a small group of thoughtful, committed citizens can change the world; indeed, it's the only thing that ever has." I'm going to borrow Mead's quote and adapt it for our purposes: "Never doubt that a small group of thoughtful, committed pro-life philanthropists can change a pro-life pregnancy center; indeed, it's the only thing that ever will." Again, remember this: almost all of a center's revenue comes from investments (e.g., donations) by committed pro-life investors like you. Therefore, as I said earlier, a center's investors can yield tremendous influence over a center, *if the investors commit to actually yielding that influence*.

You've likely seen in the for-profit world the actions a group of investors will take when they are dissatisfied with the results or strategic direction of the company they are invested in. Just do an internet search on the phrase "investor revolt" to find some of the more famous examples. As you read some of the stories about investors revolting, note the key to investor groups actually having success at influencing company leadership to change direction is related to the percentage of ownership the investor group has in the company. The higher the percentage of ownership, the greater the power to influence change. There is power in numbers.

I believe this to be the case for pro-life pregnancy centers as well. Let me illustrate using a fictitious example. Suppose there are ten total investors in a pro-life pregnancy center, each investor giving the same amount, so each has a 10 percent share. Yes, I know no one can legally own a "share" of a nonprofit, but I propose this "mental move," if you will, in order to bring focus to the fact that "money talks" in business, and that goes for nonprofit pro-life pregnancy centers as much as it does for for-profit organizations. Now if only one of the ten investors demands the center evaluate performance based on market share metrics, it is unlikely the center will change its focus from trying hard to actually keeping score using market share metrics.

However, for every additional investor who gets on board with the plan to measure performance based on market share, it ups the pressure on the center's leadership team to change its focus. Think about what would happen when the center's board of directors is facing, let's say six out of the ten investors, demanding the board change its focus to evaluating the center's performance based on market share metrics. Additionally, consider the board's reaction if those same investors also put some teeth into their demands by stating they would no longer invest in the center unless the center changed its strategy to focus on measurable market share gains. Now you've got the board's attention because there's no way the center can risk losing 60 percent of its revenue.

And yes, the center's leadership can try to replace the six investors with other investors who are more amenable to the trying hard approach, but finding pro-life investors is not easy, and the new prospective investors are likely to ask questions that will lead to a discussion of why the majority of the center's current investors are pulling their investments out of the center.

It's All about the Numbers

The point of our fictitious example is to demonstrate that if they are willing to group together and demand change, a group of pro-life philanthropists who invest in a pro-life pregnancy center can influence the leadership of the center to start keeping score and focusing on achieving a consistent increase in market share, as measured by the number of lives saved from abortion relative to the number of abortions performed at Planned Parenthood.

I believe this can be accomplished at any pro-life pregnancy center, if the investors in the center have the courage to do it. Assuming they do, and a change is made at the center, you'll know it's heading in the right direction strategically when you hear the executive director of the center say something like Bridget VanMeans said about Thrive, "First of all, we're very evidence-based, because all good businesses are."

Yes! Yes! Yes! I would like to create a poster with Bridget's quote on it and ask every executive director of every pro-life pregnancy center in the United States to hang it on the wall in their offices, directly facing their desks so that they had to look at it constantly to be reminded that all good businesses keep score. Over time, you want the leadership team at the center you invest in to say something similar to what Bridget said about ThriVe: "At ThriVe, we're very outcomes oriented. We are proud to say that we know we have reduced Planned Parenthood's numbers. When we started the ThriVe model, our Planned Parenthood competitor clinic was doing about eight thousand abortions a year. Last year, they did twenty-four hundred. So we've helped drop their business by close to 70 percent." And then imagine the executive director at the center you invest in showing you a graph like the one Bridget can show ThriVe's investors: "We have a bar graph that shows Planned Parenthood's number of abortions against our number of women who chose life. And you can see a beautiful, exact marriage between the descent of Planned Parenthood's numbers and then the ascent of our numbers." That is what winning the market share battle, and eventually the market share war, looks like. That is what pro-life investors want all pro-life pregnancy centers across the country to achieve.

Chapter Eighteen BOTTOM LINE

The PLBI is not currently structured in a way that holds pro-life pregnancy centers accountable to winning the market share battle against Planned Parenthood. For the typical pro-life pregnancy center, both the board of directors and the team operating the center are deeply emotionally invested in trying hard and being passionate about the pro-life cause—not necessarily about measuring success by keeping score using market share metrics. However, remember that almost all of a center's revenue comes from investments (e.g., donations) by committed pro-life philanthropists. Therefore, those philanthropists can yield tremendous influence over a center. If a group of a center's philanthropists—a group that accounts for a substantial amount of the center's donation revenue—has the courage to demand the center change its strategy, to the point of being willing to pull their investments out of the center if the center doesn't change its strategy, then there is a chance that the center's board of directors will implement a new strategy that focuses on the center achieving a consistent increase in market share, as measured by the number of lives saved from abortion relative to the number of abortions performed at Planned Parenthood.

CHAPTER NINETEEN: CAPITAL STAYS WHERE IT IS WELL TREATED

Capital goes where it is welcome and stays where it is well treated. Walter Wriston

The late Walter Wriston, former chairman and CEO of Citicorp, once said, "Capital goes where it is welcome and stays where it is well treated." In the for-profit world, I think that quote reasonably describes how capitalism moves money to its highest and best use. In the nonprofit world in general, and in the PLBI specifically, I don't think there is a good mechanism that directs pro-life philanthropic money to its highest and best use. I think the second part of Wriston's quote about capital, "and stays where it is well treated," is the key missing piece in the PLBI. "Well treated" implies that money invested in pro-life pregnancy centers is earning the ROI the pro-life investor seeks: saving as many preborn human lives from abortion as possible.

Unfortunately, there currently exists no objective source of information about pro-life pregnancy center performance that pro-life philanthropists can use to direct their money into high-performing pro-life pregnancy centers, as well as take their money out of pro-life pregnancy centers that consistently show poor performance. Remember that as pro-life philanthropists we define a center's performance as measurable increases in market share versus Planned Parenthood.

Grow the Winners by Starving the Losers

This may sound a little harsh, but if an objective source of information existed comparing performance of all the pro-life pregnancy centers, I believe the poorly performing centers would eventually be forced to go out of business as the operating funds supplied by philanthropists would dry up over time. The upside to the demise of the poorly performing centers would be that the high performing centers would then have additional growth funds available to expand their operations, and thereby in the aggregate, win more battles against Planned Parenthood. My assumption is that given the opportunity, pro-life investors would rationally decide to place their capital into centers that earn the greatest ROI defined as the most number of preborn human lives saved from abortion per dollar invested.

To visualize what such an objective source of information about center performance might look like, think about the way the stock market operates. I realize the example I'm about to give is a gross oversimplification of how the stock market actually works, but for the sake of our discussion, I just want to paint a very simple picture. Generally speaking, investors buy or sell stocks of companies based on reported operating results, which indicate likelihood of future success. When companies report strong operating results, they are rewarded by investors purchasing more of those companies' stocks. What about companies that report poor operating results? Investors who hold stock of those poorly performing companies tend to pull their money out of those stocks by selling their shares and then investing the proceeds of the sale into the stocks with good operating results.

In general, this back and forth of investors putting money into companies that perform well (winners) and pulling money out of companies that perform poorly (losers) will provide more capital for the winners to expand their operations and will reduce capital available for losers to operate and/or expand operations. If a company continues to perform poorly over the long term, then it is likely that operating capital available to it will eventually dry up. Essentially, the company will be starved out of existence—creative destruction through capitalism in action.

A Pro-Life Pregnancy Center Stock Market

With that admittedly overly simplistic explanation of the stock market as background, let's imagine a special pro-life pregnancy center "stock market" exists that lists all existing pro-life pregnancy centers across the country. Further, imagine that all pro-life philanthropists—from those who could invest only a little to those who could invest a lot—had access to this special pro-life pregnancy center stock market and could choose which centers to invest in, and could also trade in and out of centers based on reported performance results. And finally, imagine this special pro-life pregnancy center stock market was the only means available for pro-life pregnancy centers to get access to operating funds.

Question: In our pro-life pregnancy center stock market scenario, as a pro-life philanthropist, what criteria would you use to decide which center(s) to invest in? Of course, I'm sure you would have your own specific criteria for choosing which centers to invest in, but I'm willing to bet one of your key decision criteria would be the number of preborn human lives a given center successfully saved from abortion. In other words, you would make your investment decisions based on a center's results.

Now imagine a scenario where not only you but all pro-life philanthropists used the same decision criteria for deciding which pro-life pregnancy centers to invest in. Further, imagine that our pro-life pregnancy center stock market required all pro-life pregnancy centers to report both their lives saved numbers and their market share numbers on a regular basis—let's say quarterly—to both current and prospective pro-life philanthropists. Over time, what do you think would happen in this scenario? My prediction is the pro-life pregnancy centers showing the strongest performance numbers would receive an ever-increasing amount of funds from pro-life philanthropists, while funds flowing to under-performing centers would decrease or cease altogether. Does that process sound familiar? Correct, just like the stock market.

"E Pluribus Unum": One from Many

Pushing the pro-life pregnancy stock market scenario a step further, after the poorly performing centers were starved out of existence, I believe the next phase would involve the winning centers competing to attract sufficient funds from pro-life philanthropists to expand their pro-life pregnancy center **business models** to a regional and then a national footprint.

Notice I bolded the words "business models" above. Now we're talking about the evolution of the PLBI transforming from a conglomeration of thousands of very small independent single facility pro-life pregnancy center organizations into one, or perhaps several, multilocation pro-life pregnancy center organizations that successfully compete against Planned Parenthood on a national scale. As investors, if we seek to maximize ROI—meaning saving as many lives from abortion as possible and eventually winning the market share war against Planned Parenthood and the abortion industry—I believe we should urgently pursue this transformation of the PLBI.

We would certainly seek such an ROI-maximizing transformation opportunity in the for-profit world, wouldn't we? Think about it. In the for-profit world, as investors seeking to maximize financial return, it is almost inconceivable that if we owned a business model that proved very profitable in one city, say here in Dallas where I live, that we would not then desire to expand that model to other cities, assuming the business model lent itself to being scalable. And that's especially true, and in my opinion makes it a moral imperative, if that business model was proven effective at saving human lives.

For example, let's imagine you and I co-own a for-profit hospital in Dallas that saves ten times more human lives than any other hospital of comparable size in the country. How did our hospital achieve such astounding results? Last year, researchers at our hospital discovered the one and only cure to lung cancer. So we now have a life-saving product in very high demand, so naturally, as the owners of the hospital we would profit very handsomely from that product that cures lung cancer. But our total profit potential would be severely limited if we decided to only offer the cure at our hospital in Dallas! Putting aside our moral duty to expand distribution of our lung cancer cure product, solely from the perspective of maximizing financial ROI, wouldn't we take our lung cancer cure to as many hospitals as possible around the nation as quickly as possible? I think we would.

So in the PLBI, why hasn't an ROI-maximizing (greatest number of preborn human lives saved from abortion) transformation happened yet? After all, you saw with ThriVe that there already exists at least one pro-life pregnancy center business model that won the market share war at a local level against Planned Parenthood. I think the crux of the matter is lack of awareness. Currently, there is no mechanism that informs pro-life philanthropists about successful pro-life pregnancy center business models. (Had you ever heard about ThriVe and its success against Planned Parenthood before you read this book?)

If such a mechanism existed, whereby all pro-life philanthropists were informed about pro-life pregnancy center business models that were achieving measurable market share gains against Planned Parenthood, I believe those philanthropists would move heaven and earth to help expand the operations of those centers. Imagine if that happened!

For example, can you picture how impactful it would be if by the end of this decade there emerged three proven-effective (as measured by market share against Planned Parenthood), nationally recognized (branding!!) pro-life pregnancy center organizations, each having multiple successful facilities established in the twenty largest cities in the United States? Now I don't know if three organizations is the right number, but whatever the right number, the point is that these market share focused, nationally recognized pro-life pregnancy center brands would cause some serious problems for Planned Parenthood's abortion business. And serious problems for Planned Parenthood's abortion business means many preborn human lives saved that otherwise would have been lost—exactly the ROI that pro-life philanthropists demand.

Chapter Nineteen BOTTOM LINE

Currently there is no objective source of information revealing the market share performance of individual pro-life pregnancy centers. If such an objective source of information existed, then pro-life philanthropists could direct their philanthropic capital into high-performing pro-life pregnancy centers, as well as take their money out of pro-life pregnancy centers that consistently performed poorly. Such a change would transform the PLBI from a conglomeration of thousands of very small independent single facility pro-life pregnancy center nonprofit organizations into one or perhaps several multilocation pro-life pregnancy center nonprofit organizations that could successfully compete against Planned Parenthood on a national scale.

CHAPTER TWENTY: BE MORE DEMANDING PART 1: YOUR PRO-LIFE INVESTING PHILOSOPHY

There is nothing wrong with changing a plan when the situation has changed. Seneca

More people should learn to tell their dollars where to go instead of asking them where they went. Roger Babson

Know what you own, and know why you own it. Peter Lynch

In the concluding two chapters of this book, I want to talk with you about your financial investments in pro-life organizations. Specifically, I want to invite you to be more demanding with your pro-life philanthropy. What do I mean by "be more demanding?" Two different things.

First, I use "be more demanding" as a play on words to mean shifting more of your total pro-life investments into the PLBI (pro-life pregnancy centers that strive to increase demand for choose life services), and out of pro-life organizations that primarily focus on legislative initiatives and culture change (organizations that primarily seek to restrict supply of abortion services through the overturning of *Roe v. Wade*). Again, I am not saying investments in pro-life organizations that focus on restricting supply of abortion services are not important. They are vitally important.

What I am saying is that those investments will not win the war against Planned Parenthood and the abortion industry. Not even close. If that statement doesn't make sense to you, please reread Part I of this book. Therefore, I believe the more impactful investment in the long run is an investment that increases demand for choose life services. So this first aspect of "be more demanding" involves rebalancing your pro-life philanthropy portfolio to put more of your investments in to the demand side—the PLBI—rather than the supply side. I cover this meaning of "be more demanding" in this chapter.

The second meaning of "be more demanding" happens after you've committed to rebalancing your pro-life investment portfolio more heavily toward the PLBI. Once you've decided to do that, you have some very important investment decisions to make. What will your pro-life investment decision criteria be for deciding which pro-life pregnancy centers you will invest in? I recommend that you only invest in centers that are willing to be held accountable to achieving success against Planned Parenthood, as measured by market share—and that you demand proof of results from a center that it is in fact winning the market share battle. I cover this second aspect of "be more demanding" in the next and final chapter of this book.

Playing the Supply Side

Currently, many pro-life philanthropists put all or the majority of their pro-life investments into organizations focused on the supply side of pro-life. Recall when I say "supply side" I mean investments that restrict or eliminate the abortion industry's ability to supply abortion services. Here's a relatively recent real-life example of how pro-life investments on the supply side aim to restrict the supply of abortion services.

During the 2020 elections, Planned Parenthood launched the biggest electoral effort in its history. It invested about $45 million to help elect pro-abortion presidential, congressional and state-level candidates. How did the pro-life movement counter Planned Parenthood's historic investment? The pro-life organization called Susan B. Anthony List upped the ante by launching the largest effort in its history—a $52 million campaign to support President Trump's reelection bid. The two organizations combined invested close to $100 million over the issue of abortion supply—Planned Parenthood aiming to elect legislators who would support laws to maintain and/or expand supply of abortion services, and Susan B. Anthony List aiming to elect legislators who would support laws to restrict and/or eliminate supply of abortion services.

Turning to Susan B. Anthony List's $52 million investment, where did that money come from? It came from pro-life philanthropists who donated it to Susan B. Anthony List. And do you think those philanthropists expect a return on their investment in Susan B. Anthony List? I believe so. The ROI in this case would be lives saved from abortion based on the expectation that Susan B. Anthony List's efforts would lead to the election of legislators who would then successfully pass laws restricting the supply of abortion services.

How could we measure that ROI? To estimate what the maximum ROI might look like, let's use as an example what would be a huge pro-life victory on the supply side—the overturning of *Roe v. Wade*. Recall from Chapter 2 that research estimates overturning *Roe v. Wade* would result in 100,000 lives saved from abortion annually. To keep our ROI example very simple, in my calculation I'm just going to use the number of lives saved in one year. So, $52 million saves 100,000 lives from abortion in one year, which is a cost of $520 per life saved from abortion ($52 million/100,000).

How does this supply-side ROI compare with the ROI of an investment of the same size on the demand side, meaning an investment in the PLBI? Well, let's use ThriVe Women's Express Healthcare as an example and assume there were multiple ThriVe Women's Express Healthcare centers around the country, and that the annual investment required to operate their centers to their max potential was exactly $52 million, the same amount of the investment made by Susan B. Anthony List. We can calculate the ROI—lives saved from abortion—of the $52 million investment if we know ThriVe's cost per life saved from abortion. Fortunately, we do know that number. It's approximately $1,200.

So our supply-side investment yields a cost per life saved from abortion of $520, and our demand-side investment in ThriVe yields a cost per life saved from abortion of $1,200. From this perspective, it appears an investment in the supply side achieves a result that is about 2.3X better than an investment in the demand side ($1,200/$520 = 2.3). Hands down a win for supply-side investments, right? Not so fast.

Don't Forget about Risk

An astute investor has to consider the probability of success in any investment he or she makes. In other words, how much risk exists in the proposed investment? In our example comparing a supply-side investment (Susan B. Anthony List) to a demand-side investment (ThriVe Express Women's Healthcare), we are evaluating two organizations that are not start-ups or in an early growth phase. Start-up and early growth phase organizations both carry substantial investment risks, whether supply-side investments or demand-side investments.

Both Susan B. Anthony List and ThriVe are in their mature growth phases, so we can evaluate an investment in their current operations without worrying about start-up risks. That said, the supply-side investment in Susan B. Anthony List appears to generate a significantly better ROI than the demand-side investment in ThriVe. However, *in terms of investment risk*, there's an enormous difference between the two investment opportunities because the demand-side ROI of $1,200 to save a life is guaranteed. In other words, a $1,200 demand-side investment in

ThriVe is put to work in a system that is already proven to work as promised. Therefore, there is almost zero risk that your $1,200 investment will not save a life from abortion. Such a guaranteed ROI is extremely compelling from an investment standpoint, especially when you remember what that ROI is: saving the life of a unique human being made in the image and likeness of God.

What about the risk of the supply-side investment? As you likely already know from experience, a supply-side investment that seeks to restrict access to abortion by way of electing legislators to change abortion laws is highly uncertain. In other words, the risk on your investment in the supply side is extremely high—it is likely your investment will achieve very little return, and possibly zero return.

But just for a moment, let's not be so pessimistic about the risk of a supply-side investment. Let's assume the $52 million investment made by Susan B. Anthony List did not lead to the elimination of *Roe v. Wade*, but did lead to some smaller successes in restricting access to abortion at the local level in some states. Let's assume the $52 million supply-side investment resulted in 10,000 lives saved from abortion instead of 100,000 lives saved. In that case, our ROI—number of lives saved from abortion—drops by 90,000 lives, which causes our cost per life saved on the supply-side investment to balloon from $520 per life saved to $5,200 per life saved ($52 million/10,000).

Rebalance towards Proven Impact

Here's the point. I'm not suggesting that pro-life philanthropists should pick *either* a supply-side investment *or* a demand-side investment. I'm recommending a portfolio that invests in *both*. However, if you are a typical pro-life philanthropist, it is likely you are currently placing most of your investments in the supply side and much less in the demand side.

I am asking you to do the exact opposite—place most of your investments in the demand side and much less in the supply side. Yes, please invest in supply-side organizations that prove they are making headway in the decades-long efforts to get *Roe v. Wade* overturned. But remember that politics is the primary driver of success or failure of such laws initially being passed, and then also being maintained over the long term. Therefore, pro-life supply side investments are highly speculative. Yes, the potential ROI (lives saved from abortion) of those investments is very high, but the risk is that the ROI for those investments will be very small.

What happens when investors experience very low ROI year after year, or decade after decade? They eventually abandon ship. And this appears to be the case with many pro-life philanthropists. I have spoken with many former pro-life philanthropists who invested exclusively in pro-life supply side investments for years, and in some cases decades. They eventually stopped investing because they did not see the Pro-Life Movement making significant progress in getting laws passed that restricted abortion, especially the overturning of *Roe v. Wade*.

If those same philanthropists had instead invested heavily in pro-life "demand-side" investments, I believe they might have stuck with their supply side investments for longer. Here's why. Going all in on the highly speculative supply-side investment in pro-life can yield very low ROI year after year, eventually frustrating and wearing down an investor, who then gives up and throws in the towel. On the other hand, demand-side investments in the right pro-life pregnancy centers offer the philanthropist a frequent guaranteed ROI: proof of lives saved from abortion.

Verified ROI from pro-life demand-side investments can provide both the emotional satisfaction and the logical justification for a philanthropist to not grow weary with their long-term speculative pro-life investments in the supply side. That's why I'm a proponent of a portfolio of both investments in the demand side of pro-life (the PLBI), and investments in the supply side of pro-life (overturn *Roe v. Wade*), but with the majority of your investments placed on the demand side.

Let the Buyer Beware

Let's say you've decided to rebalance your pro-life investment portfolio with a heavy emphasis on pro-life demand-side investments. Congratulations! You have so many pro-life pregnancy centers to choose from—there are approximately twenty-five hundred to three thousand pro-life pregnancy centers in the United States. But as with most investments, *caveat emptor*—let the buyer beware—applies. And with that warning in our heads, let's move on to our final chapter and our second meaning of "be more demanding"—demanding proof of results from a pro-life pregnancy center that it is winning the market share battle against Planned Parenthood.

Chapter Twenty BOTTOM LINE

Supply-side investments that seek to restrict access to abortion by way of electing legislators to change abortion laws are extremely risky from an ROI perspective—it is likely your investment will achieve very little return. On the other hand, demand side investments in the right pro-life pregnancy centers will give you a guaranteed ROI, whereby you will receive frequent proof of lives saved from abortion—sometimes even on a weekly basis. Therefore, you should rebalance your pro-life philanthropic investment portfolio to put the majority of your investments in to the demand side—the PLBI—rather than the supply side. Frequent and verified ROI from your pro-life demand-side investments can provide you with both the emotional satisfaction and the logical justification to not grow weary with your long-term speculative pro-life supply side investments.

CHAPTER TWENTY ONE: BE MORE DEMANDING PART 2: YOUR PRO-LIFE INVESTING DECISIONS

Buy not on optimism, but on arithmetic. Benjamin Graham

Having information on investing is one thing. Knowing what to do with it is something else entirely. Don Connelly

In this final chapter, I cover what to do once you've committed to rebalancing your pro-life investment portfolio more heavily toward demand-side investments in the PLBI. I recommend you only invest in centers that are willing to be held accountable for achieving success against Planned Parenthood, as measured by market share—and that you *demand proof of results* from a center that it is in fact winning the market share battle. Please keep those thoughts at the front of your mind as we venture through this chapter.

NOT One and the Same

First, to set the stage for rebalancing your pro-life investment portfolio, let's briefly review some of the macro-level issues we discussed in Part I of this book. I do this because if you've been involved in pro-life for some time, then these issues likely affect how you view both the Pro-Life

Movement and the PLBI. Remember that many pro-life philanthropists who acquired wealth by executing successful business strategies do not use their acquired business acumen when evaluating whether a pro-life pregnancy center can compete effectively against Planned Parenthood.

What could explain this? I have interacted with many pro-life philanthropists over the years so I believe I have some insights into this phenomenon. Simply, I believe many pro-life philanthropists do not view any aspect of the pro-life universe as operating under the description of a competitive industry. Instead, pro-life philanthropists view all of the pro-life universe as a human rights movement. In other words, they don't make a distinction between the Pro-Life Movement and the PLBI. The unfortunate consequence of this is many philanthropists view the PLBI as contained within the Pro-Life Movement. They tend to view pro-life pregnancy centers as human rights ministries, and though some philanthropists may still expect the centers they fund to achieve measurable impact of some kind, in my experience almost no philanthropists demand centers win more clients than Planned Parenthood, with success measured by consistent increases in market share.

I do not believe pro-life philanthropists are making a deliberate choice to view pro-life pregnancy centers as ministries instead of viewing them as competitive organizations. They are simply accepting, without question, how the centers position their organizations in the minds of the philanthropists. And because the vast majority of pro-life pregnancy centers are led by those who have strong credentials as human rights advocates in the Pro-Life Movement, rather than as successful business leaders, the leaders of those centers proclaim boldly to pro-life philanthropists that their centers are an important part of the Pro-Life Movement.

I believe this is a critical mistake because, again, the Pro-Life Movement focuses on the right to life of the preborn human being, whereas the PLBI focuses on influencing the decision maker, the pregnant woman, in her choice between competing services: abortion services or choose life services. I am not claiming that leaders of pro-life pregnancy centers deliberately make this market positioning mistake. What I am claiming is that centers should classify themselves as competitive businesses that are not contained within the Pro-Life Movement, but instead are motivated by it. With a correct understanding of pro-life pregnancy centers as competitive businesses, pro-life philanthropists would then hold centers accountable for measurable market share gains against Planned Parenthood.

So Many Investment Options! Nope

With that short reminder out of the way, let's get to the exciting part—finding a pro-life pregnancy center to invest in! You might think that would be easy given there are somewhere between twenty-five hundred and three thousand pro-life pregnancy centers in the United States. But we must tread very carefully. *Caveat emptor* must be your guiding principle. Here's a hard truth pro-life philanthropists don't like to hear: the vast majority—I estimate more than 90 percent—of these pro-life pregnancy centers are *not* competing against Planned Parenthood. The vast majority of those centers are actually what we call "Pregnancy Resource Centers," also known as PRCs. The emphasis here is on the word "resources," which you can generally define as material assistance of some kind.

When you dive deeper into the operating philosophy of a typical PRC, it quickly becomes clear that its primary mission is to provide material assistance to those women who are already likely to carry their pregnancies to term. In other words, PRCs primarily serve women who are not actively seeking abortion services. Even if an executive director of a PRC tells you they compete against Planned Parenthood, you shouldn't take her statement at face value.

This Is Only a Test

How do you know if a center actually competes against Planned Parenthood? The simplest way (granted, not the easiest way) is to ask a woman to mystery call a center and pose as a woman who is pregnant and seeking an abortion. After some very brief initial conversation with the call intake person at the center, the mystery caller should say something to the effect of, "I am looking for a clinic that handles abortions." If you are dealing with a PRC, it is very likely the immediate response of the call intake person at the PRC will be something like this, "I'm sorry. We neither perform nor refer for abortions." Your mystery caller can then go ahead and hang up, which is exactly what abortion-seeking women in real life do when they hear that response from a PRC. The difference is that in real life, the abortion-seeking woman's next call will likely be to a Planned Parenthood facility that will be all too happy to schedule her for an abortion.

So in essence, the PRC did exactly what it said it wouldn't do—by throwing away the one opportunity it had to skillfully guide the abortion-seeking woman away from Planned Parenthood, it instead indirectly referred her for an abortion at Planned Parenthood. Please do not invest in a PRC if you want to have any measurable impact on shutting down Planned Parenthood. Don't worry, the PRC will be fine without your investment. There are plenty of philanthropists who want to support the provision of material assistance to pregnant women who are very likely to carry their pregnancies to term, but who need some financial help.

I assume that you, however, are not interested in investing in a PRC, but instead in a pro-life pregnancy center whose mission is to serve women who are actively seeking an abortion. If your mystery caller happens to connect with such a center, she will know right away because she won't hear the response, "I'm sorry. We neither perform nor refer for abortions." Instead, the call intake person at the center will begin to build a relationship with the woman by asking questions, and eventually will attempt to encourage her to come in to the center for an appointment. In other words, the call intake person will engage in a sales conversation. If your mystery caller discovers such a center, it should go on the top of your list as a high potential contender for one of your demand side pro-life investments.

The Question to Ask

But perhaps mystery calling your local pro-life pregnancy center is a bit more than you want to chew. I understand. Fortunately, there is another way to find out if a center is a PRC that you want to avoid investing in, or is instead a sales-focused pro-life pregnancy center that you want to place on your list of investment candidates.

You can simply meet with the executive director of the center and ask this question. "Last year, how many abortion-determined women did your center successfully encourage to change their minds about getting an abortion?" You must use that exact term: abortion-determined. The term is well known in the pro-life pregnancy center world to mean a woman who desperately wants an abortion, and the sooner the better. If the executive director doesn't answer your question very quickly with specific numbers of how many abortion-determined women changed their minds and chose life, and instead begins talking about all the women they served with various services, you are likely dealing with a PRC. PRCs typically do not have in place any of the operating strategies and tactics required to compete effectively and win abortion-determined clients away from Planned Parenthood. Yes, PRCs provide a valuable service to a certain group of women. It's just not a service that will make a dent in lowering demand for abortions.

Will the Real Competitors Please Step Forward?

Let's return for a moment to my claim that more than 90 percent of the pro-life pregnancy centers are not really competing against Planned Parenthood. Assuming for a moment my claim is accurate, I'm sure you're wondering just how many pro-life pregnancy centers actually do compete effectively against Planned Parenthood. Every additional year I work in the PLBI—as of this writing my seventh year—my estimate of the number of pro-life pregnancy centers that are a competitive threat to Planned Parenthood decreases.

I understand that's probably not very encouraging to you, but it goes a long way toward helping you understand why Planned Parenthood's annual abortion numbers have consistently increased year after year. Honestly, I would estimate fewer than fifty centers across our country have even a basic understanding about how to compete effectively against Planned Parenthood. Pessimistic? Perhaps, but of course, I'm open to any pro-life pregnancy center contacting me to prove with real numbers that they are winning the market share battle against Planned Parenthood.

Nonetheless, the good news is that competitive pro-life pregnancy centers do exist. And I now assume that you want to find one to invest in. Awesome! Let's dive in to how to find one.

Please Save Me from Myself

To start, I am going to assume your preference is to find a competitive pro-life pregnancy center that operates locally—in your city, or in your state if you live in a rural area. What should you do first? Inoculate yourself! Not from any communicable disease, but from your own emotions. You see, when you start meeting with executive directors of pro-life pregnancy centers, you will confront two very difficult challenges. First, the vast majority of executive directors are genuinely awesome people who are passionately pro-life, and that makes them very likeable. You will naturally want to support such awesome people! Second, an executive director will almost certainly share with you a recent heartwarming story of a baby saved from abortion after the mother of the baby came to the center. These types of powerful save stories will naturally make you want to support such life-saving work!

But you have to take a deep breath, fight against your natural inclinations, and ignore your emotions for now. And you may think that's easy to do, but be careful. Let me share with you a true story that demonstrates that even the hardest self-proclaimed "by the numbers" types of people can go soft when emotions run high.

A Shark Goes Soft

By this point in the book you know I love the TV show *Shark Tank*. The vast majority of the time, the sharks on *Shark Tank* base their investment decisions on objective numbers and do not allow themselves to be emotionally moved by the stories and presentation skills of the entrepreneurs seeking the sharks' investment funds.

However, on rare occasion, even the sharks cave in to their emotions. On one episode, billionaire Mark Cuban made an investment in a business that by his own admission couldn't be justified by the numbers. Here's how that happened. Two sisters presented the sharks with an opportunity to invest in their "stick-on decorations for t-shirts" business. For example, one "stick-on" was a bowtie you could stick on your t-shirt so that, in a humorous way, you looked like you were wearing a tuxedo. The product was fun, but sales and profit numbers for the business were not very good, so predictably, each of the sharks took their turn panning "the numbers," and one after another responded with the words the entrepreneurs presenting on *Shark Tank* hate to hear: "I'm out."

But the two sisters were *very* personable and likable. When each of the sharks said, "I'm out," you could see they were doing it almost apologetically, like they really wanted to help out the two sisters out of compassion. In the end though, the sharks still let "the numbers" control their final investment decisions.

And then Mark Cuban did something extraordinary. After he had criticized the business for having no future potential, he suddenly and unexpectedly offered the sisters $200K to purchase the entire company. He told the sisters in a very straightforward manner that he saw no potential in the business, but he wanted to help them by getting them out of the business so they could pursue a more worthwhile venture. The sisters, after some hesitation and with tears flowing down their faces, accepted Mark's offer. I think they knew that Mark was right about his assessment of their company's potential. Not willing to fully admit that he made an investment decision based on emotions alone, Cuban still justified his decision with logic saying, "I can somehow find a way to use those products with the Dallas Mavericks." (He owns the Dallas Mavericks NBA franchise.)

What Was I Thinking?

Later, upon reflection, I was interested in my own reaction to what had transpired between Mark Cuban and the two entrepreneurial sisters. Purely from a numbers perspective, I should have scolded Mark for caving in to his emotions. But that was not my reaction at all! In fact, I was overjoyed for the two sisters and my admiration for Mark Cuban grew because of the generosity he had shown those two entrepreneurs.

But wait a minute!! What about the numbers?? Objectively speaking, investor extraordinaire Mark Cuban had made a poor investment decision, yet there I was, deeply emotionally moved and applauding him for making a terrible business decision. What gives? I think the answer is simple: we human beings are not calculators. We are spiritual beings living a human experience, and as such we highly value experiences that make us feel good about ourselves. And we are willing to invest hard-earned money to get those experiences. Top of the list for such experiences is helping others who need help. Mark Cuban's investment in the two sister's company will almost certainly not pay off financially, but the investment was worth it to Mark for the emotional fulfillment it gave him personally to help out the two sisters.

How does what Mark Cuban did apply to pro-life philanthropists investing in pro-life pregnancy centers? In the same way that Mark Cuban acted toward the two sisters, many pro-life philanthropists who are seasoned business professionals, and who would be very unlikely to invest in a for-profit business without understanding, and agreeing with, its marketing and sales strategy, will freely give their hard-earned money to pro-life pregnancy centers based solely on liking the executive director and being moved by a powerful story of how the center saved a baby's life from abortion.

So please don't think what happened to Mark Cuban can't happen to you as well. You will very likely be drawn emotionally to the team members who work at pro-life pregnancy centers, even if they can't prove with market share data that their center is a competitive threat to Planned Parenthood. Investing in that pro-life pregnancy center might make you feel great, but is your investment in the center necessarily a good thing, objectively speaking? If your investment in the center doesn't fuel market share gains against Planned Parenthood, I think the answer is no.

Reverse the Order

So I recommend you don't even give your emotions the opportunity to lead you into a poor investment of your pro-life philanthropy funds. Instead, approach each pro-life pregnancy center investment opportunity as if you were a professional for-profit investor. Professional investors are astute. They recognize they are human, and therefore as susceptible to getting carried away by their emotions as any other human being. To inoculate themselves against their emotions, before an investment opportunity presentation even begins, professional investors wisely ask the presenting team to present its objective data first.

I experienced this back in the dotcom boom in the late 1990s when I was in charge of marketing for a high tech start-up company that was raising money to develop a new wireless technology. I went on the road with members of our executive team to present our "case for support" to both individual private investors and investor groups that wanted to invest in high tech start-ups. I learned very quickly that when you present your opportunity to investors, it is similar to the *Shark Tank* TV show in one respect, but completely different in another respect. The similar part is you prepare a presentation for investors that contains both the emotional story about your product's potential and the objective data (your *pro forma*) that estimates future demand and profit potential of your business. However, when it comes to the actual presentation to prospective investors, unlike on *Shark Tank* where the order of presentation is first the emotional story, and then the objective data, in the private investment world the prospective investors often demand that you switch the order and start with the objective data first. Before they decide if they even want to hear the emotional portion of your product presentation, they first want to understand the "numbers."

As the marketing guy on the team, of course, I hated this because there were times when our start-up's *pro forma* numbers did not meet a particular investment group's requirements and they said "we're out" even before I got my chance to present. It was like getting pumped up to play in a game and then the game got cancelled right as I was about to take the field. In the real world, I believe the Sharks on *Shark Tank* likely follow the "numbers first" process as well, but in the land of Hollywood, a numbers-first process would make for terribly boring reality TV.

Back into the Shark Tank

My point is this: You must lead with a center's objective data first before you engage any of the executive director's emotional stories. Let's return for a moment to our *Shark Tank for Pro-Life Pregnancy Centers* scenario we looked at in Chapter 17. Let's change up the show a little. In our revised show format, when pro-life pregnancy centers present their cases for support, you and your fellow sharks now require them to start with their objective numbers before you allow them to present their emotional stories. Your number one investment criteria before you allow a center to move on to the next step and share their centers' emotional stories? A center's market share gains versus Planned Parenthood.

Now imagine that all of the pro-life pregnancy centers across our country came on your show, and each center began its presentation with how many client wins it had against Planned Parenthood versus how many client losses it had. Most centers would have to say something like this, "Last year, in our competition against our main competitor, Planned Parenthood, for every one hundred prospective clients who were seeking an abortion, we had one client win compared to Planned Parenthood's ninety-nine client wins, so our market share was 1 percent." I can hear both your and your fellow sharks' responses to those centers: "I'm out."

The Wrong Objective Data

So there you are on the *Shark Tank for Pro-Life Pregnancy Centers* show, and following each center's presentation of its numbers, over and over again you're saying "I'm out." After a while, you'd likely start getting depressed and think to yourself, "it can't be this bad, can it?"

Then you have an idea. You've heard there's a more experienced pro-life philanthropist who has been investing in pro-life pregnancy centers for years, so you decide to bring him on the show. Great! Perhaps you'll learn something from him! The next show begins, and your guest philanthropist takes his seat next to you. The executive director of the first presenting pro-life pregnancy center comes on stage. You are ready to ask the executive director your go-to question about the center's market share numbers, but being the gracious host you are, you invite your guest philanthropist to begin the questioning.

He obliges and begins his inquiry by asking the center executive director, "What percentage of your annual budget is spent on program?" You think to yourself, "Wow, now that seems like a sophisticated investment question!" The executive director responds, "Our annual budget was $1,000,000, and we spent 90 percent of that on program, and 10 percent on fundraising and administration." On hearing that, your guest investor almost falls out of his chair with delight and says to the executive director, "Ninety percent on program! Impressive! Congratulations!"

You, on the other hand, don't even know what "program" is, so when it's your turn to question the executive director, you ask your typical question about the center's market share numbers in its competition against Planned Parenthood. The executive director hesitates, and then replies sheepishly that their center saved 100 lives from abortion last year, while the local Planned Parenthood conducted 9,900 abortions, so the center's market share was 1 percent. As you've become so accustomed to doing by now when you hear answers like that, you immediately say, "I'm out."

Your guest philanthropist, on the other hand, ignores your response and tells the executive director that he is happy to invest $100,000 in the center to help it expand its operation. You are scratching your head at your guest philanthropist's decision. Why would he invest in a center with such low market share numbers against Planned Parenthood? What does he know that you don't? You decide to wait patiently until the show is over to ask him, thinking perhaps you'll gain more insight into your guest philanthropist's investment philosophy.

The show continues, and the next pro-life pregnancy center executive director walks on stage, and again, you let your guest philanthropist begin the questioning. This time as well, he asks the exact same question, "What percentage of your annual budget is spent on program?" It's now becoming clear to you that this is your guest philanthropist's "go-to" question. The center executive director responds, "Our annual budget was $1,000,000, and we spent 70 percent of that on program, and 30 percent on fundraising and administration." Your guest investor slowly leans back in his chair, this time with no smile on his face, and says, "I'm out."

Now you're starting to understand your guest philanthropist's investment criteria has something to do with these percentage breakdowns of how a center spent its funds on program, fundraising, and administration.

From the perspective of your guest philanthropist, it appears that the more a center spent on program, and the less it spent on fundraising and administration, then the better the investment opportunity.

To give credit where credit is due, you like that his investment decisions appear to be driven by measurable data, not by emotions! However, you still have no idea what "program" is so even though your guest philanthropist is already out, you go ahead and ask the executive director your typical "go-to" question about the center's market share results versus Planned Parenthood. The executive director gets excited about your question and responds confidently that their center saved 1,000 lives from abortion, while the local Planned Parenthood conducted 9,000 abortions, so the center's market share was 10 percent. She adds that they achieved a 2 percent market share increase versus Planned Parenthood compared to the previous year.

You think to yourself, "Now we're talking!" Of course, you would like for the center to have achieved an even greater market share, but after hearing a seemingly endless stream of "1 percent market share" results from the executive directors of other centers, 10 percent seems downright amazing! In addition, the center appears to be achieving increases in market share on an annual basis! You tell the center executive director you will happily invest $100,000 in the center to help expand its operation.

You've Been 990'd!

The show ends, and you lean back in your chair reflecting on what just happened. You're wondering to yourself, "Who made the better investment decision, me or my guest philanthropist?" Please be proud of yourself because you did. Here's why. For your investments, you said no to a center that spent $1,000,000 to save one hundred lives from abortion, and yes to a center that spent the same amount to save one thousand lives from abortion.

Your guest philanthropist, on the other hand, did the exact opposite. For his investments, he said yes to a center that spent $1,000,000 to save one hundred lives from abortion, and no to a center that spent that same amount but saved one thousand lives from abortion. Both centers had the same annual budget of $1,000,000, and your guest philanthropist said no to a center that saved nine hundred more lives from abortion than the center he said yes to. The ROI math is simple: the center you invested in historically saves one thousand lives for $1,000,000, while the center your guest philanthropist invested in historically saves one hundred lives for $1,000,000.

You think to yourself, "How on earth could my guest philanthropist make such a profound investment error?" Easy. Like many philanthropists, he based his investment decision on information contained in an IRS form called a Form 990.

How Precious Investment Funds Get Misallocated

Form 990 is a financial document nonprofit organizations are required by law to file with the IRS every year. The IRS makes a nonprofit's Form 990 available to the public for inspection. The document details, among other things, how a nonprofit organization used all the money it received. Total funds spent by the nonprofit are divided into three categories: program, fundraising, and administration.

Unfortunately, and I mean *very* unfortunately, many philanthropists use data in the Form 990 as the sole criteria for making their philanthropic investment decisions. I cannot emphasize strongly enough what a profound error this is. I don't know how it happened, but somewhere and somehow, someone who was not thinking clearly advised philanthropists that the more a nonprofit spends on "program" as a percentage of its total expenditures, the better. In other words, many philanthropists believe the money a nonprofit spends on program equates to the desired ROI the philanthropist seeks. This belief is extremely common among nonprofit philanthropists, from small dollar donors all the way to those who give millions of dollars annually. Can you see the problem? The problem is that just because the nonprofit spent money on program, it doesn't necessarily mean that expenditure achieved the ROI desired by the philanthropist.

Let me demonstrate what I mean by using an example from the for-profit world. Imagine you have before you two small for-profit retail flower shops—Shop #1 and Shop #2—and you've decided you are going to make an investment in one of them. Both shops have great locations, great products, great processes and procedures. As a matter of fact, they are practically identical in their particulars. However, there is one thing you can't figure out. Shop #2's profit and loss statement shows that, on average, it has consistently generated two times the financial profits of Shop #1 over many years. As you dive deeper into the details of each shop's financial statements, you notice something strange.

Year after year, Shop #1 had spent a very large sum on many things having to do with its products—it bought twice the variety of flowers as Shop #2, including some very rare flower types from South America, along with hiring flower experts to tend and care for those special types of flowers. Yet Shop #1 didn't spend much money on advertising or on hiring and training skilled sales staff. You calculate that Shop #1's expenses break down as follows: 90 percent spent on product-related items, 5 percent on advertising, and 5 percent on administration.

Turning to Shop #2, you conduct the same analysis. You notice Shop #2's expenses break down as follows: 70 percent spent on product related items, 20 percent spent on marketing and advertising, and 10 percent spent on administration. You now start to understand the major difference between the two shops. Shop #1 is very product-focused. So much so that it seems to have forgotten that the objective of the business is to generate profits for its investors. And that can't happen without sales, which can't happen without marketing and advertising.

Compared to Shop #1, Shop #2 doesn't spend as much on its flowers, but it still has excellent products that its customers love, and those customers know about Shop #2's products because it consistently advertises about those products. Shop #2's expenses are more balanced toward generating a greater number of sales than are Shop #1's. This leads to Shop #2 having significantly greater sales and profits, and is therefore a much better investment than Shop #1. I think any astute investor would see the mistake that Shop #1 is making in terms of how it spends its money. Shop #1's expense outlays are completely out of balance, with a significant over-investment in product related expenses.

The point? I hope you see the parallel between our two for-profit flower shops, and nonprofit organizations that spend enormous amounts on program, but deliver little in terms of the actual results the philanthropists desire from their investments. Please burn this deeply into your mind: *A nonprofit organization's program expenses do not necessarily equate to the results the organization's philanthropists seek.* Of course, it is possible that a nonprofit's program expenses equate to results, but my point is you cannot determine that solely from data presented in a Form 990. If you rely solely on a Form 990, you can easily make the same investment mistake the guest philanthropist made on your *Shark Tank for Pro-Life Pregnancy Centers* show. Remember: Invest in a nonprofit based on its proven results, not on how much it spends on program.

What Result Are You Investing In?

Let's get back to our *Shark Tank for Pro-Life Pregnancy Centers* show. Being the kind person you are, you decide to charitably show your guest philanthropist the error of his ways. After you do so, you are shocked at his response. "But the pro-life pregnancy center I invested in saved one hundred lives from abortion while only spending $100,000 in marketing and administration! They're much more efficient at spending their money!" You think to yourself, "Efficiency? As investors we want effectiveness first, then efficiency!"

Now you've had enough with the wayward thinking of your guest philanthropist. You reply, "Who cares how efficient a pro-life pregnancy center is if it's not effective? Is a Planned Parenthood abortion facility more worried about a pro-life pregnancy center competitor that is efficient and takes away only a few of Planned Parenthood's clients, or one that is effective and takes away many of its clients?"

You're on a roll so you continue, "What should matter most to philanthropists like you and me is a center's total number of lives saved from abortion. Once a center is succeeding in that area, then we can look at efficiency, but even so, not in the way you look at it. Efficiency should be measured as a pro-life pregnancy center's total expenses divided by the total number of lives it saved from abortion. So for example, the center you invested in required $10,000 ($1,000,000/100) to save one life from abortion, whereas the center I invested in only required $1,000 ($1,000,000/1,000) to save one life from abortion."

You finish the conversation with your guest philanthropist by emphasizing as charitably as possible, "Your investment of $100,000 in the pro-life pregnancy center you invested in will save ten lives from abortion ($100,000/$10,000), whereas the pro-life pregnancy center I invested $100,000 in will save one hundred lives from abortion ($100,000/$1,000). The center I invested in is both more effective and more efficient. Please explain to me again why you think the center you invested in is the better investment."

Your guest philanthropist's reaction to your question? Hopefully, stunned silence, and some deep reflection about how relying solely on information presented in the Form 990 to make investment decisions has the potential to grossly misallocate philanthropy dollars—taking funds that could have been invested in pro-life pregnancy centers achieving very high ROI, and giving it instead to centers with very low ROI.

Now that you know how to find a competitive pro-life pregnancy center to invest in, what do you do if you can't find a viable investment candidate in your local city, or even in your entire state? I propose to you three options, from easiest to hardest, and we'll cover those next.

Easiest: Go Outside Your Boundaries

I have worked with a few pro-life philanthropists who were not able to identify any competitive pro-life pregnancy centers in their local markets. My advice to them was simple: if it's not a high priority for you to invest in a local pro-life pregnancy center, then find and invest in a competitive pro-life pregnancy center in a different city or state. My emphasis when I offer that advice is simple: a human life in another city or state is as cherished in God's eyes as a human life in your local community. If you also choose the path of investing in a center in another city or state, of course, you will use the exact same investment criteria we have already covered.

If you're not sure where to begin your search, please contact me through my website at BrettAttebery.com. From time to time, I learn about pro-life pregnancy centers that are having success against Planned Parenthood, as measured by market share, and I would be happy to connect you to those centers.

Harder: Demand a Change

Let's say you decide it is a high priority for you to make your investment in a pro-life pregnancy center located in your city or state. Further, let's assume you have spoken with the leadership teams of all of the pro-life pregnancy centers in your community, and none of them passed your investment criteria test (remember: market share gains versus Planned Parenthood!). You still have options, though pursuing them requires a much greater commitment on your part. These options are founded on something that is very important for you to remember: money talks.

You are a business professional so I'm sure you are already aware that money talks, but specifically, how does money talk concerning investing in a local pro-life pregnancy center? I'll use an example from the for-profit world to demonstrate. Think about what happens fairly often to public for-profit companies (owned by stock holders) that consistently underperform. The stockholders—the owners of the company—explicitly make their displeasure known directly to a company's board of directors and its executive team.

If a large enough block of a for-profit company's stockholders band together to demand a change in the company's leadership and strategy, those stockholders have sufficient leverage to force a change. I'm sure you've read before in the financial news how disgruntled investors of a public company successfully forced a change in the company's management. Such so-called investor revolts don't always work, but sometimes they do. You're probably thinking, "Yes Brett, but a nonprofit is different because no one can legally own a nonprofit." And you're right about that.

However, just like a for-profit, a nonprofit cannot operate without money. And in the case of a pro-life pregnancy center, pro-life philanthropists provide the vast majority of that money. Therefore, in the same way stockholders wield significant leverage over a for-profit company, philanthropists who fund the operations of a pro-life pregnancy center also wield enormous leverage over the center. The question is, are the philanthropists willing to use that leverage? And more specifically, are you willing to use that leverage?

If you identify a local pro-life pregnancy center that is consistently underperforming in terms of market share, are you willing to do the work to bring this to the attention of other like-minded philanthropists who fund the center? If so, are you then willing to (1) organize those philanthropists who, together with you, provide the majority of the center's financial support, (2) demand the board of directors change both the center's strategy and its leadership team, and (3) tie continued funding of the center to your demands being met?

Does the thought of doing something like that make you uncomfortable? I would think so. The whole approach sounds pretty heavy-handed, doesn't it? That's because it is. Undoubtedly, pursuing such an approach would be stressful, and some, maybe all, of the good-faith folks on the center's board of directors and leadership team would not have nice things to say about you and your fellow philanthropists. However, I ask you to keep in mind the following: if the pro-life pregnancy center is like most centers, it saves the lives of 10 babies for every 990 preborn babies the local Planned Parenthood brutally slaughters. In my mind, that sobering metric demonstrates that a change at the center is an imperative, and if you keep that metric at the forefront of your mind, it should help you and your fellow philanthropists get over the discomfort of demanding change at the center and staying the course to see it through.

Hardest: Do It Yourself

But certainly, leading or participating in a philanthropist revolt at a local pro-life pregnancy center would not be fun, to say the least. And just like investor revolts in the for-profit world, a philanthropist revolt is not guaranteed to succeed. So let's assume you either lead or participate in a philanthropist revolt toward a certain pro-life pregnancy center, and it doesn't succeed, or perhaps you just don't want to get involved in such a thing in the first place, but you still strongly desire to play a role in the emergence of a highly competitive pro-life pregnancy center in your local city or state.

What to do? Well, if you've been around a while, you've likely experienced in your personal life or in your business dealings a situation where even with the assistance of others, no matter what you tried, in the end you just couldn't get something completed that met your standards. When that happens, you can either decide to settle for what you consider subpar, or you can take the reins and do it yourself.

How does this apply in terms of you investing in a local pro-life pregnancy center? Well, if you can't influence an uncompetitive pro-life pregnancy center in your local community to change, you have the option of starting your own pro-life pregnancy center. I know the thought of doing that might initially give you a heart attack, and I don't want to give you the impression it would be easy. However, starting your own pro-life pregnancy center, while certainly not easy, would probably be easier than you think.

Here's why. If you decide to start a pro-life pregnancy center, you don't have to figure out on your own how to compete effectively against Planned Parenthood. Instead, you can follow a pro-life pregnancy center blueprint for success that already exists. This is similar to what happens in the for-profit world, when an investor "buys" a franchise license of a proven business model—to name just one I'm sure you're familiar with: McDonalds. Why do investors buy franchises? Because the investor believes it significantly lowers the risk of the investment to buy into a turnkey business system that has already proven in other markets that it can generate a positive ROI. And if you're wondering, yes, there exist such turnkey business systems in the PLBI.

For example, as of this writing, I know that ThriVe Women's Express Healthcare (covered in detail in Chapter 12) is actively seeking to expand its successful business model into other cities. In addition to ThriVe, there currently exist a few other pro-life pregnancy centers that have successful turnkey business systems, and there will likely be more emerging in the future, so if this is a path you are considering pursuing, please contact me through my website at BrettAttebery.com and I will provide you with up-to-date information on such opportunities.

While the DIY approach would likely be the most challenging for you in terms of bringing a truly competitive (as measured by market share gains) pro-life pregnancy center to your local city, remember that such a center would also have the potential to earn the highest ROI—meaning the greatest number of preborn human lives saved from abortion. In addition, if a sufficient number of pro-life philanthropists in large and medium-sized cities around the country invested in proven pro-life pregnancy center turnkey business systems, in the aggregate that could become part of a wave—a pro-life pregnancy center business model movement—that tips the scales toward shutting down Planned Parenthood nationally. Can you imagine how awesome it would be to have your name associated with that accomplishment!?

Through a Different Lens

As we come to the end of this final chapter, and the end of this book, at the risk of being too repetitive, I want to make one final appeal to you: Remember that you must view pro-life pregnancy centers as competitive organizations if you want to help them win, as measured by market share, against Planned Parenthood. As I know from my own experience working directly with many pro-life pregnancy centers, it can be difficult to make that mental shift.

So I want to share with you a mental trick I use when I feel myself slipping back into evaluating a center based on my emotions (I love the team members!) rather than the center's results as measured by market share gains against Planned Parenthood. This mental trick is deceptively simple, but it works for me, and because you are a business professional, I think it might work for you as well. The mental trick I use is to simply pretend the pro-life pregnancy center I'm evaluating is a for-profit company, not a nonprofit organization. When I make that mental shift, suddenly, there's no chance I'll think of my potential investment in the center as philanthropy with no strings attached. Instead, I expect, better said I "demand," a return on my investment.

Specifically, I demand the center achieve market share gains against Planned Parenthood. And I am very happy to forgo investment in one center when another center proves it is achieving better market share results. I recommend you try this mental trick and then ask yourself what you think would happen at pro-life pregnancy centers in your local community if all pro-life philanthropists adopted the same for-profit mindset when evaluating which centers to invest in. Of course, it's hard to know for sure exactly what would happen, but I believe it's very likely each center would attempt to significantly up its game in terms of gaining ground, and dare I say winning, against Planned Parenthood, as measured by market share. Why? Because each center would then have to compete for philanthropy funds based on demonstrated results, not on emotional appeals.

What Profit in This?

I understand if you think my proposed mental trick goes too far or is a bit too radical, especially if you are thinking of "profit" as money. Thinking about a pro-life pregnancy center seeking to maximize financial return would certainly be an extreme departure from current practice. But I'm not really thinking about profit in the sense of financial return. I'm thinking of a center earning profit in the sense of generating meaningful, measurable results that benefit someone. Under that definition of profit, pro-life philanthropists would seek opportunities to maximize profit by investing in pregnancy centers that offer the most competitive choose life benefits to women facing unexpected pregnancies.

By bringing that type of "for-profit" attitude into a nonprofit investment opportunity, the philanthropist would then be less interested in the emotional storytelling of a center's executive team, and more focused on evidence of proof of success, in other words, a pro-life pregnancy center's measurable market share gains against Planned Parenthood.

Chapter Twenty-One BOTTOM LINE

The vast majority of the twenty-five hundred to three thousand pro-life pregnancy centers in the United States are not really competing against Planned Parenthood. Most centers are actually what we call

PRCs, and their primary mission is to provide material assistance to those women who are already likely to carry their pregnancies to term. You must weed out PRCs until you find "investable" pro-life pregnancy centers that are actually having success encouraging abortion-determined women to change their minds and choose life for their preborn babies. Do not use a center's IRS Form 990 data as a decision variable in your analysis, as a center's financial accounting results, especially its "program" spend, may not be relevant at all to its actual success at competing against Planned Parenthood for abortion-determined clients. After conducting thorough due diligence, you may find that no competitive centers exist in your local community. If so, you have three choices: (1) Easiest: Invest in a center outside your local community, (2) Harder: Organize philanthropists who fund a center in your local community to leverage their influence to demand the center's board of directors change the center's strategy to become more competitive, (3) Hardest: Start your own pro-life pregnancy center using an existing, proven successful pro-life pregnancy center turnkey business system. Remember that you must view pro-life pregnancy centers as competitive organizations if you want to help them win, as measured by market share, against Planned Parenthood.

EPILOGUE: I LEFT MY NETS

> *He said to them, "Come after me, and I will make you fishers of men." At once they left their nets and followed him.* Matthew 4:19–20

> *The most ambitious project is misguided if it does not foster at the same time the development of the virtue, character, and personal excellence of all those involved in it.* Alexandre Havard

> *You are the light of the world. A city set on a mountain cannot be hidden. Nor do they light a lamp and then put it under a bushel basket; it is set on a lampstand, where it gives light to all in the house. Just so, your light must shine before others, that they may see your good deeds and glorify your heavenly Father.* Matthew 5:14–16

So we've come to the end of our time together. I am grateful to you for engaging with me in this discussion about the business of pro-life, and I hope you found the ideas in the book enlightening and fruitful. But more than anything, my hope is that you will now decide what story you want to write in this great struggle against the evil of abortion. What role do you want to play in this drama? And then crucially, once you've decided what role you want to play, what will you then do? I implore you, please do not just sit on what you've learned in this book. Don't make it just an intellectual exercise. Put what you've learned into action.

I want to share a quote from Greg Cunningham that was passed on to me from pro-life apologist Scott Klusendorf. Greg said of pro-lifers: "Most people who say they oppose abortion do just enough to salve the conscience but not enough to stop the killing." Ouch. That hurts. Does Greg's claim have merit? I believe national polling data proves his claim is accurate.

For example, remember from the data we looked at in Chapter 4 that in Gallup's 2020 poll on attitudes about abortion, 19 percent of adult Americans said that abortion should never be legal under any circumstances. So how many adult Americans is 19 percent? If we use 2020 census data, as of July 1, 2019, there were 255,042,109 Americans who were eighteen years old or older. Nineteen percent of 255,042,109 would equate to 48,458,000 Americans who believe that abortion should never be legal under any circumstances.

So what do you think? Are 48,458,000 Americans actively engaging their 3T assets to try to, as Greg Cunningham put it, "stop the killing"? Of course, no one knows exactly how many of those 48,458,000 Americans are actively doing something with their 3T assets that goes beyond doing "just enough to salve the conscience," but I don't believe it's a very high percentage.

To give you some context of why I don't think so, take for example one of the largest pro-life organizations in terms of number of donors: Students for Life of America. I believe Students for Life of America has approximately 100,000 pro-life individuals who support them financially. One hundred thousand donors would equate to 0.2 percent of the 48,458,000 pro-life Americans who profess they believe abortion should be illegal in all circumstances. Not 2 percent, but 0.2 percent. Using that as a proxy, I think it's a fair assertion that most of the 48,458,000 individuals are not engaged in any significant way in the fight to end abortion. I believe if all 48,458,000 pro-life Americans were already actively engaging their 3T assets in pro-life programs, I doubt an abortion industry would even exist in this country.

Going All In

Of course, the fact that you have read this book very likely means you already are or soon will be one of the pro-life Americans who prioritizes investing their 3T assets into pro-life programs that aim to win the war against abortion. And my hope is that after having read this book, you feel equipped to invest your 3T assets in a way that will have even greater measurable impact on saving lives from abortion. I want to strongly encourage you in your efforts to up your game! But I also want to offer you a cautionary tale based on my own experience of what I did after going all in on pro-life following my "road to Damascus" moment at a Rachel's Vineyard retreat in 2013, which I shared with you the first part of that story in the prologue of this book.

Let me pick up that story where I left off.

Recall that during the Rachel's Vineyard retreat for abortion healing, I asked the Lord to use me to help young women and men not make the same mistake my girlfriend and I had made decades earlier when we made the decision to abort our own child. It is not an understatement to say that I emerged from the Rachel's Vineyard retreat believing with every fiber of my being that the Lord had called me to a new mission in life. In line with my new belief, I decided to abandon everything that had previously been important to me in order to pursue the mission of fighting against the evil of abortion. I think back on that "going all in" decision as a "leaving my nets" moment. It reminds me of the complete and total commitment some fishermen made to Jesus long ago: "He said to them, 'Come after me, and I will make you fishers of men.' At once they left their nets and followed him" (Matthew 4:19–20).

Following the retreat, I immediately began pursuing my new calling. I started a digital magazine called *Pro-Life Magazine*. I started a nonprofit called Maria's Choice that raised funds to help women who were thinking about getting an abortion because they faced economic hardship. Through both of those endeavors I attracted the attention of the leadership team of a nonprofit called Heroic Media, who invited me to join their team, which I did in early 2015, enabling me over the years that followed to become an expert about the inside workings of the PLBI. And that inside industry experience led to me writing this book you now hold in your hands.

And Who Is My Neighbor?

Now if I read that quick summary and it was about someone other than myself, I would probably think, "Wow. What a story! That's so heroic!" And some people do say that to me. But because the story is about me, I know the details of the "story within the story" that they don't know about. And I can assure you, in hindsight, key parts of my story are not heroic at all.

Before I get into the details of why not—and again, I'm only doing so because I want to offer it as a cautionary tale to you—let me set it up with this Bible passage you are likely very familiar with, the Parable of the Good Samaritan:

> There was a scholar of the law who stood up to test him and said, "Teacher, what must I do to inherit eternal life?" Jesus said to him, "What is written in the law? How do you read it?" He said in reply, "You shall love the Lord, your God, with all your heart, with all your being, with all your strength, and with all your mind, and your neighbor as yourself." He replied to him, "You have answered correctly; do this and you will live." But because he wished to justify himself, he said to Jesus, "And who is my neighbor?" Jesus replied, "A man

> fell victim to robbers as he went down from Jerusalem to Jericho. They stripped and beat him and went off leaving him half-dead. A priest happened to be going down that road, but when he saw him, he passed by on the opposite side. Likewise a Levite came to the place, and when he saw him, he passed by on the opposite side.
>
> But a Samaritan traveler who came upon him was moved with compassion at the sight. He approached the victim, poured oil and wine over his wounds and bandaged them. Then he lifted him up on his own animal, took him to an inn and cared for him. The next day he took out two silver coins and gave them to the innkeeper with the instruction, 'Take care of him. If you spend more than what I have given you, I shall repay you on my way back.' Which of these three, in your opinion, was neighbor to the robbers' victim?" He answered, "The one who treated him with mercy." Jesus said to him, "Go and do likewise." Luke 10:25–37

The part of the parable I would like you to focus on is when both the priest and the Levite "passed by on the opposite side." Until recently, I had always interpreted the actions of the priest and the Levite as being completely uncaring concerning the victim lying in the street. And of course, it is possible that interpretation is entirely correct. However, based on my own experience I think there is another possible interpretation. Could it be that both the priest and Levite were actually very caring individuals, but were so singularly focused on the pursuit of their missions to serve *some* of God's children that they completely forgot that *all* of God's children were their neighbors?

In other words, is it possible that instead of allowing God to lead their hearts and minds with the Great Commandment at all times and at all places, the priest and Levite instead kind of "took the reins" on their own and jumped in the pilot seat to pursue their own course with a "Thanks God, but I got this now" attitude, at least subconsciously? (To learn more about how common this phenomenon is among people of goodwill, please do an internet search for this study: "From Jerusalem to Jericho": A Study of Situational and Dispositional Variables in Helping Behavior).

You're probably wondering what led me to that possible interpretation of the actions of the priest and the Levite. The insight came in hindsight as a result of a very painful personal experience resulting from my decision to drop everything in pursuit of my new mission. In the course of abandoning *everything* to pursue my mission, I came perilously close to abandoning *everyone*. Like the priest and the Levite, I too "passed by on the opposite side" by failing to properly love the most important persons that God had so generously placed in my life: my wife and children. The details of how that played out would require writing another book, so let me quickly summarize what happened.

First, some background. When my wife and I married in 1991, we agreed that I would be the primary breadwinner for our family. That agreement enabled my very talented wife, who could have developed her own successful career, to focus on committing herself full time to raising our family. And she did a remarkable job at that! Mostly due to my wife's sacrifices, our three kids developed into amazing individuals, now adults pursuing their own missions. So when my wife and I mutually agreed that I would be the primary breadwinner that worked well for us for many years.

However, I completely abandoned our agreement following the Rachel's Vineyard retreat when I embarked on pursuing my pro-life mission full-time. I had no plan for how I would generate sufficient financial income to support our family. As a result, toward the end of 2014, our family's financial reserves were completely depleted.

My response to that challenge? Instead of taking responsible action to do something to earn income to get us back on track, my response was to double down and dive even deeper into abandoning my agreed-on responsibility to financially support our family. Eventually, this led to declaring personal bankruptcy and deciding unilaterally that our family would continue to live, subsist really, on very minimal income.

Looking back, I recall with deep regret that I did not care much about how the decision to declare bankruptcy affected my wife and children. It seems crazy to me that I actually went forward with that bankruptcy decision—doing it not out of necessity, because with my professional background I was very employable, but out of a purely self-centered choice.

Maybe I thought I was impressing God with my commitment. Whatever the motivation, what is clear to me now is that I deeply idolized my new pro-life mission, and what I mean by idolizing my mission is that for some reason I believed God was okay with me abandoning my responsibilities as a husband and as a father in order to commit myself to full-time pro-life work.

What I understand now is that my actions violated the virtue of prudence—the action of making right decisions. I learned painfully that passionate pursuit of a mission does not mean one should make rash and reckless decisions in other important areas of one's life. Looking back, it is now very clear to me how I could have pursued my new pro-life mission *and* fulfilled my responsibilities as husband and father. Simply, I was selfish. And as a result, my actions ended up being very unjust toward my family members.

Interestingly, I didn't clearly understand this until very recently when my friend Pierre Koshakji introduced me to the concepts of virtuous leadership taught by Alexandre Havard. When I reflected on what I had done through the lens of those concepts, the scales fell from my eyes and I could see the mistakes I had made that deeply affected my family in a negative way. (I highly recommend author Alexandre Havard's teachings on virtuous leadership. Please start with his book *From Temperament to Character: On Becoming a Virtuous Leader*, as well as checking his website about the Virtuous Leadership Institute at https://hvli.org.) So that's my cautionary tale for you if you are motivated to go all in on pro-life with your 3T assets. I applaud you for your decision, but please do not forget about the other "neighbors" the Lord has called you to love, and make sure you love them authentically.

What Is Authentic Love?

What does it mean to love someone authentically? I don't believe it means the sentimental syrupy feel-good emotion of what many would call love. My definition of authentic love is the one Bishop Robert Barron often uses: "Willing the good of the other as other." The silver lining from my failure to "love my neighbor as myself" in terms of my relationship with my family was that the Lord taught me a lesson about what authentic love is. My approach to love now looks more like what you and I covered in Chapter 10 when we looked at the framework of Maslow's hierarchy of needs.

From the perspective of that framework, I want my family members to achieve self-actualization. And though they are ultimately responsible for striving to achieve self-actualization and I can't do that for them, what I can do is ask myself constantly, "What can I do to empower them to achieve self-actualization?" In other words, while respecting their free will, what environment can I create around them that facilitates their personal pursuit of self-actualization?

And to push that even further, looking at it through a virtuous leadership framework (see above about resources from author Alexandre Havard), what environment can I create around my family that facilitates them achieving greatness in their lives?

And then the final step, what environment can I create around my family so that their light shines before others and "gives light to all in the house?" As Jesus says, "You are the light of the world. A city set on a mountain cannot be hidden. Nor do they light a lamp and then put it under a bushel basket; it is set on a lampstand, where it gives light to all in the house. Just so, your light must shine before others, that they may see your good deeds and glorify your heavenly Father" (Matthew 5:14–16). So if you challenged me to sum up all of that into one word, I would use the term *empowerment*.

Daily and Continuous Contact

And so with the idea of empowerment in mind, for my last word to you in this book, I want to encourage you to do something courageous. I want to encourage you to be willing to do pro-life differently, and dare I say do pro-life better, even if doing so leads to you having to endure some criticism from other pro-lifers.

My objective in the preceding pages of this book was to persuade you that you will have much more impact at saving lives from abortion by investing a much larger share of your 3T assets on the "increase demand for choosing life" side of the PLBI than on the "fight for human rights of preborn babies" side of the Pro-Life Movement. That reprioritization moves the majority of your 3T assets over to the daily front-line battles of organizations in the PLBI, and away from organizations in the Pro-Life Movement that work primarily to change laws and change culture.

Participation in the Pro-Life Movement does not necessitate your direct involvement with those who are the victims of abuse of justice and human rights, whereas your participation in the PLBI does. Now your direct involvement in the PLBI doesn't mean you have to work at a pro-life pregnancy center. It means the 3T assets you invest are in some way affecting the front lines of the PLBI. Such a change in orientation of your 3T assets reminds me of a quote from Mother Teresa. She said, "In the world, there are some who struggle for justice and human rights. We have no time for this because we are in daily and continuous contact with men who are starving for a piece of bread to put in their mouth and for some affection."

For those who are active in the pro-life world, I think there is currently a substantial imbalance between the number of pro-lifers who primarily, as Mother Teresa said, "struggle for justice and human rights," and the number of pro-lifers who primarily are—if I change Mother Teresa's words for the specific context of a woman facing an unexpected pregnancy—"in daily and continuous contact with women who are starving for something that will help them overcome their fear of an unexpected pregnancy." And then if you'll allow me to add an idea that pushes the idea even further, "and empowers them to achieve the unique mission God has called them to." I believe that last part about empowerment is a critical piece of the puzzle for ending abortion. It is a piece I did not understand for a very long time.

Let me take you back to the story of my Rachel's Vineyard experience to demonstrate that. When I was at the Rachel's Vineyard retreat for abortion healing in 2013, I was offered the opportunity to share with the other retreatants the details of the story of how I had lost a child to abortion and the role I played in the abortion decision. Of course, sharing the details of that story made me very emotional, as I'm sure you can imagine.

What surprised me though was what I said that made me breakdown emotionally. It wasn't the abortion itself per se. It was the fact that I had failed to protect my girlfriend and our preborn son in the incredibly vulnerable circumstances they suddenly found themselves in. I abandoned both of them at a time when I should have stepped up to protect and provide for them.

You might say to me, "Yes, Brett, but you came to that realization thirty years after the fact, after having helped raise your children with your wife." That would be a fair comment, I think. It might be true that as a completely dependent immature teenager at the time, I couldn't offer my girlfriend and our child what I did not myself possess—security. That being the case, my girlfriend would have needed others to help her. But what kind of help would have been sufficient for her to change her mind about abortion and choose life, especially considering I was not providing for any of her needs in her situation?

Naturally, there is danger in playing mental games of "what if," but I think doing so might provide some valuable insights. For example, what if someone had entered into our story and offered my girlfriend basic security and material provision—the lower levels of Maslow's hierarchy of needs—if she decided to choose life? Would that have been enough for her to change her mind about abortion? Of course, I don't know the answer to that for sure, but I think the answer is no, that it wouldn't have changed her decision. As necessary and good as basic security and material provision are, they're not empowerment as I defined above: self-actualization, personal greatness, letting your light shine before others.

But what if someone had entered into our story and had offered my girlfriend various credible paths to empowerment that included her choosing life for our child? I still don't know if it would have changed her decision, but I feel confident in saying it would have increased the chances of her choosing life for our preborn son. And I'm not saying that as a complete guess. After I committed to full-time pro-life work, my girlfriend, who I had not spoken with for thirty years, found out about it and sent me a letter expressing her support for what I had decided to do. In that letter, she reflected on what we had done to our preborn child so long ago, and there were suggestions in her reflection that if certain fears had been taken care of, maybe the decision would have been different.

Again, I'm just speculating, of course. Nonetheless, I think that insight is crucially important because I believe we can apply it to many cases of women experiencing unexpected pregnancies. At the core of their beings, women experiencing unexpected pregnancies are seeking purpose for their lives; seeking self-actualization; seeking greatness; desiring to let their lights shine before others so that they may glorify their heavenly Father. Just like all of us.

I want to leave you with this thought, because I don't think it is a question we pro-lifers ask ourselves often enough, if ever, in the ongoing struggle to end abortion: "How do we end abortion even if abortion remains legal forever?" I think many pro-lifers assume abortion has to be illegal in order for the vast majority of women to choose life instead of choosing abortion.

I don't believe that's true because remember, even when abortion is legal, women experiencing unexpected pregnancies still have a choice between two competing options—abortion services and choose life services. I believe offering women a pro-life "choose life product" that empowers them to achieve self-actualization and personal greatness is the key to ending abortion.

My prayer is that you and I and the nearly 50 million other Americans who, according to the Gallup poll, are pro-life in all circumstances will work without ceasing to continually improve the attractiveness of that empowering pro-life product, and by God's grace that we will offer it skillfully and persuasively, daily and continuously, to women facing unexpected pregnancies who in their hearts so desperately want that product.

I look forward to co-laboring with you in that mission.

May the Lord bless you and keep you,

Brett

ACKNOWLEDGMENTS

This book has my name on it as the author, but I believe in many respects that it was cowritten in spirit by so many. Writing a book is truly a team sport! I owe a deep debt of gratitude to those who have accompanied me on this journey, especially My Heavenly Father, my Lord and Savior Jesus Christ, the Holy Spirit, Holy Mary, all the angels and saints, my child Jesse in Heaven, my mother, Sharon, in Heaven, my father, Raymond, my wife, Eri, my children Kevin, Rachel, and Sean, my dearest friend of forty years Don Greiner, my child Jesse's mother who prayerfully and silently supports my pro-life work, my Rachel's Vineyard retreat director Evelyn Walsh, my Respect Life group at Mary Mother of the Redeemer Catholic Church in North Wales, PA, and especially to its former leader Bob Reynolds who helped me get started in pro-life advocacy, Maria Malone and Jenny Wetherill Galiani of Adoption Is a Loving Option, Brian Follett who offered me the opportunity to join Heroic Media, the Heroic Media team past and present, especially Kevin Fitzpatrick, Karen Garnett, Jordan Long, Evan Woolsoncroft, Elaine Russo, Kenzie Muckway, Sam Meier, Marie Wood, Mike Perkins, Mike McMurray, Marissa Cope, Renona Palone, and Joe Young, my fellow members of Heroic Media's board of directors past and present, especially the chairman of the board, Pierre Koshakji, who opened my mind and heart to an elevated view of life through virtuous leadership, and also Bishop Joseph Strickland, Jay Lamy, Anne O'Brien, Ed Mello, Bridget VanMeans, Jeff Kassing, and Jim Coffey, all of Heroic Media's generous benefactors, all of Heroic Media's pro-life pregnancy center partners, and last but certainly not least my good friend and spiritual coach Christopher Scroggin.

I would also like to offer a special note of appreciation to those who helped edit this book, as well as provided invaluable suggestions for improving its content, especially Don Greiner and Jonathan Frase, but also many others, including Shellie Greiner, Cindy Stone, Neil Fusco, Jose Lanuza, Maria Malone, Doug Heulitt, Jeff Kline, Matt DiTeresa, Ken Horton, Bridget VanMeans, Bob Reynolds, Ed Mello, Pierre Koshakji, and Tim Watkins.

I am grateful to all of you, and pray that our Lord will continue to generously bless you!

In deep appreciation and gratitude,

Brett

ABOUT THE AUTHOR

Brett's journey into full-time pro-life work began when he entered the Catholic Church in 2004. As he deepened his understanding about the Church's teaching on the sanctity of life, Brett had to confront a tragic event from his distant past. When he was just a teenager, his girlfriend at the time became pregnant, and together Brett and his girlfriend chose to have their own child aborted.

Upon entering the Church, Brett firmly believed that God had forgiven him for that terrible mistake, but it still weighed heavily on his conscience for many years, so in 2013, Brett decided to seek healing at a Rachel's Vineyard Retreat. During the retreat he experienced a powerful outpouring of God's healing grace. In gratitude, Brett asked God to use him in some way to help young women and men not make the same mistake he had made so many years earlier.

God did not wait long to answer Brett's prayer. Shortly after the Rachel's Vineyard Retreat, Brett founded *Pro-Life Magazine* and also launched Maria's Choice, a crowdfunding website that raised money to benefit pregnant women who felt pressured to choose abortion because of lack of financial resources.

These initiatives attracted the attention of the leadership team at Heroic Media, who invited Brett to join their executive team in 2015 as vice president of marketing, tasking him with leading Heroic Media's efforts to save babies' lives from abortion by using targeted internet advertising. In 2020, Brett became president and CEO of Heroic Media, and in 2021, he joined Heroic Media's board of directors.

Brett graduated with a BA double major in French and economics from Tulane University, and he earned an MBA with a concentration in marketing and operations from the Wharton School. He also earned an MA in international studies from the University of Pennsylvania in collaboration with the Japanese language program of the Wharton School's prestigious Lauder Institute.

Brett was born and raised in Oklahoma City, Oklahoma, and now lives in McKinney, Texas. He enjoys tennis, golf, ballroom dancing, and hunting.

You can contact Brett through his website at BrettAttebery.com.